small-plot, high-yield gardening

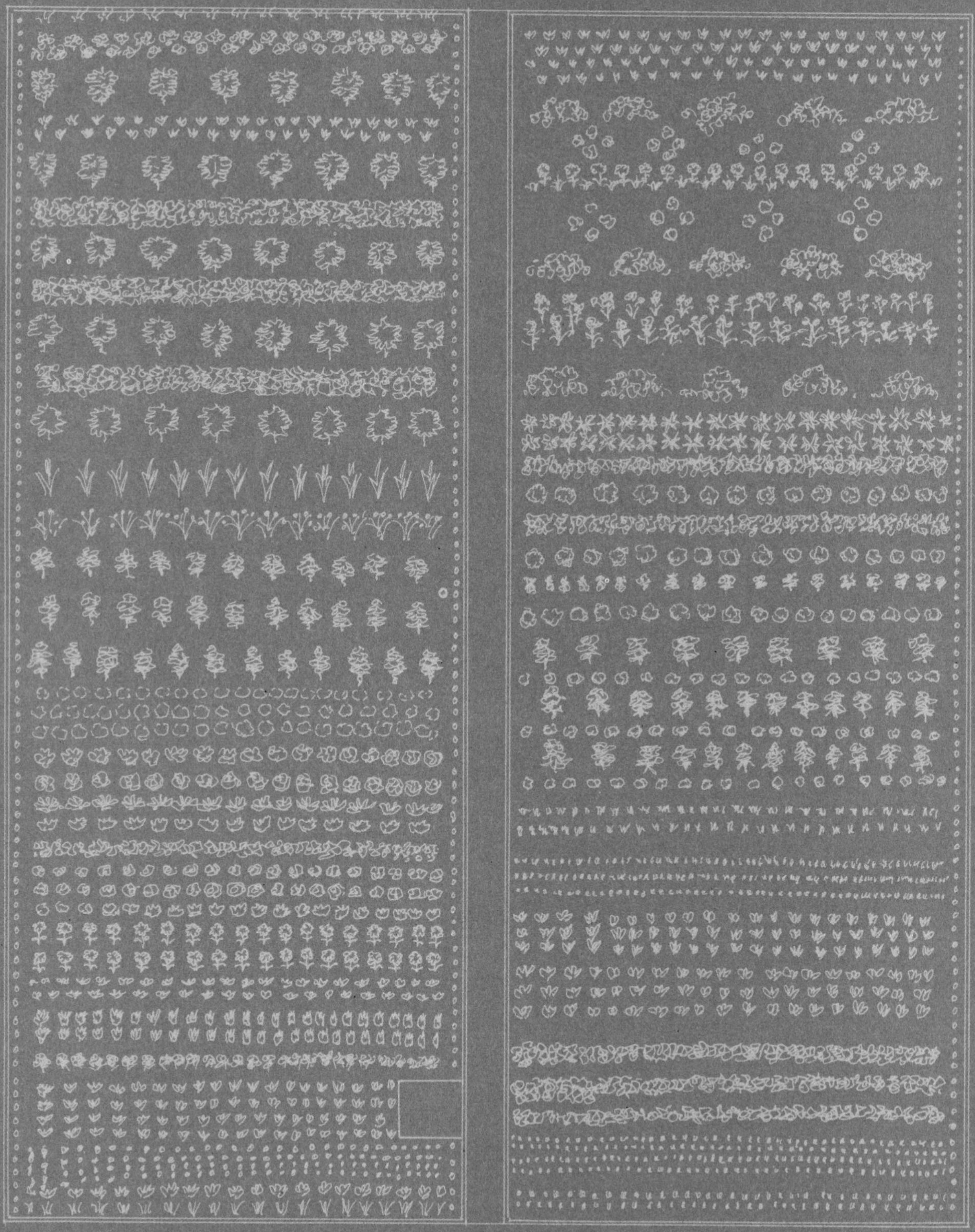

small-plot, high-yield
gardening

grow like a pro, save money,
and eat well from your
front (or back or side) yard
100% organic produce garden

Sal Gilbertie and Larry Sheehan

TEN SPEED PRESS
Berkeley

Copyright © 2010 by Sal Gilbertie and Larry Sheehan
Garden plans © by Sal Gilbertie; executed by Akiko Aoyagi Shurtleff.
All rights reserved.
Illustrations on pages vi, vii, 1, 7, 34, 50, 57, 62, 65, 74, 80, 106, 126,
130, 145, 148, 156, 163, 165, 168, 189, and 199 by Cheryl Graham ©
istockphoto

The excerpted lines on page 72 are from "Build Soil," reprinted from
The Poetry of Robert Frost, edited by Edward Connery Latham.
Copyright © 1936 by Robert Frost. Copyright © 1964 by Lesley Frost
Ballantine. Copyright © 1969 by Holt, Rinehart and Winston. Reprinted
by permission of Holt, Rinehart and Winston Publishers.

Published in the United States by Ten Speed Press, an imprint of the
Crown Publishing Group, a division of Random House, Inc., New York.
www.crownpublishing.com
www.tenspeed.com

Ten Speed Press and the Ten Speed Press colophon are registered
trademarks of Random House, Inc.

Library of Congress Cataloging-in-Publication Data

Gilbertie, Sal.
   Small plot, high yield gardening : grow like a pro, save money, and eat
well from your front (or back or side) yard organic produce garden / Sal
Gilbertie and Larry Sheehan. — Rev. ed.
       p. cm.
   Includes index.
   "Originally published in the United States under the title Home
Gardening at Its Best by Atheneum, New York, in 1977."
   1. Vegetable gardening. 2. Organic gardening. 3. Small gardens.
I. Sheehan, Larry. II. Title.
   SB324.3.G56 2010
   635—dc22

                                    2009038119

ISBN 978-1-58008-037-8

Printed in Canada

Design by Katy Brown
Front cover photos: top right © Kate Mitchell/Corbis;
top left © Image Werks/Corbis

10 9 8 7 6 5 4 3 2

To my parents,
who first taught me to love the soil.

CONTENTS

I. Gardening at a Glance

You Don't Have to Be Italian to Grow Good Peppers

I have a customer who is the consummate "gardener from the old country." If he eats a delicious peach, he saves the pit and plants it somewhere in the yard. He has a one-third-acre lot in the middle of town, but if he eats a dozen good peaches in the season, he'll plant a dozen peach trees.

Some of the peach pits do germinate, and one or two occasionally survive the ravages of the neighborhood kids and dogs, and my friend eventually gets peaches off them. But when one of the trees dies in the spring, does he cut it down? No. He plants pole beans at the base of the trunk. By summer the branches of the tree are covered with thousands of dangling beans. So he gets another crop out of the tree, dead or alive.

It is in this man's make-up to grow things, not because he is Italian, but because he grew up in a family who happened to have a garden.

I've noticed that many of our visitors to Nana's Garden, which is on the grounds of our garden center as a kind of demonstration plot, have an inferiority complex about gardening because they're not of Italian or Yankee heritage.

In my part of the country, East-Coast Yankees and older Italians are believed to have the proverbial green thumb.

I tell our visitors that good gardening is not in the genes. It's in the jeans—the pants you wear when you have to work hard at something. It's the product of knowledge and experience, and if you didn't grow up with a gardening background, you're going to have to acquire the knowledge and experience on your own, with the help of friendly neighbors, neighborly friends, and books like this one.

Offhand, I can think of a veritable melting pot of outstanding gardeners among our customers—a Swede who specializes in early peas, a Scot with a knack for lettuces, an African-American who grows an amazing variety of medicinal herbs, a Greek who raises giant Spanish onions. . . .

Obviously, vegetable gardening is not, cannot be, and should not be a contest among races, religions, and creeds. No one is born with a green thumb. Anyone can learn to garden successfully.

All that aside, in case you ever want to win an argument about who may be the best gardeners in the world, I suggest you consider the implications of a list compiled by the United Nations ranking countries according to agricultural output per acre. It reveals that many of the nations small in geographical size are in fact the most productive in their farming techniques.

The Top 10:
> Republic of China (Taiwan)
> United Arab Republic (Egypt)
> The Netherlands
> Belgium
> Japan
> Denmark
> Germany
> South Korea
> Sri Lanka
> Norway

I'd just like to know what happened to the Italians.

Why Bother?

The ostensible reasons so many of my customers are turning to vegetable gardening are to save money and to eat better.

Why *are* vegetables so expensive?

There are fewer farmers growing them, mainly. Not long ago, New Jersey—known as the "Garden State"—announced it had lost tens of thousands of its traditional truck-farming acreage to soybean-farming enterprises. A single big-cash crop like soybeans happens to be a lot easier for a farmer to manage than a mess of vegetable fields. With world population expected to exceed 7 billion any minute now and to reach 9 billion by the year 2040, there is going to be a lot more pressure on farmers who are in the business of growing varied crops to either sell their land or convert their fields to the big basic crops.

Truck farms are also being lost to real-estate developments all over the country, which is nothing new but it's continuing to erode the supply of fresh vegetables. As most such farms tend to be located fairly near their outlets in metropolitan areas, they're naturally regarded as attractive and potentially valuable building sites.

There are fewer farmers, period. The rural life that Thomas Jefferson and the other Founding Fathers extolled and promoted has practically disappeared. As late as the 1880s and 1890s, some 25 percent of Americans lived on farms. Today less than 1 percent do. We have more people living in prisons than on farms these days.

The most recent Census of Agriculture, conducted by the United States Department of Agriculture (USDA) every five years, shows some hopeful signs, however. The number of farms in America peaked in 1935, at 6.8 million, and declined for several decades after that. In the last two decades, it has leveled off between 2 million and 2.5 million.

The number of small farms increased by 4 percent from 2002 to 2007, with most of the new farms being part-time operations. Although often disparaged as "farmettes" or "hobby" farms, they represent a significant amount of farmland saved from disuse or development. Another encouraging sign: there were 18,200 organic farms in 2007, compared with about 12,000 in 2002.

Within the farming community, the balance of power continues to shift from small to humongous. Consider the fact that about 900,000 of the nation's farms generated $2,500 or less in sales per farm in 2007. In contrast, 5 percent of total farms—about 125,000 operations—accounted for 75 percent of agricultural production. Not surprisingly, those operations receive the majority of government farm subsidies. In 2001, for example, a mega-operation called Tyler Farms in Arkansas received $8.1 million in subsidies—90,000 times more than the median farm subsidy of $899—and nearly equal to the total of farm subsidies to all farmers in Massachusetts and Rhode Island combined.

BIG OIL, MEET BIG SOIL

But there is also good news on the good-food front. The Community Supported Agriculture (CSA) movement, started in 1984, now has more than 3,000 small farms growing food crops for subscriber families who pay a fee in advance to the farmer, then collect fresh organic produce—usually on a weekly basis—throughout the growing season. Many of these CSA farms also offer organic meat products to their members. (Sales of organic poultry and dairy products soared in the 1990s.) Each CSA farm represents acreage saved from development and another farming family saved from extinction.

There was a 40 percent increase in farmers' markets between 2002 and 2006 (totaling 4,385 markets nationwide at the end of 2006). And nothing epitomizes the glories of fresh local fare better than a good farmers' market. Shoppers at the farmers' market in Seattle, for example, can take home the Ozette, a fingerling Spanish potato; the Geoduck, a clam-flavored mollusk; the Pluot, a cross between a plum and apricot; and bushels and bushels of that staple of the Pacific Northwest, sour pie cherries.

Apart from supplying their customers with glorious produce and a wide range of locally made food products, farmers' markets often feature free performances by local musicians and the handiwork of local craftspeople and artists. A farmers' market is a vital gathering place for the community it serves, a place where people make friends with farmers, home chefs and restaurant chefs alike find delectables for their menus, and everyone chews the fat about everything under the sun.

Also making gains in recent years are food co-ops, community gardens (despite the loss of federal funding in the 1990s), and a national USDA-funded farm-to-school program, designed to get local produce into local schools as part of the effort to deal with the epidemic of obesity and diabetes among our children. (Kids aren't the only fatties. Our fast-food-and-agribusiness-based diet has led to a population in which 65 percent of all adults are overweight, and 30 percent of them are clinically defined as obese. Yikes! Hold off on those second helpings.)

The demand for home-grown food has led to a new cottage industry: vegetable gardeners for hire. Two organic gardeners in the metropolitan Portland, Oregon, area, for example, have made a business of maintaining backyard gardens for some forty customers who range from food-stamp recipients to lawyers and other professionals. The pair tend, weed, and water each garden and deliver a harvest basket to each client's back porch once a week throughout the growing season.

Then there's the Slow Food movement, founded in Italy in 1986 to combat the dark side of fast food and to preserve one region's unique cuisine and associated food plants, seeds, domestic animals, and farming practices. Today Slow Food has 83,000 members with chapters in over 122 countries. In the United States there are 16,000 members, including Berkeley, California, restaurateur and food activist Alice Waters, and respected food writers Michael Pollan, Eric Schlosser, and Corby Kummer.

Nationwide, we are down to 2.2 million farms from a high of nearly 7 million prior to World War II. It doesn't take an expert economist to see that with fewer farmers growing vegetables, the consumer is going to end up paying higher prices for the produce. This is what has been happening.

High prices might not be so bad if the vegetables sold in the typical supermarket were worth it.

Certain vegetables are constitutionally unfit for mass marketing. It is not the fault of the big food conglomerates that peas, corn, and asparagus invariably leave their flavors somewhere in transit or on the vine because they are harvested too early. Such vegetables you must eat in or near the garden to savor their true qualities.

Other vegetables have lost their old-fashioned virtues in the process of being adapted to the needs of large-scale farming. Wholesale seed catalogs don't even mention flavor in listing varieties available to big growers. I just picked up one at random and read through eighteen detailed accounts of different peppers. Only two entries bothered to describe the taste.

Commercial varieties of lettuce and tomato have been bred and selected not so much for bite and taste and afterglow, but for their ability to grow to a uniform size, so they fit into the supermarket package, and for sturdy skins, so they get to the store with a minimum of cracks and blemishes.

I'm not sure there's hard evidence that chemically grown, genetically modified, mass-packed, and shipped store-bought vegetables are *significantly* less nutritious and contain *dramatically* less valuable fiber content than home-grown vegetables. However, if you blind-tested ten gourmet diners with a series of choices between the two, I'm willing to bet that all ten of them would pick the home-grown vegetables—and ask for seconds.

Mass-produced tomatoes taste flat unless you sprinkle salt on them. Mass-produced strawberries taste bland unless you sprinkle sugar on them. That's another minor savings if you grow your own: you don't have to spend as much on ketchup, mustard, and other condiments, and all the sauces used to give flavor to flavorless foods.

Some of my customers have started gardens because they've observed that their youngsters will actually eat good fresh vegetables. Not long ago, *Consumer Reports* analyzed the offerings at a sampling of all our leading fast-food chains—the ones where youngsters like to eat.

The study showed that the nutrients most commonly in short supply in a meal served up at McDonald's, Kentucky Fried Chicken, or Hardee's were biotin, folacin, pantothenic acid, vitamin A, iron, and copper.

Guess where your kids can get those nutrients? From fresh fruits and vegetables.

Apart from chains like Whole Foods, health-food stores often carry fresh vegetables, but the choice is usually limited to a few items, piled in there between the towering banks of vitamin jars, and for most budget-minded shoppers, the prices for organic foods are just too high.

Deprived of quality, on one hand, and of economy, on the other, it's not surprising that many families and individuals have turned to home gardening. Let me state the bind in another way.

We've reached the point where there is no way that large-scale growers—using chemical fertilizers, insecticides, pesticides, fungicides, and herbicides, and raising varieties suited to mechanical handling and processing—are going to be able to offer significantly better vegetables than are already on the market.

And it is equally unlikely that growers using nonchemical farming techniques on a smaller scale will be able to offer lower prices for their produce. In fact, I've noticed that even prices at farm stands, those traditional bastions of bargains, have skyrocketed.

All this leads me, somewhat indirectly, to the key question that every newcomer must face before the first assault on the earth in spring: should you garden organically, or should you garden chemically?

It is quite possible to garden productively on a small scale without the use of chemicals of any kind, as I've tried to demonstrate to customers in Nana's Garden. And I believe there is much more personal satisfaction to be gained by growing vegetables organically.

In recent years evidence has mounted that a lot of other people feel the same way. There has been a quiet counterrevolution in support of organic farming and gardening practices, a desire on the part of growers and consumers alike to take control of their food supply. Recent volumes like *Fast Food Nation* by Eric Schlosser, *In Defense of Food* by Michael Pollan, and *Animal, Vegetable, Miracle: A Year of Food Life* by Barbara Kingsolver have made Americans more

Organic Gardening, Energy, and the Environment

The Florida Extension Service has calculated benefits of organic gardening that go well beyond an individual's fresh harvest from the humble backyard vegetable patch. In the 1990s, in the entire state of Florida some 7,000 acres of land were dedicated to vegetable gardens. If only yard compost and animal manures had been used to condition and fertilize the soil in these gardens, it would have replaced between 25,000 and 50,000 tons of 6-6-6 chemical fertilizer. Each pound of nitrogen fertilizer manufactured from natural gas uses 31,870 BTUs, so each ton of chemical fertilizer replaced by yard compost and animal manures represents a savings of 456 gallons of diesel fuel in equivalent energy. If all inorganic fertilizers used in Florida's vegetable gardens were replaced in this way, the potential savings in diesel fuel could be in the range of 684,000 to 1,368,000 gallons per year.

aware of the rusty links in a national food chain largely controlled by corporate agriculture. Consumers are now more cognizant of the healthful and environmentally friendly alternatives offered by small, independent local growers and providers, including families who have decided to grow their own produce not only for reasons of better taste and nutrition, but to save money too—a motive not to be scoffed at in hard economic times.

The growing popularity of the various movements and organizations described earlier in this chapter attest to a broad underlying support for a new and better way of feeding ourselves. It's great to grow organic, but it's even better to grow *productively* organic—harvesting our peas and spinach, beans and broccoli, and corn and tomatoes as fast and as bountifully as we can. That's what this book is all about.

Chemical gardening is easier, and just as productive over the short run, regardless of what the more outspoken advocates of organic gardening may say on the subject.

However, as odd as it may sound, organic gardening teaches the *science* of gardening better than *chemical* gardening does. Dishing up 5-10-5 fertilizer from a 50-pound sack hardly stretches the mind or taxes the imagination. Building up the nutrients in your soil by organic means can—and does.

Attacking bugs or soil-borne disease with the appropriate insecticide or fungicide is a simple matter of spraying and hoping you don't kill too many bees and other beneficial critters in the process. Preventing these problems from occurring in the first place is a complex proposition involving thoughtful garden design, proper soil-enriching methods, and various other sound gardening techniques.

But why bother?

The answer to that is there appears to be another, deeper reason why more and more people are turning to vegetable gardening, and in this lies the attractiveness of the organic approach.

It's important for people to save money and to eat better—and maybe to get their teenagers to swallow something containing vitamin A.

But—if I read my customers right—it's also important for them to make contact with something as solid, vital, and challenging as the home-gardening experience. Verlyn Klinkenborg, who lives on a farm, said it well on *The New York Times* editorial page on February 15, 2009. "Part of the [economic] crisis we face is a sense of alienation and powerlessness," he wrote. "You don't meet many alienated gardeners, unless it's been a terrible woodchuck year."

Gardening brings people in touch with the realities of land and sky, heat and cold, rain, wind, and drought, and the life cycle itself. If you are lucky enough to be able to watch things grow naturally, these are wonders that are free for the asking.

As a devotional activity for mind and body, gardening beats TV, and it beats joining the therapy-of-the-month club.

People are tired of secondhand entertainment and self-absorption, fed up with the synthetic nature of many of the products and services in our culture generally, and anxious to exercise more control over their own lives.

Pardon the brief lecture, but that, it seems to me, is why they bother.

Productivity Is Growing $7,486 Worth of Fresh, Organic Produce

How many ripe tomatoes should you get off a single tomato plant? I ask that question whenever I talk to groups of would-be home vegetable gardeners.

Most people guess one or two dozen. Occasionally someone will boldly declare, "Fifty—but I know that's high!"

As a matter of fact, that's low. If your garden has a rich soil, your plants are properly spaced, and they get plenty of sun, each of your tomato plants should provide you with 60 to 90 tomatoes, minimum. One year I made a point to keep track of how much fruit I got off one of our plants. I harvested 158 good-sized tomatoes. That doesn't count a dozen green tomatoes I plucked off the same plant before the first killing frost in the fall.

I stake my tomato plants because I don't have the space to let them sprawl in all directions. Most home gardeners don't, either.

Another time I planted a pole bean for my then five-year-old son. I set it in a 2' x 2' elevated bed in a sunny spot and stuck a pole in the center. We watched it grow up the pole, and as the beans appeared, we started counting. We picked a total of 265 beans off the one plant. That's about half a bushel of green beans from a single seed. I'd never taken a census of beans before, either. I'm not sure Sal, Jr., was impressed, but I certainly was.

My point is, using sound gardening techniques under the right growing conditions, anyone can and should expect a bountiful harvest from his or her vegetable garden. From a single pepper plant, you should get 25 to 30 peppers. From a cucumber vine trained to a fence or trellis, you should get 50 cukes. From a 25' row of bush beans (the row you'd plant from a standard seed packet), you should get more than half a bushel of snap beans.

These estimates are not inflated. Indeed, the good veteran gardener will reap a bonus in many cases, thanks to the practical savvy that comes with being long in the tooth. He'll get 40 peppers per plant, 75 cucumbers per hill, and a bushel of green beans from the row.

I stress productivity here because it underlies my entire approach to gardening. When I was an infant, my mother—the Nana of Nana's Garden—used to carry me strapped to her back as she worked in our gardens and greenhouses. I got the distinct impression at a very early age that if there wasn't good production in the gardens, there'd be nothing to eat.

I guess I haven't shaken my very first impression about gardening. And I'm making the assumption that readers of this book are interested in getting the greatest quantity of fresh vegetables possible from the space available to them.

Now there are people who garden strictly for the fun of it. I had a wonderful customer for years who never cared about getting a lot of anything out of her vegetable patch. She always sent for the rarest and most difficult seeds you could grow. She was interested in the patterns she could create in her garden with different plantings. She would arrange a dozen baby-head cabbage in the shape of a heart, and sow ruby lettuce into a colorful knot pattern surrounded by flowering kale. Her garden was a canvas, and she was an artist creating all sorts of designs on it. This book would not be for her.

For those who do want to garden productively in limited space, there are three things to be noted right off the bat.

First, pick a spot for your garden that enjoys at least two thirds of the sunlight available per day. On the longest day of the year—June 21st—the sun is in the sky for about 15 hours. Your home garden site should get 10 hours of that sun. Early and late in the growing season, when the days are shorter—on April 1st and September 1st, say—your garden should get 8 of the 12 available hours of sunshine.

Newcomers to gardening are sometimes deceived by reading articles on growing vegetables in only 5 to 6 hours of sun. If you receive 6 hours of sun on the longest day of the year, it means you'll be getting only 4 hours of sun early and late in the growing season, when vegetables, though growing at slower rates, still need the sun.

Crops such as tomatoes never get to the fruit-producing stage under insufficient sun. You'll get plenty of vine and leafy growth, but few if any tomatoes.

Trying to grow tomatoes in an area with only 6 hours of direct sunlight per day is as futile as waiting for water to boil in a kettle you've set on "low."

Farmers, you will notice, do not locate their fields in 5 to 6 hours of sun. They plant away from the shade of trees and buildings. Why should a home gardener try to achieve something never attempted by people who have to grow things for a living?

If you can't get full sun, pick the spot where you get the most sun possible, even if you have to smother some of the lawn to do it. If all else fails, you can still grow plants that appreciate some shade, like lettuce.

Second, give your plants room to grow. This aspect of gardening is consistently underplayed in popular literature on the subject. In fact, the smaller the garden plans offered, the more vegetables seem to be featured in them.

Newcomers overcrowd their garden plots because they don't really appreciate the potential for growth and productivity that plants have. Not realizing they could get 12 eggplants off a single bush properly cared for, they double up and even triple up on the space available to them.

Instead of getting 12 eggplants from the 1 bush, they get 2 eggplants from 3 bushes that have not had the room to grow properly. And eventually they may write off growing eggplant as lunacy.

Third, don't grow corn, potatoes, winter squash, pumpkins, or melons unless you really have the extra space those particular crops require, or are prepared to cut down greatly on the variety of vegetables you're going to grow in your limited area.

On pages 224–225 you will find a plan for a general vegetable garden occupying approximately 3,000 square feet. In this relatively small area—a tennis court requires more space—enough vegetables can be raised to supply the needs of an average family of six for a year.

The more than 50 vegetables included in this plan produce efficiently in relation to the growing space they require. According to experts at Kansas State University, each vegetable requires anywhere from 5 to 15 square feet of space to supply the needs of the average person. By contrast, melons, winter squash, potatoes, pumpkins, and corn require 70 to 100 square feet to satisfy the same average eater.

The 2009 market value of the produce from this 3,000-square-foot garden, incidentally, is a whopping $7,486. (A chart on pages 216 to 218 in the Appendix itemizes the anticipated yields and the retail value.) Even if your garden is half the size, or smaller, your savings in dollars will be substantial.

That figure makes an impressive dent in the food budget for any family—and it is a conservative estimate.

I should add quickly that you're not likely to save that amount in your first year or two of gardening.

I have a realtor friend who managed to lose a bit of money—no easy task in raising vegetables—in his first venture into gardening. The following year the bottom fell out of the real-estate business generally, and he had a lot more time on his hands. He applied himself to the garden project and ended up supplying his family with an abundance of fresh produce.

Not only that, his vegetables took half a dozen ribbons at the local grange fair in the fall—to the consternation of some of the long-time exhibitors.

Finally, be aware that the bigger your garden and the better you get at gardening, the greater the burden you may put on the person who happens to be responsible for using, preserving, or freezing the fruits of your labors.

Come August and September, when tomatoes, eggplant, and squash begin to occupy all available counter space in the house, productivity will have its perils unless there is an amicable working relationship between gardener and chef. And if they are one and the same, scale back your output accordingly.

Alternatively, make a lot of new friends by sharing your abundance. Consider a CSA-type program of your own on behalf of a neighbor who may not be able to garden. Your local food banks would be delighted to receive your extra fresh produce. Our new community garden has two plots dedicated to food bank donations.

Or you may have to get out the Mason jars and preserve the excess harvest yourself.

Rabbits and Raised Beds

All gardeners have their distinctive techniques. I don't mean basics like full sunshine and proper spacing. I mean tricks or methods that set them apart from other gardeners. I'd like to let you in on mine, to show you how, when applied in conjunction with many basic techniques, they have helped three generations of my family get the most out of our vegetable plots. They are summed up in the chapter heading.

Rabbits: Those traditional enemies of Mr. McGregor and the rest of the world's salad gardeners happen to produce the most effective natural fertilizer for garden soils that is generally available. I wouldn't presume to force the use of rabbits on any newcomer to gardening. But as you'll soon learn, they're easy and economical to care for, and really more like pets than farm animals.

Raised Beds: I am less flexible about this. I would urge all new gardeners—and any veteran gardeners who've had mediocre results in their vegetable patches so far—to seriously consider elevating their gardens, because it greatly increases the chance for success and productivity.

In my case, rabbits have been an indispensable resource. There are alternative manures and soil amendments available to organic gardeners, but let me briefly make my case for the bunnies. I use nothing but rabbit manure to feed my plants. I spread it over the old garden in the fall, sprinkle the new garden lightly with it in the spring, and use it to side-dress some crops during the growing season.

Unlike most manures, rabbit manure is easy to collect and apply, being available in small, dry, nearly odorless pellets. More important, it is rich in nitrogen, phosphorus, and potassium, three elements essential for plant growth that no garden soil can do without.

No other common animal manure has the well-rounded nutritional content that rabbit manure has. Sheep manure, for example, is rich in nitrogen, but lacking in potassium. Horse and cow manure are low in phosphorus. Even if you had access to these bulkier forms of manure, to enrich your soil fully you would have to apply bone meal or dried seaweed, or a chemical version of these, along with the manures.

I raise several dozen rabbits to supply the manure needs of our model vegetable garden in Westport, our herb gardens, my own garden at home, and the many other growing projects that are part of our nursery operation.

Home gardeners wouldn't need such a pack. Once, for data-gathering purposes, I isolated three of the rabbits (normal-sized animals of 6 to 8 pounds, not dwarf varieties) to keep track of exactly how much manure they produced. It came out to about 6 bushels a year, or 3 wheelbarrowfuls, per rabbit. The manure from those three rabbits was all I needed to take care of Nana's Garden. So for every 500 square feet of garden, I always figure one rabbit. I've checked with commercial rabbit growers who sell or give away their manure to farmers, and they've confirmed that ratio. If anything, it's low, not inflated. Of course, you can never have too much good manure. Any surplus can always be used to feed your flowers, berry bushes, fruit trees, and shrubs. Sometimes I make manure tea with the surplus. I drop a spadeful of the manure into a five-gallon can, mix with water until it dissolves, and then apply to plants in the garden where needed. If you want to impress friends and neighbors with the size of your delphiniums or foxgloves, fertilize them with manure tea, and stand back.

Our business as growers dates back almost ninety years. My father raised rabbits and my grandfather raised them before him, for the cheap but effective fertilizer they supplied. We've tried chemical mixes, other animal manures, and various combinations thereof. But nothing has produced the bounty in our gardening projects that the rabbit manure has.

When the first showman pulled a rabbit out of his hat, he didn't know just how magical that creature could be. Your local feed store or county extension service are both good sources of information on raising rabbits.

Now, about the raised beds: I use these in all my gardens for the many benefits they afford the garden and the gardener. Perhaps the most important benefit is the greater yield you will achieve with this approach. In a traditional home garden, according to Ohio State's extension service, good management of crops may produce about 0.6 pounds of vegetables per square foot. Records of production over three years in a raised bed at Dawes Arboretum near Newark, Ohio, indicate an average of 1.24 pounds per square foot, more than double the conventional yield.

The best way to achieve elevated growing areas is to build perimeters for them with safe, durable materials. Any reasonably waterproof material that can provide a solid means of elevating and containing the garden area would do the job. It could be concrete blocks; logs of white oak, fir, juniper or locust; 2" x 12" cedar or similar hardwood planks; or some variation on the fiber-plastic building materials that have become available in recent years. Even makeshift materials like recycled barn beams, old diving boards, dismantled sandboxes or slides, and the like may also fit the bill. But avoid railroad ties and utility poles treated with creosote, which may leach into the soil to harmful effect.

You can avoid the expense and effort of creating beds with building materials if you like. The simplest raised bed is soil mounded to a height of 12" to 20" between two parallel furrows or irrigation ditches. Furrows also provide convenient walking space between planting rows. Not long ago, I employed this method in designing teaching gardens for a new school in my hometown of Easton, Connecticut. (The garden plan appearing on pages 234–235 depicts this raised-bed method.)

I believe that the raised bed is the most practical solution for growing vegetables productively in areas from 100 up to 3,000 square feet, which covers the range of gardens the typical family would need or desire.

Because I am making such a claim for the general utility and effectiveness of the elevated garden, let me list all my reasons why.

1. **It makes it easier to put the garden in full sun where it belongs.** Often people try to grow vegetables in old garden areas near which trees and bushes have grown up over the years. They do that to avoid the backbreaking labor of cutting up the lawn or digging out rocks in a sunnier location elsewhere. But you can erect a raised bed right on top of chopped-up sod or gravel.

2. **It gives you complete control over your growing medium.** What you are doing, in effect, is filling a giant sandbox with the exact soil mix your vegetable plants will need to flourish. The feeding range for the roots of your crops is greatly enlarged. Even if at the outset you must haul in topsoil, peat moss, sand, and manure to fill your new garden bed, it will pay off in extra produce at harvest time in the very first year. These don't have to be separate; soil mixes are available by the

cubic yard and truckload at a pretty reasonable price. We've brought in a local 3-way mix of topsoil, sand, and compost, and the plants are flourishing. Preexisting deficiencies and problems in the garden site won't impede or destroy the growth of the varieties you decide to plant. In situating ground-level beds, you need to be aware that nearby shrubs and trees can compete with crops for water and nutrients in the below-ground soil for a distance about equal to their height. Raising the garden eliminates this threat as a factor.

3. **It's easier to work.** You won't achieve an ideal growing medium overnight, but in the course of a year or two you will have the opportunity to gradually improve the tilth, or texture, of the soil until it is light and consistent throughout. Good tilth aids retention of the oxygen and water that plants need in the soil along with the nutrients. You'll be able to hand-till and cultivate a garden as large as 3,000 square feet because the soil will be so light and easy to work and the planting rows themselves will be easily accessible from either side.

4. **It improves drainage.** Water drains off the four sides of a raised bed as well as straight down. The added 8" to 12" of soil in good tilth automatically facilitates passage of excess moisture. Seeds and seedlings will rot in soggy or mucky ground. In a raised bed, you can eliminate depressions where water collects or high points where water is lost too quickly by building up one side more than another. And even if the surrounding ground is on a pitch, there won't be any soil erosion within the confines of the elevated garden. Also, your soil can be worked a bit earlier in the spring, because the sun warms it up faster when it's raised. This is a big plus in northern latitudes of the country.

5. **It's much easier to control grass and weeds growing around the perimeter of the garden.** Ordinary fences have more loopholes than a book contract. With a raised garden surrounded by a barrier, weeds are less likely to intrude. An

occasional stomping or trimming will keep them from ever growing up over the barrier.

6. **It creates an effective defense against many crawling insects, slugs, and snails,** which might otherwise devour your tender shoots and plant leaves. These creatures are lazy and usually choose not to mountaineer up 90° surfaces.

7. **It creates an effective defense against burrowing animals.** The mole has wits as dim as his sight. He'll turn around if he bumps into so much as a nickel in the course of his travels—this is why he seems to tunnel in pretzel patterns. Sinking your 2" x 12" cedar planks into the ground to a depth of about 2" all around will usually keep such creatures from feasting on vegetable roots or causing earthquakes in your new seedbeds.

8. **It makes it easy to fence in your garden,** in case you have to defend the place against preschoolers, or neighborhood cats and dogs, or skunks and rabbits from a nearby glen. Nowadays deer are Public Enemy No. 1 for gardeners in many locales, and fences can deter them. You won't have to dig post holes or drive stakes; simply nail your fencing to the solid perimeter material.

9. **It is neat.** The elevated garden can be an attractive feature placed anywhere in your yard, front or back. This helps if you have an aesthetic sense about the home landscape, or if you suspect that your neighbors do. Neatness generally stimulates better gardening, anyway.

10. **It is economical,** for a combination of reasons stated previously. It sets you up to get maximum yield from whatever you plant and to prepare and maintain the soil without having to rent or buy any heavy equipment.

Raise a couple of rabbits. Raise your garden. Raise your productivity. It's as simple as that. Almost.

More on Garden Architecture

The elevation of my gardens is the most distinctive feature in their design and, next to placing gardens in a sunny location, the most important.

There are three other features I try to include in the design of any vegetable garden, and I'd like to summarize them now. They promote healthier soil and growing conditions and so aid productivity in their own special ways.

LAY OUT THE GARDEN IN STRAIGHT ROWS
A neat garden pays off in two ways.

First, in planting the garden neatly, you'll use your available space more efficiently. Crooked rows force some plants too close together, and others too far apart.

You don't have to become a fanatic about neatness. I have one customer who lines up his long rows of tomato stakes with surveyor's equipment. Stand behind the stake at one end of a row and sight down it, and you won't see another stake.

With reasonable care and without too much fuss, you'll be able to plant according to the specifications of the different crops. You'll economize on seed and on space, and build a garden that's nice to look at, too.

The second benefit of the neat garden is that it makes it easier to cultivate and water plants when they need it. If you plant in a hit-or-miss pattern, you'll probably end up stepping on vegetables and starving some while you drown others. If the garden is designed neatly at the outset, you'll probably tend it properly throughout the growing season. Careless design invites negligence and indifference later on, and vegetables will not produce well in the wild state.

As you cultivate the garden, the soil around young plants remains properly aerated and free from weeds that compete for soil nutrients and sunlight. It also gets you inside the garden more often. So you'll stay abreast of caretaking and of any problems that may develop. You'll be more likely to know when it's time to hill the beans, or pluck the suckers off the tomatoes, or cut the lettuce before it goes to seed.

The well-run farms are generally the neat ones. Drive out into a rural area someday and you'll see what I mean. In early spring you'll catch the "neat" farmer out in the fields already, plowing under green manure (a grassy crop planted in the fall) and exposing the soil to the sun so it warms up sooner for an earlier planting. This farmer's barns and outbuildings and fences will, as a rule, be clean and in good repair.

Now try to find a ramshackle farm—one that needs paint, and maybe has the hull of an old Pontiac upside down in the barnyard. The farmer presiding over this estate won't even be in sight. Last year's cornstalks are still standing in the fields. Farming here is behind before it's even begun.

Lay out your garden rows on an **east-west axis** if at all possible. This way the sun, rising in the east in the morning and setting in the west in the evening, will pass over the garden in such a way as to shine evenly on all the plants in each row. Simply by locating your taller plants on the north side, as the days become shorter in August and the sun begins to fall toward the south, you won't have to worry about them shading shorter plants in the course of the day.

USE ONIONS TO GUARD THE GARDEN PERIMETER

Members of the allium, or onion, family of plants can act as a deterrent to a number of insects and pests that might otherwise cross over into your garden and cause trouble. White onions, yellow onions, Bermuda onions, Egyptian onions, shallots, leeks, garlic, and garlic chive all possess the same off-putting characteristics for bugs, and in most regions of the country there are no serious threats to the alliums from pests or disease.

I discovered the trick some years ago when I made a delivery to one of my customers. She had two small garden plots in her yard—an old one, and a new one a short distance away. To create a pleasing effect, she had planted chives all along the edge of the new garden.

It was July or August, I remember, for there were vegetables ripening in both patches. But there was one striking difference.

The old garden was crawling with aphids and cucumber beetles, and the insects were having a field day. But the brand-new garden, within its circle of alliums, was bug-free.

Since then, I've always planted onions of some type along the borders of my gardens as well as throughout. I don't think the onions alone are responsible for our relative freedom from insects and other pests. In fact, no general problem like bugs can have just one cure-all. The solution lies in applying a combination of good gardening techniques, and I've said as much when preaching the onion border to all my customers.

My mom used garlic chive for her borders. It's small, self-perpetuating (if you dig it up in the fall every year, break up the cloves, and replant), and quite attractive when in flower. The blossoms draw a lot of bees into her garden in the summer.

Any of the onions will do the job and provide you with a useful crop at the same time. The disadvantage in most "companion planting" of nasturtiums and marigolds and such is that you sometimes end up raising more companions than you do the vegetables you wanted to grow in the first place. Border-planting of alliums skirts that problem, and helps discourage the bugs, too.

DIVIDE THE GARDEN IN HALF

There are two reasons for splitting your garden in half with a walkway down the center.

The practical reason is that it creates shorter rows and provides you with more flexibility in planning. Shorter rows are neater and easier to maintain and irrigate, and you can get a greater variety of crops into your garden with them. The smaller root and leafy crops, like beets and spinach, can be planted quite effectively in short rows that are close together.

The more important reason is that side-by-side plots make it possible to rotate crops from year to year without having to resort to the protractor and compass. With two plots you can simply "flop" your garden map every year and meet the needs of crop rotation for most of the vegetables.

Why rotate crops at all?

Vegetables are living organisms planted in a soil that also consists of living organisms, and their interaction over a long period of time tends to bring out the worst in both parties.

Different vegetables take up different amounts of each nutrient, along with the trace elements contained in good soil, too. Beets need potassium to do well. If you planted beets in the same corner of the garden every year, eventually your beets would deplete the area of its potassium content. Even if you replenish the garden every year with manure or compost, that particular spot is going to come up short in potassium, and your beets are going to start coming out looking like radishes.

By moving the crop to a different location every second or third year, your beets will continue to get all the potassium they need.

Vegetables affect the presence of disease and fungi in the soil if the same varieties are grown there year after year. A steady succession of cucumber crops in one spot will encourage mosaic, a fungus that not only will destroy the cucumber crop when it appears, but will linger in the soil in that spot for many years to come.

Crop rotation is simply a preventive technique for keeping the soil rich in all plant nutrients and disease-free. A lot of the mental gymnastics that go along with crop rotation are eliminated when you plan the home garden in equal halves from the start.

Grow into Gardening

Because of the time and expense involved in serious gardening, I would like to suggest that newcomers consider applying themselves to the craft in an orderly and not overly ambitious manner.

I am prompted to propose a kind of three-year plan for becoming a full-fledged home gardener, because I have seen so many beginners fall flat on their furrows trying to do it any faster. That's why I suggest building a 400-square-foot garden for your first growing season, then adding to it in subsequent years. My garden plans depicted elsewhere in the book, the result of such an expansion, include a plot of approximately 1,500 square feet—big enough to feed a family of four with a few cousins thrown in.

A sensible game plan will save beginning gardeners much frustration. Many a novice has marched into our garden center on a sunny spring day and bought $80 to $100 worth of seeds and seedlings for a 10' x 10' area that has not yet been prepared and that gets half a day's sun provided the Winnebago isn't parked in the driveway and shading it.

This makes for a rough introduction to gardening. Next year, the novices appears at the shop in a new guise.

They have decided to become a specialist in one crop—usually tomatoes—on the hunch that if monoculture works for the big Midwestern grain farmers, it will work for them. Or they don't come back at all.

My three-year plan does not consist of hard-and-fast rules, or timetables that must be rigorously adhered to. I am merely tracing the broad phases of development that lie before you, and suggesting the order in which you should be able to tackle them with the best chance of success each step along the way.

YEAR ONE: Have your soil tested to find out if it's too sweet or too sour or if it's low in any nutrients required for good plant growth. Plan a small area for planting and give yourself plenty of room for everything you plant within that area. Remember, many people do just the opposite—tackle too big an area and then jam it with every crop under the sun. Acquaint yourself with the special growing conditions for your locale, and be sure to choose hardy, low-risk vegetables to grow.

Grow any of these vegetables from seed:

- Radishes
- Beans
- Beets
- Lettuce
- Parsnips

Grow any of these from seedlings or sets:

- Tomatoes
- Bell Peppers
- Onions

Build a compost pile from available vegetative waste materials and kitchen scraps. Expand the garden at the end of the season, if desired, and improve the condition of the soil.

YEAR TWO: Add maximum-production techniques.

- Feeding and/or conditioning soil for specific crops

- Border-planting of onions and garlic

- Interplanting

- Succession planting

Plant some of the harder-to-grow vegetables: ————————————————

- Peas

- Carrots

- Celery

- Cucumbers

- Squash

- Start some late crops from seed in a spare patch of the garden where early-season vegetables, such as radishes and lettuces, have completed their growing cycle. Plan to preserve/store some of your harvest. Expand the garden at the end of the season and improve the condition of the soil.

YEAR THREE: Plan a major general garden, using your available space and growing season to the maximum.

- Start some seed indoors.

- Build a cold frame.

- Experiment by planting at least one new crop or different variety. Expand the garden at the end of the season to the size that will meet your needs for the foreseeable future.

Breaking Even in the First Year

A longtime customer of mine named Leon Hunt used to say, "There's not a man on earth who can take care of a one-acre garden." By that, the veteran gardener meant, "Don't underestimate the work it takes to grow vegetables successfully."

Let's look more closely at the investment that serious gardening demands in money, time, and energy.

First, it's important to be realistic. Not a week goes by in the growing season without something to do or think about in the garden. If you are serious about raising vegetables, the time-and-motion study I provide here won't scare you off. Instead, it will give you a clear picture of the scope of the work involved and of the rhythm of the gardening year, and so, I hope, it may help you to organize your first efforts a little better.

Gardening literature generally minimizes the time factor and misconstrues the money side. I would like to be as candid as possible about both, in the belief that if you understand the precise practical challenge involved, you'll be much more likely to make a success of your own gardening venture.

I have one customer for whom money is no object. She sends her chauffeur 100 miles to our garden center to pick out all the largest potted, ready-to-fruit vegetables.

I have another customer for whom time is no object. He wouldn't dream of spending less than an hour in his garden before going to work every day, and this routine of his goes on from April to September. He patrols his garden when there's nothing else to do. He knows every pebble in the patch.

Most gardeners are limited by their bank account and also by the free time at their disposal.

Nevertheless, at first glance it would seem that—economically, at least—you would be foolish *not* to garden if you have the place to do it.

My 3,000-square-foot garden is designed to yield vegetables with an average retail value of $7,486, as I reported earlier. Total cost of the seed to plant that garden comes to about $295.

That works out to a return on your investment in seed of roughly 2,000 percent. You don't need *The Wall Street Journal* to tell you that's a good deal. But now let's look at your investments in other raw materials.

Let us suppose you had to start from scratch in building your garden the first year.

To create a raised, 400-square-foot garden where rocky or otherwise poor soil conditions have prevailed can be an expensive one-time investment.

The easiest way to build a raised bed is with 2" x 12" untreated lumber, as pressurized lumber is not suitable for organic gardening (or any gardening for that matter), due to the amount of toxic chemicals used in the manufacturing process. I suggest untreated spruce, as it is the least expensive and will last six to eight years.

In our area, untreated 2" x 12" spruce sells for about 90 cents a foot, bringing the cost for setting up a 20' x 20' garden perimeter to approximately $75. The cost of lumber could be substantially higher for hardwoods such as hemlock, white locust, and red oak—as much as $5 per foot.

To form the garden and hold the lumber in place, use 4" wood screws to secure the corners of the garden, and purchase ½" steel rebar, cut in 24" sections. Drive the rebar into the ground every 4' to secure the borders. The cost of the rebar should add another $25 to the project.

Filling the garden would require 10 yards of topsoil at $33 per yard and about five yards of compost at $45 per yard in our area, for a total cost of about $550. Prices for these materials vary by region. In California, for example, soil can be purchased for $19.50 per yard, compost for $16 per yard. Prices vary within regions as well, with metropolitan areas more expensive than rural areas. Lime and fertilization would add an extra $50 dollars to the bill.

Total cost of materials to set up a 400-square-foot raised garden in our area is about $550 to $600.

If you choose to eliminate the wood perimeter and build the garden by tilling an area and simply adding compost to build its elevation, you would need about 8 yards of compost plus the lime and fertilizer at about half the cost.

Larger gardens would cost the same proportionally—figure on $1,000 to $1,200 for a 750-square-foot garden with a wood perimeter, and $600 for one without a border. A 3,000-square-foot garden would cost about $4,000 with the wood materials, and about $2,000 for a borderless garden.

High as this sum may seem to you, bear in mind that you would get it back in fresh vegetables in the first year. Naturally, the less you have to fork out initially, the sooner your gardening enterprise will be in the black and the better everyone will feel. This may be even easier than you think.

Many gardeners wouldn't have to buy all or any of the topsoil, which is the most expensive single item in the budget. Some areas have plenty of topsoil. And within a yard area, topsoil depth can vary considerably.

Access to some local stable manure would also cut down on the initial investment. Nowadays there is so much equestrian activity that there may well be a horse stall in your own neighborhood. There are more horses in America today than at the time of Wild Bill Hickok, and they're no longer primarily found in rural areas, so their manure and associated bedding materials could well be a resource for many gardeners. Aged manure contains fewer weed seeds than the fresh stuff.

I haven't included the cost of basic gardening tools—rake, hoe, spade, wheelbarrow, and garden hose—in the gardening enterprise because they are probably part of your basic lawn and yard-care equipment already.

Of course, if you have a special hankering for tools and gadgets, you could spend a small fortune. One of my customers plows back all the profits from his highly productive garden into hardware. If he has a bumper crop of tomatoes, he translates it into its current retail value, then goes out and spends that amount on a gadget for the garden, especially if it's something that runs on batteries.

Now for the investment of *time*.

The actual person-hours demanded by home gardening is shrouded in mystery for all but those who have actually done it, and they know least of all how much time everything really takes, because they like doing it.

The job is spread out over such a long period of time that you'd need to punch a clock to keep track of all the bits and pieces of effort donated to the cause. And how to compute the hours spent daydreaming about the garden while en route to work, or standing in line at the bank for the cash to buy that beautiful English spade fork you saw at Smith & Hawken? Also, how to figure in the cheap labor you have managed to exploit in the form of children under age ten (who love to pick peas or dig potatoes if you make a contest of it) or friends and relatives who made the mistake of visiting the day you're turning over the garden for the first time?

I sat down to calculate how much work really goes into a garden the size of our 3,000-square-footer. This is a bigger plot of land than most home gardeners would farm, so don't fall off your chair as you review my month-by-month workload—geared, of course, to my particular growing seasons, frost dates, and ways of doing things.

Here's the breakdown:

January

- Sorting through catalogs, reading, planning, ordering seeds and supplies, drawing up the garden plan = 6 hours

February

- Sorting incoming seeds, preparing indoor sowing media and window space, more planning = 2 hours
- Sowing first crops indoors = half hour

March

- Spreading manure and compost = 2 hours
- Tilling with a machine (add 9 hours if you till the whole garden by hand) = 1
- General preparing = 1 hours
- Spring cold-frame work = 1 hours
- Sowing and tending crops indoors = 3 hours

April

- More cold frame activity = 4 hours
- Sowing, tending, and planting crops outdoors = 10½ hours
- Thinning and staking peas = 2½ hours

May

- Last of spring cold-frame work = 2 hours
- Sowing and planting last of major crops = 10½ hours
- Thinning and harvesting = 2 hours

June

- More sowing and planting = 3 hours
- Thinning, hilling, staking, and tying = 4 hours
- Harvesting = 3 hours
- Cleaning up after early harvests = 2 hours

July

- Sowing and planting succession crops = 5 hours
- Tying and hilling = 1½ hours
- Harvesting = 3 hours
- Cleaning up = 3 hours

August

- Sowing and planting fall crops = 4 hours
- Thinning and hilling = 1½ hours
- Harvesting = 4 hours

September

- Sowing and thinning = half hour
- Harvesting = 5 hours

October

- Harvesting = 4 hours
- Planting for next spring = 2 hours
- Cleanup = 4 hours

November

- Harvesting = 1 hour
- More cleanup = 4 hours

- Fall cold-frame work = 2 hours

- Spreading manure and compost = 2 hours

- Covering crops to remain in ground = 1 hour

December ——————————————————————————————

- Ordering seed catalogs, extension service literature, and so on
  = 1 hour

- Harvesting remaining leeks, endive, and so on, and placing in
  storage = 1 hour

In these calculations I haven't even bothered to try to account for all the time required to cultivate, water, fertilize, weed, and protect the garden. I figure this miscellaneous maintenance work would come to 15 minutes every day per 500 square feet of garden space. Time would vary according to individual expertise and experience. And the total doesn't include the time spent in the kitchen *after* harvesting—with a really big garden, there might be quite a bit of preserving and freezing to do.

If you are tackling a smaller garden area, one in the range of, say, 400 to 500 square feet, count on spending 2 to 3 hours per week working in the garden from April 15 to October 15 (the approximate growing season in my area). Add 2 more hours in the months of April and May to account for the time it takes to prepare your soil, sow seed, and set transplants.

Anyway, a few noteworthy matters are evident from this effort to do a time-and-motion study on gardening, and I could have told you about them without going to all this trouble.

Novices think there are two jobs involved in gardening:

- Planting

- Harvesting

But actually there are six:

- Planning

- Preparing

- Planting
- Maintaining
- Harvesting
- Finishing up

In the first year everything takes longer, especially planning, planting, and preparing. There is an outside chance that harvesting will not take longer, but that is only if you've been particularly careless or unlucky.

The bigger the garden, the more work there is. One-crop gardens take much less time than gardens with multiple crops. Patio gardens and container gardens often take more time than people realize, simply because their smaller soil base requires more frequent watering and fertilization.

So, as the saying goes, there's no such thing as a free garden. And I would have been less than honest if I did not make it clear early on that the maximum productivity I'm talking about depends in large part on your willingness to work in the garden a fair amount. But it is work you will enjoy.

How to Read Seed Catalogs

Seed catalogs are informative, entertaining, inspirational, and free.

They become available annually in that generally bleak December to January period when nothing is growing anywhere except in southernmost Florida, Texas, and California. Some catalogs also issue supplemental editions at intervals during the year, while others maintain an Internet presence with frequent updates and changes as the growing season progresses.

Send for these for the first time about the same time you mail your Christmas cards. Pick up a year-end issue of a magazine like *Organic Gardening* or *Horticulture* and you'll find dozens of free-catalog offers and coupons in among the ads. If you have Internet access, you will find dozens of catalogs on line. Or you can go by the address list of major catalogs in the Appendix. Some of the leading flower-and-vegetable seed merchants also carry young fruit and nut trees, berry bushes, strawberries, and perennials such as asparagus and rhubarb, and any or all of these items may also figure in your gardening plans now or later.

There's a rich mix of Americana, salesmanship, color, and facts contained in these catalogs. And by studying them with more than passing interest, you can improve your gardening IQ in several departments.

If you're a novice, you'll get to know all the vegetables simply by looking at the pictures. At last you'll be able to tell the difference between Bermuda onions and Spanish onions, celeriac and Swiss chard, zucchini squash and summer squash, Indian corn and sweet corn, kale and kohlrabi, globe artichokes and Jerusalem artichokes, spinach and New Zealand spinach, rutabaga and turnips, and parsnips and parsley. Beginners often mix up these last two for some reason. They come in to buy parsnip seed but ask for parsley, then return a few months later wondering why they have all this parsley growing in their garden.

By taking a bit more time to read here and there in the catalogs, you'll also get to know more about the immensely varied growing habits of vegetables.

You'll see that peas are frost-hardy and grow best in cool weather, whereas okra is frost-sensitive and thrives in the heat. You'll find out that some beans climb poles and others like to grow in bush form. You'll discover that vegetables have different maturity dates. Radishes are ready to eat in 25 days from sowing, whereas carrots take 90 days or more to fill out. Tomatoes, America's most popular vegetable, are available in varieties that mature as early as 55 days from transplant, and as late as 100 days. Most vegetables also come in a choice of sizes and colors. Burpless Hybrid cucumbers grow 10" long, whereas West India Gherkin cucumbers mature at 3"—perfect for pickling. You can raise yellow tomatoes and white eggplant if you like. There are red cabbages and green cabbages, green beans and yellow beans, yellow beets and red beets—and when it comes to peppers, every color in the rainbow is represented.

Nowadays, you'll also find that many vegetable varieties are available in dwarf forms. Seed growers have responded to the increase in the number of gardeners who by choice or circumstance are raising their food crops in smaller spaces or in containers. Tomatoes, cucumbers, squash, and many other varieties that thrive in confined areas have been developed by seed company hybridizers. Their names alone suggest their compact growing habit. At our garden center in Westport, for example, we offer Baby Bell eggplant, Pickle Bush cucumber, and Windowbox Roma tomato, among many other good things that come in small packages.

Incidentally, some standard-size vegetables, especially leafy crops such as lettuce, can be grown in smaller areas by spacing them more closely together, then harvesting them on the early side, before they reach full size. In fact, lettuces grown this way are often more tender and flavorful than their "adult" counterparts.

Like dwarf and compact varieties, heirloom vegetables have become popular in recent years. These are open-pollinated plants that have been grown and handed down from generation to generation, just like a family's heirloom grandfather clock. Heirlooms often come in unusual shapes and colors, and they have some disadvantages when compared with modern varieties. They produce less consistently and are more prone to disease and more perishable when ripe. For these reasons, many commercial growers have avoided heirloom vegetables, although some specialty growers have begun to offer them at premium prices, not only at farm stands and farmers' markets but also in grocery stores.

I'll never forget the time I visited Louie and Virginia Saso at their herb farm near Sacramento, California, in 1990. He showed me his "acre of paradise," a lovingly tended orchard of heirloom varieties of apricots, peaches, plums, nectarines, and other fruits. From the 1940s through the 1960s he had been able to sell these juicy, delicious varieties commercially, but that business went into decline with the introduction of fruit that looked better and lasted longer in produce bins, although in a taste contest Louie's fruit was the winner. A grafter extraordinaire, Louie proudly showed me a peach tree with five different varieties of the fruit growing on it. Yet hybridization had driven this master grower out of the fruit business.

I myself am a proponent of maximum productivity in the garden, but sometimes taste trumps practicality, as anyone will attest who has taken a bite of a flavorful heirloom tomato, for example. Indeed, if heirlooms belong anywhere, it's in the home garden, where they can be given individual TLC to minimize their shortcomings and celebrate their virtues. Which is why we offer a dozen heirloom tomato varieties for sale in the spring at our garden center, and another dozen or so Old World Italian tomato, pepper, eggplant, and zucchini plants.

One of our heirloom tomatoes is called Mortgage Lifter, a pink-skinned variety that produces large, meaty, and sweet fruit. Customers think I carry it for its name, so evocative of economic downturn, and not for its wonderful taste. In fact, this tomato came into being in West Virginia during the Great Depression. A fellow named M. C. Myles, known as "Radiator Charlie," who had his own financial woes in the early 1930s, developed the hybrid by crossing

Beefsteak, German Johnson, and several other tomato strains. He used a baby's ear syringe and pollen from the plants to cross-breed the granddaddy of heirloom plants. He sold seedlings at $1 each, and in six years he was able to pay off his $6,000 mortgage.

Heirloom vegetables are not just a gardening fad. Today, virtually all the seed catalogs carry at least a sprinkling of them. People enjoy including heirlooms in their gardens as a way of honoring and preserving our diverse garden heritage, and, of course, because they taste good. One seed dealer in Missouri's Ozark Mountains has gone so far as to establish an online museum featuring hundreds of vintage garden catalogs and magazines for gardeners to peruse and enjoy. Baker Creek Heirloom Seed Company, with its catchy motto, "Groovy seeds for all your needs," started in 1998, sending out its first catalog to 550 gardeners. It printed nearly 100,000 for 2009—and ran out before the end of January of that year.

The largest nongovernment seed bank is located on 890-acre Heritage Farm in Decorah, Iowa. Seed Savers Exchange, a nonprofit member-based organization, was founded in 1975 by Diane Ott Whealy and Kent Whealy. Their collection started modestly, with seeds gleaned from two plants from the garden of Diana's grandfather. The plants, Ott's Morning Glory and German Pink Tomato, were originally brought from Bavaria by his parents in the 1870s. Today, Seed Savers Exchange maintains some 25,000 endangered vegetable varieties.

Even as we embrace the vegetable varieties of our forebears, dynamic new forces in our culture are introducing us to previously unknown foods and flavors. The surge in our Hispanic population, and the parallel expansion of Mexican and Tex-Mex restaurants, has led to a rapid growth in interest in Mexican cookery and the inclusion in our gardens of such south-of-the-border favorites as cilantro, jalapeño peppers, ancho chiles, and tomatillos.

Asian varieties of vegetables and herbs are also enjoying growing popularity. Several factors are behind this development. There's been an increase in American travelers to the Orient, mainly to Japan, China, Hong Kong, Singapore, Indonesia, India, and Korea. Tourists invariably sample the cuisines of other cultures and take home fond memories of some of the dishes they've tasted. Also, the immigration of entire families from the Far East to the United States, especially on the West Coast and in large cities like Houston, along with the appearance of noodle shops and other Asian fast-food eateries, has accelerated the

Garden Catalog Lingo at a Glance

Novice gardeners may find it helpful to understand the special vocabulary that seed dealers and growers use to characterize their offerings in the pages of their catalogs.

Latin Names. Professional botanical identifications of plants are always given in Latin. Practically speaking, vegetable gardens are more interested in the traits offered by the varieties under the Latin rubric. The potato's formal name is Solanum tuberosum, but we select it for our gardens by its street names—such as French Fingerling, Russian Banana, Yukon Golf, Red Cloud, Cranberry Red, All-Blue, and so on.

Size. Seed descriptions include estimates of the height and width to which a given plant will grow in your garden. "Compact" usually means the plant grows more tightly and uniformly. "Dwarf" or "Mini" indicates smaller—sometimes much smaller— than standard.

Days to Maturity. This is the time from when it is planted outdoors to time of harvest. When direct-seeding peas and beans, for example, it means from the time of sowing. When setting out transplants of tomatoes or peppers, it means from the time the transplant is planted in the soil.

Exposure. "Full Sun" means the plant needs at least 8 full hours of direct daylight per day. "Partial Sun/ Partial Shade" means the plant will grow in 4 to 6 hours of sunlight per day. "Full Shade" means the plant needs less than 3 hours of direct sun per day.

Annual. A plant identified as an annual generally lives for only one year and is killed by the first strong frost.

Biennial. Biennial plants develop only their foliage in the first year, then flower and go to seed during the next growing season. Parsley, for example, is a bountiful provider of foliage for your cooking needs in its first season. Allowed to remain in the garden over the winter, it produces seed quickly in the spring and has no further leaf production.

Perennial. Perennials live for three or more years, often not flowering for the first season or two. "Tender" perennials, or perennials grown in areas colder than their recommended hardiness zone, are often treated by gardeners as annuals. In Zone 4, for example, rosemary and bay laurel die back to the ground after sustained freezing and must be replaced the following year.

Hybrid. Hybrid plants are crosses between two or more plants. Seed from hybrid plants will produce a not always desirable variety of offshoots with an assortment of traits from each parent plant. Hybridization itself sometimes sacrifices the more desirable qualities in plants—flavor in vegetables, for example, and fragrance in flowers like roses—in the quest for other qualities, like uniformity and durability for shipping.

Open-Pollinated. These are plants that have stabilized so that when you sow seed from the plant, the resulting seedlings will be identical to the parent plant in all important respects.

Heirloom. Heirloom varieties are all open-pollinated plants that have been handed down for generations. They usually taste better than hybrid varieties but are often less durable and productive in the garden.

Resistant. When resistance is claimed for a seed or plant, it implies that a variety has a certain amount of resistance when exposed to a disease-causing pathogen, such as a fungus, bacteria, or virus.

Tolerant. When tolerance is claimed for a seed or plant, it implies that a variety will perform relatively well when it is exposed to environmental stresses such as hot weather, cold weather, or drought.

Certified Organic. These are seeds harvested from plants that have been grown organically, that is, without chemical fertilizers and pesticides.

demand for crops such as napa cabbage, bok choy, bamboo shoots, water chestnuts, daikon radish, ginger root, bean sprouts, lemongrass, Chinese long bean, watercress, winter melon, and many other crops once considered exotic and now being adopted by restaurant chefs and the public. These varieties are now well represented in most U.S. seed catalogs.

Shopping through the seed catalogs in winter is better than buying your seeds off the racks in the spring for two reasons.

First, you have the leisure to compare varieties and consider the seed dealer's recommendations for growing each variety. Descriptions may occasionally slip into purple prose. ("Every succulent ear of corn has 16 rows of tender sweetness.") Seed dealers give proprietary names to their products. For years, Burpee has offered "Big" and "Better" varieties, as in "Big Boy Tomato"; Park Seed uses "Whopper" to distinguish its favorite tomato, pepper, eggplant, and melon varieties. Stokes has an "Early Bird" selection of peppers with names that denote their different colors—Canary Yellow, Dove White, Blue Jay, Blackbird, and Oriole Orange. Beyond the distinctive nomenclature, seed catalogs seldom fudge on such vital data as maturity dates, size, average yield, taste characteristics, resistance to particular fungi or diseases, and suitability for different climates and soil conditions.

The point is, all these factors take time to sort out, especially if you're still new at the game, and it's easier to do this at home. Only a real wizard could make an intelligent selection standing in the middle of the hustle and bustle of the typical garden center in spring.

Second, you have a vastly superior selection of seed varieties to pick from in the seed catalogs. Even large garden centers with many racks of seed packets from their main suppliers can't compete with the plethora of choices available via mail order and the Internet.

In their 2009 editions, for example, Johnny's Selected Seeds of Maine listed 68 different kinds of tomatoes and R.H. Shumway's of Wisconsin offered 49 tomato varieties and 30 types of sweet corn. The Burpee catalog for that year offered numerous bean varieties in these categories: green bush, yellow bush, purple bush, filet bush, Italian bush, soybean, lima, and pole. Elsewhere it listed 26 radishes in a rainbow of colors—white, red, red-and-white, pink, scarlet, purple, and lavender—and almost as many shapes—short and fat, lumpy and long, icicle-thin, and perfectly round. And it offered 28 hot peppers of varying degrees Fahrenheit, including "customer favorites," hot lemon heirloom, jalapeño, ancho, habanero, Zavory, and Biker Bill Hybrid ("the hottest we've ever tested").

The first time you sit down with a stack of catalogs, your eyes are likely to glaze over from this embarrassment of riches. But eventually you will appreciate the wide range of choices.

Seed packets do not cost substantially more off the racks than they do through the mail, nor is the seed at stores inferior in any way. But there is always the possibility that the type of seed you want won't be available from your local sources, or that it may sell out by the time you get around to shopping.

You need not be concerned about how much you pay for your seeds, as vegetable seed is surprisingly cheap. For $100 you could plant an acre of head lettuce, no matter what catalog you buy from. If you're a bargain hunter, you'll often find that smaller, less renowned seed companies give you more seeds per packet for the money. But you would probably have to order from a number of different seed companies to get a bargain on every single variety you wanted to plant, and the cross-checking and page-flipping might not be worth it.

Generally, you pay more for hybrids—the seeds that have been developed to resist various diseases, to produce earlier and bigger—and the newest hybrids are always the most expensive. New hybrids are protected by patent, like inventions; after a certain period of time has elapsed, other seed companies can get in on the action and offer those hybrids for as little as half the price of the original.

Price variations in seed also reflect how much money different seed companies invest in their hybridization trials, and also how much they spend in advertising and in producing the catalogs themselves. Some catalogs are printed on cheap stock, others are slick productions with thousands of full-color photographs.

By the way, not all hybrids attain the distinction of being picked up by other seed dealers, as were Burpee's Big Boy and Big Girl tomatoes, for example. Some hybrids obtain little or no public acceptance, and others become strictly regional favorites.

Some technical innovations in seed-sowing have had mixed results. Embedding seed in biodegradable tapes or disks makes it easier to distribute tiny seed like lettuces or carrots more evenly and efficiently. In my experience these products do not attain the same high germination rate I obtain when sowing seed in the tried-and-true fashion. The pelleting of such seed looks more promising, however. Pellets are made of inert materials and clay and do no harm to seeds or soil. As the pellets absorb moisture, they split open, allowing the seed to germinate. New gardeners, who are usually shocked to see how miniscule are the flakes that pass for lettuce and carrot seed, may be willing to pay the higher price that pelleted seed commands.

Buying seed in quantity, possible only by ordering through the catalogs, can save you a few dollars. But unless you plan to use all of the seed right away, or really know how to store the leftover seed properly, or have a neighbor to share the seed with, this practice doesn't make sense for the home gardener.

I suggest that you order a lot of the catalogs in your first couple of years of gardening, just for the fun of it. Eventually, you'll probably settle on one or maybe two of them to order from consistently, going by price, or the selection of varieties suitable for your region, or the kind of quality and service you've received in the past.

Another reason to shop by catalog is to take advantage of promotional coupons and seasonal specials. This applies especially to online versions of the catalogs, so conducive to daily adjustment of terms and deals. As a lifelong retailer, I can tell you that cash flow is a beautiful thing in the months of February and March. Seed companies will do almost anything to get your business at this time of year. With a minimum order for seeds in the range of $25, Burpee will send a free bag of organic fertilizer, and Farmer Seed of Minnesota will dispatch free bulbs and daylilies. Other companies simply give cash discounts or include packets of flower or vegetable seeds with your early order.

Seed dealers are scientists first, merchandisers second, or maybe it's the other way around. In any case, there are lots of offers for the thoughtful gardener to consider in the world of seed catalog shopping. The venerable Stokes (founded 1881), for example, offers its Wedding Favor Forget-Me-Nots program—flower seed packages printed with the message, "Let the memory of our Special Day blossom in your garden," along with space for the newlyweds to print their own names and the date of their wedding. Price: $1.25 per packet, minimum order 25—and that's still a lot cheaper than the five-tiered wedding cake.

Lately, seed dealers have begun to stress more "how-to" in their vegetable sections, no doubt in response to the resurgence of interest in backyard gardens generally. Most of them now offer fairly detailed cultural information on all the crops, in layperson's language rather than in the farmer's technical shorthand. Some have added special illustrated sections devoted to planning and growing gardens of all kinds. With typical Yankee forthrightness Stokes reviews all the materials used for starting seed indoors. Thompson & Morgan includes "nourishment content charts" for each vegetable as an aid to those who shop with vitamins and minerals in mind.

Stokes also has an "Ask the Expert" feature permitting customers to e-mail questions about their gardening problems and challenges to a panel of knowledgeable growers. Farmer Seed offers its "Garden Planner," to which gardeners can submit specifications about their needs and desires and receive practical suggestions in return. Other seed companies provide tips on cooking with herbs and vegetables. Nichols Garden Nursery of Oregon has a blog called "The Gardener's Pantry" (http://nicholsgardennursery.wordpress.com/), in which recipes are posted for everything from roasted beets to barbequed pinquito beans.

The sheer readability of some catalogs should not be overlooked. Seed dealers that go back years and years often proudly include their checkered company histories along with their product descriptions. In recent years, Burpee has maintained an online photo album featuring hundreds and hundreds of pictures of its customers and their gardens. I came back from a recent perusal of this site with some favorite images: a small boy standing next to a 10½' sunflower; close-ups of vegetables in the garden of one Dwayne Bauknight, including a shot of Dwayne's cat "on mole patrol"; a tricolor collie with a carrot in its mouth; a close-up of Paul Marincic's specimen beefsteak tomato along with the blue ribbon it was awarded; and beautiful shots of the hummingbirds and butterflies in the garden of one Patricia Landry.

The smaller seed merchants can't afford to produce lavish volumes, or maybe they just prefer not to take the Madison Avenue approach. But their catalogs also have charms—black-and-white snapshots of warehouses and trial fields, views of satisfied customers holding up heavy cucumber yields, and photos of the owner's broadly smiling nephew or granddaughter about to tear into an ear of corn, to name just a few.

It's good to read the catalogs to find out what not to try to grow, too. Almost all of them reserve at least a page for such novelty plants as dwarf banana trees and gourds shaped like penguins, none of which aid the cause of garden productivity very much.

And there are always pages featuring the latest implements for home and grounds. Among my favorites in this category are the towering luxury hotels for purple martins—the birds with the insatiable hunger for mosquitoes—and traps for catching raccoons and other pests without hurting them. I've never seen these guilt-free traps advertised with tips on what to do with the animals once you've caught them, however.

And of course there are the flowers—which always take up more pages than the vegetables, because there are more of them, and also because there is a greater profit margin in selling them. I include flowers in some of my garden plans, as will be seen shortly, not only for their beauty, but because their very presence motivates gardeners to step into their gardens more frequently, and thereby encourages them to stay abreast of what is going on with their vegetables, which are the real money crop.

Another advantage in growing flowers is that it ensures that our gardening efforts are devoted not just to filling our stomachs, but to satisfying our souls as well.

Other Sources of Gardening Savvy

There are a number of other sources of gardening information, besides seed catalogs, that you're going to encounter by chance or design in your foray into vegetable gardening.

Let's look at the most common sources and point out how to make use of them most effectively.

LOCAL GARDEN CENTER

Not to toot my own horn, but a potentially great source of information is a garden center that caters to the small vegetable gardener. You have to find the experts on the staff, not the part-time help with their eye on the clock, or the kid who carries the peat moss out to your car.

Many places specialize in flowers and house plants, or in trees and bushes for landscaping, not vegetables. Of course, any kind of grower automatically knows quite a bit about conditions for gardening in his area. But most of them won't have the patience or desire to spend much time with you once they know you're only good for two $3.49 seed packets.

Some in the general nursery trade are a bit cynical about their vegetable trade. A couple of years ago, I went to a meeting of growers from all over the country. I suggested to one of the leaders that the group create a small guide to growing vegetables that we all could pass out to our customers, so newcomers to gardening didn't plant their tomatoes 6" apart, as they insist on doing every year.

"Are you kidding?" he said. "If they knew how far apart to plant, we wouldn't do half the business!"

In most garden centers, seed racks are usually set up and filled with the new year's offerings by the end of January. That's a good time to come by if you're looking for free advice, too. By spring even those places that cater to vegetable gardeners have just too many customers to give you more than a few minutes' time.

All during May, I'm too busy to stop for lunch, never mind sit down and design a fellow's complete garden for him. You might be able to corner me for fifteen minutes if it happens to be a cold and rainy day in the spring, but don't count on it. I might have a lot of work in one of the greenhouses. You'd do better dropping by in the winter, anytime after the holidays.

NEIGHBORS

The recently renewed spirit of sharing among home vegetable gardeners hearkens back to the World War II days of Victory Gardens, and earlier times when people relied more on growing their own and neighbors helping neighbors. Some neighbors are once again talking about vegetables, trading seeds, supplies, and suggestions with each other. "I'll give you two dozen of my John Bear tomato seeds for fifty frying peppers." "You let me start my eggplant in your hot frame and I'll let you have all the chicken manure you'll ever need." "I'll help you dig the trench for the asparagus if you tell me how you got so damn much zucchini last year."

Sadly, most of those who tended a World War II Victory Garden are no longer with us, but a later wave of gardeners can be tapped for advice. They are the back-to-earth Woodstock and *Whole Earth Catalog* generation of the 1970s. Not all participants in the Age of Aquarius were rebels without a cause. Many were genuinely interested in forging a lifestyle based on honest values, including natural foods; they became expert organic gardeners long before it was the fashion. So if your neighborhood includes an aging hippie with a vegetable patch, ask him or her how the garden grows.

There's an old Italian expression that my mother often invoked to explain this phenomenon: "Nobody is going to tell you that your face is dirty—because if you wash it you might look better than they do."

Unfortunately, many neighbors in our area don't get to know each other the way they used to and there are fewer opportunities to communicate. Just before Christmas, a couple of snowstorms fouled up our delivery schedule and inadvertently revealed to me how far apart people have become, at least in some of the suburbs of Connecticut.

One of our drivers took a dozen roses to a dead-end street with seven houses on it. He didn't have the house number for the addressee—we'll call her "Mrs. Brown"—so he inquired at the first house he came to. But no one there had ever heard of the Browns. He went from house to house without success, before by process of elimination he deduced where the Browns lived.

"When'd you move in?" my driver casually asked when he finally was able to hand over the roses to Mrs. Brown.

"Two years ago; why do you ask?" she said.

That same week I tried to drop off a poinsettia for a customer on my way home from work one night. Her house was dark, so I went next door.

"Say, can I leave this plant here? It's for your neighbor."

"Yeah," said the man who had answered the door, "if you get an affidavit signed by her that says it's all right."

When there is no love lost between neighbors, obviously there is very little knowledge of gardening to be shared, either. Personally, I think gardening can and does improve neighborhood relationships and friendships, but the gardens have to be there first.

Anyway, if you can locate an old-time gardener who's friendly and talkative, by all means listen to her and ask her questions, even if she's hard of hearing. Do everything she does, and you'll have a good garden.

GARDEN CLUBS

Garden clubs, 4-H clubs, and horticultural societies can be a source of helpful information. If you're a beginner, the topics at meetings may be too specialized for you to understand or care about. But some clubs organize programs devoted exclusively to vegetables, and those you could enjoy and benefit from.

Men's garden clubs tend to take a greater interest in vegetables than women's garden clubs—at least that's been my impression. There's one here in Fairfield County made up largely of men who are gardeners on big estates, and they really know their stuff. And they lack the spirit of rivalry that I sense in some of the more specialized clubs, where the issue of who has the pinkest tea rose can arouse great emotions.

Interestingly, those who can most easily tolerate high food prices—I mean the wealthiest class of people, such as those who employ my friends in the men's garden group above—never really stopped raising vegetables for the home kitchen, as did so many families, after World War II. Of course, they never had to do all the work of the garden, either. But if you've ever wondered where on the social ladder your craving for good fresh produce belongs, now you know. It is an Upstairs taste.

NEWSPAPERS AND PERIODICALS

A good, locally authored gardening column in the newspaper provides a great service, because it deals with the realities of gardening in the circulation area of that particular newspaper, so it must contain some facts or tips that pertain to you. Even if it's a mixed bag of advice on flowers, shrubs, indoor plants, and vegetables, it's worth plowing through, if only for the reminder that next month is March.

Beware of the general newspaper or magazine stories intended to inspire you to grow vegetables in areas where you get more shade than sun, or to plant pumpkins and corn as part of a postage-stamp-size garden plot. Reporters who are not gardeners themselves seem to gravitate toward those two themes in particular. They consistently oversimplify gardening techniques and underestimate the time and work involved in raising plants of any kind.

Even their dazzling color pictures are sometimes suspect, as I found out one day when one magazine happened to send a photographer down to Nana's

Garden. He needed a large number of geraniums to make part of a photo he was planning to illustrate something about patio gardening. Anyway, before he left he had broken off the flowers from the majority of the plants he had bought and stuck them in the soil in the remaining ones. I'm sure it made a nice effect for the layout—but a rather misleading one.

I myself enjoy reading some of the chatty success stories in *Organic Gardening* every month. *Martha Stewart Living* regularly addresses gardening topics in great detail. Before she moved away from her longtime residence in Westport, Connecticut, Martha was a regular customer of ours, and I can vouch for her enthusiasm for gardening and vast knowledge of the subject. I'll never forget the day I happened to be on hand for a photo shoot in one of the many gardens she had built at her home on Turkey Hill Road in town. Martha was on her hands and knees in the garden, ready to be photographed in action, when the art director called a halt to operations and instructed an underling to remove a rake from the background of the scene being shot. "Leave the rake where it is," Martha insisted. "Rakes belong in gardens."

Several other publications merit mentioning. I subscribe to *Horticulture*—a quarterly devoted primarily to flowers, shrubs, and trees—for its occasional in-depth treatment of different aspects of vegetable gardening. *Gardens Illustrated*, a British magazine appearing ten times annually, also concerns itself more with flowers than with vegetables, but its photography and artwork are outstanding. Indeed, it treats gardening as an art, with much emphasis on design and visual effect. Fabulous gardens, antique and modern, are featured in its pages, most of them in Great Britain, with occasional forays to Europe and elsewhere. Botanical information on plants is precise and detailed, as might be expected from the Brits, who have long been obsessed with their gardens. The word "eccentric" is overused when it comes to the character of the English people, but the magazine's profiles of garden experts and authorities may cause you to resort to that description. To subscribe to the magazine in the United States is a fairly expensive proposition, so you might consider taking it just for a year—the content is so rich it bears rereading, anyway, so ten issues may inspire you for several years.

Going from the sublime to the straightforward, I recommend an American quarterly called *GreenPrints*, subtitled The Weeder's Digest. Each issue offers a collection of short musings by amateur gardeners or writers who know gardeners and have been affected by them. A woman pays tribute to her mother, who gardened with great gusto into her eighties. A man procrastinates on raking his yard in the fall, estimating there are a half-million leaves on the ground, until high winds blow them all into the neighbor's yard—but that's okay, the neighbor has a "thermonuclear blower" to get rid of them. An elderly couple is given permission to adopt two children who have been abandoned by their mother, after the adoption agency gets a tour of their vegetable garden and is impressed by the couple's dedication. In short, these are uplifting pieces that remind us of the importance of gardening with heart and humor.

Another quarterly, *The Heirloom Garden*, runs about a dozen articles per issue on all aspects of vegetable varieties and history, organic cultivation, antique flowers, seed saving, and other topics. A recent piece on bok choy, by Debbie Leung, a farmer in Olympia, Washington, gives a clear description of this tasty Asian green in the Brassica family (described as "poor people's food" and similar to mustard greens), with good information on growing it as an early spring or fall crop. Topics covered in the Summer 2008 issue include produce in Mexico, tomatoes, salsa recipes, gardening in the Southwest, making herb jellies, and how to build a cold frame. The magazine has been published since 2003.

The U.S. publication *Fine Gardening*, appearing six times a year, addresses all facets of gardening, and on the occasions that it features vegetables and herbs it does so thoroughly. To say it takes its subject seriously is an understatement. For example, it has created an online pronunciation guide to botanical names in Latin. If you don't know how to pronounce peppers (*Capsicum annuum*) or black snakeroot (*Cimicifuga racemosa*) in the language of Roman emperors, just click on this site and listen.

THE INTERNET

I've already mentioned that virtually all seed companies and garden supply firms of any size have sites on line, not only useful but in many cases economical for ordering garden seeds and supplies directly. Publications aimed at gardeners also have websites. Many local nurseries and garden centers also now have a presence on line. The USDA's cooperative extension network has offices in every state, usually on or near the campus of a major land-grant university. Each office maintains a website full of valuable information on plants and techniques. Like politics, to borrow the phrase from Tip O'Neill, all gardening is local, and state extension services can be immensely helpful to gardeners as they deal with the climate and soil conditions particular to their area.

To give just one example of the breadth of information that may be useful to gardeners on line, consider the website for the National Gardening Association (www.garden.org). This is a nonprofit group, based in South Burlington, Vermont, that since 1982 has promoted home, school, and community gardening. Its website is chockfull of how-to and how-not-to ideas and information for gardeners. Some 750 gardening articles, clearly and cogently written and presented, are posted here. It has plant care guides for 100 popular perennials, bulbs, vegetables, and herbs. It has a "weed library" with color photos of every weed likely to invade your garden, from crabgrass to prostrate knotweed, along with tips for getting rid of the weeds, including the use of organic herbicides based on clove oil, acetic oil, citric acid, and soap.

Garden blogs on the Internet can be informative and entertaining—or useless and vapid. It all depends on the gardener doing the blogging. Garden Variety (http://martyross-gardenvariety.blogspot.com/), by syndicated garden columnist Marty Ross, is always fun to read. Ms. Ross wrote a wonderful tribute to her Great Aunt Monnie when that woman, a lifelong gardener and birdwatcher, died on her 110th birthday. At the graveside, she arranged for friends and relatives to scatter bird seed over Aunt Monnie's final resting place. Another well-written blog called shirls gardenwatch (http://blog.shirlsgardenwatch .co.uk/), originating in Perthshire, Scotland, is by another woman as smitten by birds as by gardens. It's illustrated with color photos of her own garden and the many public gardens she has visited in Great Britain and Europe. Closer to home, Hanna of Cleveland, Ohio, has created the blog This Garden Is Illegal (www.thisgardenisillegal.com/). What the blog's name means isn't really clear, but we do know that Hanna has a problem with deer, which she calls "overgrown garden rats with long legs." Her blog features a multiple-choice quiz that purports to identify what you would be if you were a flower. I answered the twenty questions and was turned into a snapdragon. My wife, Marie, took the same quiz and came out a canna lily (a flower she does not like!).

The garden blogosphere is a here-today, gone-tomorrow phenomenon—you may locate a favorite blog or two, but you never know how long they'll keep on blogging. All told, however, the resources on the Internet, accessible at the stroke of a key or the click of a mouse, are truly staggering. I recently Googled "tomato" and was presented with 38,100,000 entries.

And that's the problem. Too much time spent surfing the net may eat into the time you should be using to take care of your nonvirtual garden—the one in the yard, with the real soil and the real tomatoes.

COMMUNITY GARDENS

Community gardens are sets of small garden plots for people who live in apartments or for people who don't have the sun or space in their own yards to raise vegetables. Usually towns or businesses provide the acreage and a group of interested gardeners keep the thing organized.

Even if you're able to grow vegetables on your own land, you might be able to learn quite a bit by visiting a community garden, if there's one in your area. (Write to American Community Garden Association, 1777 E. Broad St., Columbus, OH 43203-2040, or visit www.community.org, for more information on this concept and how it is actually working out in different locales.)

The gardeners at such places seem to be a sociable lot—unless someone is growing corn in the plot just to the south, thereby shading the neighboring plot. And as they've all taken the trouble to set up shop at some distance from home, you know they must be serious about making things grow.

At one time, Westport had a community garden consisting of about eighty 20' x 40' plots on town land on a hill behind the local high school. In only its second year of existence, it enjoyed about 85 percent success: all but a dozen plots were fully gardened throughout the growing season.

The high location of the gardens was a problem discussed at one of the meetings of the group that I happened to attend. Various elaborate irrigation proposals were debated, but these were dismissed as an unnecessary expense. It was decided that everyone would just have to drag pails of water up the hill.

At this point an older gentleman with fine, weather-beaten features stood up and cried, "No need to carry water! Just spread more potash. That's it, potash!"

And he sat down again.

When the puzzled murmurs died down, someone else got up and explained that potassium encourages root development in plants. With stronger and deeper root systems developed as a result of heavier applications of potassium, the plants would be able to find more water for themselves.

That's what I call gardening with the head.

Ask Uncle Sam

The job of the U.S. Government's Cooperative Extension Service is to conduct research and advise the public on a wide variety of matters, mainly in the domain of raising plants and animals.

Operating through more or less autonomous state units, cooperative extension has been in business since 1914 and has accumulated a mass of technical knowledge and expertise. Much of this is useless to the average citizen starting out in gardening, but a tiny fraction of it is quite relevant and may be absolutely indispensable.

This is true especially if you're one of those millions of Americans who move to a different area every four or five years. The state service can supply precious orientations for those who have to play residential musical chairs.

The addresses and telephone numbers for the main extension service offices in each state are given in the Appendix. About the time you send for your first free seed catalogs, you should also drop a note to your own extension service headquarters requesting copies of all their published material on home vegetable gardening. (Underline "home" so you don't get deluged by technical bulletins strictly for large farming operations.) Or call your county agent, who will be listed in the phone book under "Cooperative Extension Service." Ask the agent for a list of available publications and services. The various brochures, pamphlets, and flyers are usually free to residents of the state, or available for a nominal charge. Most of them are also available on line.

What you get back in the mail seems to depend in part on the imagination and depth of the extension service staff in your particular state. Many of the services furnish quite detailed material in an interesting format and style. New York, Pennsylvania, and Illinois present excellent general approaches to vegetable gardening. The extension service at New York's Cornell University has developed a home gardening website with planting guides for fifty-eight popular vegetables. It also features an interactive "citizen science" program, which allows browsers to view ratings and read reviews of vegetable varieties submitted by other gardeners in their area before deciding what to grow in their own gardens. For something completely different, North Carolina offers a Master Beekeeper Program, the oldest continuously active program of its kind in the United States, with over 3,500 individuals enrolled at various levels of training and expertise.

Publication No. 8059 from the University of California, "Vegetable Garden Basics," is a thorough examination of what it takes to grow your own food. Extension services in Mississippi, Nebraska, and Colorado have each developed snazzy and informative fact sheets on all the individual vegetables, as well. Oklahoma offers numerous sharply focused "white papers" on different aspects of gardening. New Jersey has a handbook showing all the major plant insects in blazing color. Georgia gives the pros and cons on more mulch materials than even Ruth Stout (the high priestess of mulching in the 1960s) knew about. Illinois publishes a guide to growing plants indoors so thorough and accurate that with it in hand you could go into the greenhouse business.

At a minimum, expect to receive from your own service a precise description of the major local climate and soil conditions that will affect your plans for gardening and a current list of the recommended vegetable varieties for your region. You really should have both these areas of information firmly established before you sit down to plan your own garden.

Frost dates are a function of latitude, mainly—the farther north you are, the shorter your growing season. But there is always a range of growing seasons even within one state. You can plant beets safely as early as mid-April in eastern Nebraska, for instance, but it doesn't warm up enough to plant them until two weeks later in western Nebraska. You can start sowing seed on the Virginia coast a whole month earlier than you can in Oklahoma, even though Virginia is about a hundred miles farther north. In some parts of New York, the first frost in the fall descends on crops before September 10th, and in other parts, not until six weeks later.

The extension service keeps close records on all these annual occurrences in nature in each state and can supply you with the resultant "average date of last killing frost" in the spring and "average date of first frost" in the fall for your locale. These are the dates that will effectively bracket most garden activities in your area.

It's not a bad idea to double-check these dates by consulting veteran growers in your neck of the woods. In any case, adjust the dates by a safety margin

Hardiness Zones in the United States

The USDA publishes a Hardiness Zone map that reflects the range of temperatures in the country. The map divides North America into eleven separate zones. Moving from south to north, each zone is 10 degrees colder in an average winter. (Within zones there are areas designated "a" and "b," with 5-degree differences.) The map focuses on low temperatures rather than high temperatures simply because most plants are more sensitive to cold than to heat. The USDA map accurately identifies garden climates in the eastern half of the country, which is relatively flat. The lines between zones are drawn roughly parallel to the Gulf Coast every 120 miles. They tilt east as they approach the Eastern Seaboard. The lines also sway and swerve to take into account the special garden climates created by the Great Lakes and the Appalachian Mountains.

For half of the country, roughly through the middle of the Dakotas down to central Texas, the map is less useful to gardeners. Not just low winter temps but elevation and precipitation determine western growing climates. The weather blows in from the Pacific and becomes less humid and drier as it moves over and around mountain ranges. Cities in similar zones in the East may have the same climates and grow the same plants, but in the West there is great variation. Coastal Seattle and high-elevation, inland Tucson are both in USDA Zone 8, but their weather and their plantings are quite different. Even within your immediate growing area, significant variations in temperature and other climate factors can affect decisions about planting and caring for the garden.

Vegetable gardeners need not be overly concerned with ambiguous aspects of the Hardiness Zone Map. That's because most vegetables are annuals that kick the bucket at the end of their growing season no matter where they are.

of one or two weeks, especially the crucial spring dates, and especially if you're relatively new to the whole business. The average last frost for my locale is given as May 1st, but I work around a May 15th date to be on the safe side.

You may be surprised at the difference in temperature extremes that exist in different locations otherwise quite close to each other. Our farm in Easton is only 10 miles from our garden center in Westport, but we'll have early morning temperatures as much as 8 to 10 degrees lower than in Westport.

A climate map for your particular state will show these key frost dates a lot more accurately than the national map of climate zones that you frequently see in periodicals and other gardening literature because the national map is simply too big in scale. Anyway, too many people have their gardens exactly on those dotted lines that delineate the zones, so they can't be sure which one they're in. Many extension services include a county-by-county climate map in the literature sent out to gardeners.

Sometimes you may also get a map of the major soil types in your state if there happen to be substantial variations within your borders. That will give you an idea of exactly what lurks beneath that lawn of yours—and what, if anything, you should do about it.

Soils vary almost as much as frost dates. Florida soils usually need humus or other organic matter added to them because they're so sandy. New England soils are notoriously acid, so county agents in these parts harp on testing the soil periodically and adding lime to sweeten the ground when you have to. In some parts of Arizona, special watering techniques are recommended to reduce the excess of salts in the soil. In neighboring Nevada, soil tends to be deficient in calcium, an important element in plant growth, so calcium-rich gypsum is recommended as an additive.

There are also special pests, insects, and diseases that affect gardens in different sections. Maryland offers seventeen bulletins on pest control, including "Controlling Gypsy Moth Caterpillars with Barrier Bands" and "Got Bugs? Get Bats!"

Soil, heat, and rainfall—all these climate factors influence how well vegetables do, and they call for a host of specific gardening techniques. My dill reaches a height of 3' in summer, but in Florida it grows to 5'. In fact, almost all herbs that are grown and perpetuated as perennials in the South must be raised as annual one-shots anywhere in the North, simply because they can't survive our severe winters.

Peas—the English, or garden, peas that the Jolly Green Giant used to tramp through in TV commercials—won't grow in the sultry South, but black-eyed peas and cream peas love the warmer climate. In certain cooler, wetter corners of Oregon, tomato plants won't set fruit in spring and early summer unless you douse them with a commercial hormone preparation. In some parts you have to go around tapping the male and female blossoms of summer squash or you won't get any pollination or fruit. Tomatoes grow so vigorously in Mississippi that some gardeners succeed their first crop with a second crop, because the early ones get so big as to become unmanageable. In Montana, in contrast, there's hardly time to get the first crop of tomatoes ripened, and some gardeners clip off the uppermost young fruit toward the end of the growing season to hasten ripening of tomatoes lower on the vine.

Arizona's arid climate obviously favors plants that don't require a lot of water. Arizonans garden from almost sea level to over 7,000 feet, which poses two major problems: the hot summer at lower elevations and the cold winter at higher elevations. California is so vast and varied in terrain that its extension service has divided the state into three distinctly different growing climates. Farther north, the states of the Pacific Northwest offer gardening challenges— and opportunities—of their own. In Oregon, for example, winter gardening is possible in the mild winter areas west of the Cascades. With a little protection, cool-weather crops can be harvested throughout the winter. In addition, some fall-planted crops—notably broccoli, carrots, and onions—will grow slowly through the winter and be ready for harvest early in the spring.

The amazing array of purely local or regional factors affecting plant growth patterns has led to the development of varieties and hybrids for specific conditions. Varieties suitable for Oregon's aforementioned mild winter areas include Winter Keeper beet, Purple Sprouting broccoli, Jade Cross 'E' brussels sprouts, Danish Ballhead cabbage, Bolero carrot, Snow Crown cauliflower, Champion collards, Winter Density lettuce, Olympia spinach, and Perpetual Swiss chard.

To take one of the seed catalogs at random, here are the varieties of lima beans that were offered by Burpee in 2009:

- Florida Speckled Butter (Pole)

- Burpee's Improved (Bush)

- Baby Fordhook (Bush)

- Fordhook No. 242 (Bush)

- Big Mama (Pole)

To take two extension services at random, here are the varieties of lima beans recommended for growing in Connecticut:

- Fordhook No. 242
- Henderson
- Eastland
- Burpee's Improved

and in Alabama:

- Fordhook No. 242
- Baby Fordhook
- Henderson
- Caroline Sieva
- Florida Speckled Butter
- King of the Garden

These recommendations don't necessarily mean that any other variety will die on its feet in Connecticut or Alabama. In fact, a new or different variety may well be even more productive in some cases. But unless you can verify this from other sources, your best bet is to order one of the recommended varieties. You can be sure that these have already proved themselves extensively for gardeners in your region, or they would not be listed.

BETTER LIVING THROUGH CHEMISTRY?

Virtually all the extension services make the assumption that the home gardener desires to use—indeed, should and must use—chemical fertilizers to get good results.

Chemical fertilizers are the product of a variety of industrial processes. The combination of numbers on the packaging—"5-10-5" or "22-6-12," or a host of other combinations—represents the percentages of nitrogen, phosphorus, and potassium (or potash) contained in mix. They are also designated as N, P, and K—the chemist's shorthand for the elements. Organic soil amendments are also identified by their N-P-K content. Their numbers are always lower, but because the organic elements are absorbed more slowly by plants, they produce better long-term results.

In any event, extension service philosophy on the subject of chemical fertilizers generally coincides with that of the USDA, which administers the Cooperative Extension Service from Washington, and directs a lot of the agricultural research that goes on at our land-grant universities.

The USDA makes no apologies for its support of the use of chemical fertilizers, chemical insecticides, chemical fungicides, chemical pesticides, and chemical herbicides for increasing yields in large-scale farming. This point of view tends to hold sway throughout the extension services, too, whether the inquirer is growing vegetables commercially or not. However, I've been encouraged of late to observe a shift in this outlook, perhaps in response to popular demand. Many state extension services are now giving more emphasis to organic gardening techniques.

As I've mentioned, you can garden productively without using chemicals of any kind. Some of the extension services have acknowledged this possibility— or at least have acknowledged the desire of many individuals to try to garden nonchemically—by making available helpful guidelines on organic methods. Florida recently published a detailed treatise, "Producing Garden Vegetables with Organic Soil Amendments." Virginia has issued a bulletin on organic fertilizers, North Carolina a leaflet on composting for home gardens, and California a publication on the same subject, titled "Compost in a Hurry."

Other state services seem to have reacted somewhat defensively to the rise in interest in nonchemical gardening, and a couple of them have even printed elaborate critiques of organic methods. But the critiques take the stance that chemical farming is the only logical method for growing things because of increasing world hunger. Whether or not that stance is correct, it really has nothing to do with the home gardener.

The main reason such high-minded critiques annoy me is that in the guise of serving the public interest, some officials are in fact shunning their duty to serve the public by fairly describing the organic methods that can be used safely and successfully on a small scale. One author insinuated that improperly maintained compost piles can attract rats and that garden mulch can provide a hiding place for mice and also create a fire hazard. The innocent new gardener reading such a pamphlet might overlook the fact that these are far-fetched dangers, and thus opt for gardening with every chemical he or she can acquire.

But we don't need chemicals to get a bumper crop out of a well-gardened plot of earth, and we don't have to worry about rats and mice and gardens catching fire any more or less than chemical farmers do.

What I'm really saying is that you should make use of your extension service, but take some of the things they have to say with a grain of . . . sodium chloride.

II. How Vegetables Grow

Big Is *Not* Bountiful

When I was a kid, we had an old pear tree 20' from the garden that produced delicious fruit. One day in early fall, my Uncle Charlie was up on a ladder picking the pears near the top of the tree. The fruit at the very top was always the best, but it was also the hardest to get. Uncle Charlie reached a bit too far for one such pear on this particular day. I was standing nearby, and I saw him and the ladder teeter slowly but surely away from the tree.

"Uncle Charlie, jump!" I cried, aghast, but in the excitement of the moment my uncle held on to the ladder, and went all the way down with it—down into the middle of the squash patch in our garden, and that's what saved him. The sound of a dozen ripe zucchini going squish, and the sight of my uncle rising pale but uninjured from those bushes a minute later, his backside dripping with mashed zucchini, is something I'm not likely to forget.

Anyway, it's a fact that the fruit at the top of trees is always the juiciest and sweetest. Why? Because that's the fruit that's nearest to the sun. Which brings me to the subject of how plants grow.

Photosynthesis is Greek for "putting together with light," and it is the basic life process of all the green plants in the world, vegetables not excepted.

Chlorophyll in the plant combines with radiant energy from the sun, carbon dioxide from the air, and mineral-rich water from the soil. The result of this combining or manufacturing process is carbohydrates in a wide variety of edible forms. These carbohydrates are the basic foods for most higher forms of life. Without photosynthesis, there would be nothing to put on the table except mushrooms.

Good gardening might be described as anything that facilitates or improves the process of photosynthesis.

I realize you were probably taught all about photosynthesis back in sixth grade. I am refreshing your memory at this juncture only because I think it could help you to understand better and cope with the needs and growth patterns of your vegetables.

Why must the garden be in a sunny spot? So plants can absorb the solar energy needed in their photosynthesis formula.

Why should plants have the proper spacing? So that each of them has air circulation in order to get enough carbon dioxide (CO_2) through their pores to supply that element in the formula. (By the way, if there's any good in "talking " to plants—a practice that was all the rage years ago—it's not because the plants are listening to your sweet nothings. It's because you happen to be breathing CO_2 all over them.)

And finally, your plants must have access to moisture in the soil and to the various nutrients that the soil and moisture contains. In a drought, plants die even if they get all the sun and air circulation they need. If there's not a drought, they would still have problems if the soil was so hard and compacted that a root system couldn't develop, or so poorly drained that standing water rotted the roots away. The third basic ingredient in the photosynthesis formula would not be supplied.

Knowing why and how plants function at this basic level will help you care for your garden in many small and various ways. For example, if you see that bugs are eating holes in the leaves of your radishes, you'll react more quickly. Knowing that a smaller leaf surface will reduce the plant's intake of carbon dioxide, and so limit the growth of the radish forming beneath the soil, you'll take steps to eliminate the ravagers.

The concept of photosynthesis sheds light—if I may be forgiven one pun—on the main conditions required for productive plant growth. But it doesn't necessarily help you to grow individual vegetables productively, because plants go about achieving photosynthesis in many different ways, each way entailing different growing techniques.

In fact, if you provide the conditions for photosynthesis to take place, but then let the process go its merry way, you might well end up with nothing good to eat from your garden.

Let me explain this apparent paradox.

The drive of any living thing is to reproduce itself. The end result of photosynthesis naturally occurring in plant life is the production of seed for the next generation.

But seed is not always what *Homo sapiens* are after in *Petroselinum crispum* (parsley) or *Solanum melongena* (eggplant), or many of the other vegetables we grow. We plant corn and peas for the seed—for the kernels on the cob and the peas in the pod.

But we grow carrots for the root, asparagus for the stem, peppers for the fruit, and cauliflower for the . . . flower. It has been the business of seed dealers and growers to perpetuate the common vegetables in a manner that maximizes the quality and the quantity of that part of the different plants that the human palate likes the best.

If vegetables had been allowed to grow according to their own lights, none would be recognizable today, any more than Arabian horses would be if no one had bothered to breed them for the form of their head, gentle disposition, and endurance.

That Better Boy tomato of mine certainly would not have produced 158 tomatoes in its season of life a few years ago. A dozen tomatoes would have been quite enough productivity for it to meet its duty as a perpetuator of the species.

In other words, we facilitate the process of photosynthesis only up to a certain point. Then we step in and stop or divert the process, so we can enjoy the roots and tubers, the stems, fruits, and flowers, and in some cases the seeds, too, that make those plants desirable as a food crop in the first place.

If your lettuce bolts and your broccoli goes to flower, you've succeeded in providing the plants with the three fundamental elements required for photosynthesis to occur—sun, air, and water.

But you've failed to apply the techniques that would have prevented photosynthesis from helping the plants finish their life cycles. In these particular cases, perhaps you planted the wrong variety of lettuce for your climate, or put in the broccoli too late in the spring to prevent hot weather from rushing the plant to maturity. You've arranged for too much sun in the photosynthesis formula and the plants have gone to seed as a result, taking their good flavor and edibility with them.

Customers sometimes proudly bring their giant-sized zucchini or cucumbers into our garden center around harvest time, figuring they've stumbled on some new, award-winning approach to gardening.

Somehow, diplomatically, I have to explain to them that big is not bountiful. They should have picked that squash or cucumber long before it reached jumbo size.

Their mistake is not just that the big cuke or squash will be tough and bland when it is eaten. The real disaster is that the seeds within the fruit, having been allowed to develop fully, will have signaled "Mission accomplished!" to the parent plant.

And the plant, hearing it has succeeded in doing its bit to reproduce the species, will call it a day. It will stop producing.

Chaos in the Vegetable Kingdom?

The fifty-odd common vegetables that we use in the United States today originally came from the far-flung garden patches of the world.

Cucumbers started in India. Corn and squash were first domesticated by the Indians of Central America. Garlic is supposed to have originated in Southern Europe—Italy is my guess, naturally—and watermelon in Africa.

Some of the vegetables have been around for a long time. Peas have grown in Asia for more than 5,000 years. Others have only recently appeared on the scene, at least in a form you can eat. Tomatoes and potatoes have been cultivated for only a couple of centuries.

My point is that vegetables possess a broad range of distinctly different characteristics as a result of their diverse heritages. In terms of needs and growing habits, they all speak different languages.

Carrying this one step further, the way to get on speaking terms with all the vegetables is, first, to understand how they relate to each other generically—by "birth" or by botanical classification—and, second, to analyze the cultural factors that cause good gardeners to group certain vegetables together for practical reasons.

I think this twofold general orientation will help you appreciate the subtle differences in the life cycles of vegetables and make you more alert to the varied requirements of productive culture that we will spell out in much more detail later on for each variety.

There are eight different plant families represented in our three large garden plans—a 750-square-foot garden, a 1,500-square-footer, and a 3,000-square-foot plot that would perhaps be the ultimate kitchen garden. Any general garden would contain much the same cross-section of families.

Membership in the same family does not invariably tell the vegetable gardener a lot of useful information about raising the crop. But in many cases there are instructive similarities.

In fact, for purposes of effective crop rotation over a period of years, it is imperative to know the family groupings. That's because some of the families characteristically generate low fungus or disease tolerance in the soil if allowed to grow in the same spot every year. If you located your cabbage where your cauliflower grew the year before, you would not be meeting the aims of crop rotation, because, though cabbage and cauliflower differ ostensibly, they are in fact members of the same clan and interact with the soil in the same way.

Knowledge of how vegetables interrelate is also helpful in preventing potential problems of cross-pollination. Planting cucumbers alongside melons—both gourd family members—sometimes results in melons tasting like cucumbers.

Most families also act similarly in their absorption of the various nutrients and trace elements in the soil. And some families are susceptible to the same types of insects.

Let's quickly review the major families gathered in the garden.

Onions, shallots, leeks, garlic, and **chive** are in the *Amaryllis* or *Lily family*. We grow them all for their bulbs, stems, or both. Their early growth patterns make them safe and easy to transplant as bulbs (or "sets") or seedlings. They all repel insects rather than being susceptible to them, so they can be used as a natural pest control in the garden. They all are fast out of the gate in the spring,

The Birds and the Bees

Pollination refers to the transfer of pollen within a flower or between flowers on a plant. It is needed for many vegetables to produce. It's not important for vegetables we grow for their leaves (spinach and other greens) or for their roots (carrots, beets, radishes). But pollination is almost always needed with vegetables we grow for their fruit (tomatoes) or seed (corn).

The pollen itself is produced in the anthers (male parts) of flowers and must be moved to the pistil (female part). One part of the pistil, the ovary, develops into the seed or fruit that is eaten—corn kernels, squash, tomatoes, cucumbers.

Corn pollen is carried by the wind as it drops from the tassel to the silks of the ears. If anything prevents the wind from transferring the pollen, the result will be ears with empty rows and missing kernels. That's why corn must be planted in a block of rows rather than one or two very long rows.

In peas, beans, and tomatoes, transfer of pollen takes place within the individual flowers without the help of wind or insects. These plants are essentially self-pollinating.

In squash, pumpkins, melons, and most cucumbers, the male and female flower parts are in separate flowers, but still on the same plant. Insects, most commonly honeybees and bumblebees, transfer pollen from male flower to female flowers as they go from blossom to blossom, collecting nectar and pollen.

If you plan to collect seed from the fruits of these plants for next year's garden, cross-pollination can be a problem in summer squash, pumpkins, vegetable spaghetti, acorn squash, and small ornamental gourds, so you should not plant these vegetables close to each other in this year's garden. If you must grow several varieties of summer and winter squash in the same garden, purchase fresh seed every year.

too. That's why you may see their undomesticated cousins sprouting madly in clumps in your lawn long before the grass itself turns green or your first crocuses appear.

Peas and **beans** are in the *Legume family*. They reproduce similarly—in pod production—and they're all rich in protein, incidentally. Their seeds are large and easy to handle. Both come in both bush and climbing varieties, depending on the seed.

Lettuce, endive, chicory, celtuce, and **escarole** are in the *Daisy family*, the largest single grouping of plants in any botany book you can find. We grow them for their leaves. They are all relatively simple, shallow-rooted plants. If grown in poor conditions they may not provide you with as much to eat, but they'll give you something. That's why designers of "no-sun miracle gardens" lean heavily on them to fill out their would-be gardens.

Tomatoes, eggplant, and **peppers** are in the *Nightshade family*. They are fruit-producing plants of tropical origin, so all require temperatures of 65° F (minimum) for 10 to 15 weeks in order to mature. Potatoes are in the same family but would not seem to fit—indeed, they do not figure in our general garden plans for several reasons. But potatoes are just as sensitive to cold, and need just as much sun, as their siblings. And at a certain stage in the growing season, and from a certain distance, tomato and potato plants look almost exactly alike.

Another fruit-producing clan is the *Gourd* or *Cucurbit family*, to which belong **squash** and **cucumbers**. They also need a long, warm season to do well, and in fact are marginally more sun-loving than the previous group. They and their confreres, the pumpkins, melons, and winter squash, have spidery root systems that lack the taproot characteristic of almost all the other vegetables. Their roots must be treated with kid gloves because they're so fragile and slow to repair themselves. You could dig out a six-week-old pepper plant, manhandle it to a new location, and it would survive and produce. If you did that to a young zucchini, you would set it back severely.

Unlike the nightshade group, cucurbits depend on air movement and insects—mostly honeybees—to achieve the pollination between male and female blossoms on the plant that results in the setting of fruit. Tomatoes, eggplant, peppers, and potatoes produce blossoms that pollinate themselves. Thus, should you choose to spray your garden with poisons—many insecticides kill honeybees—you may adversely affect the sex life among your squash and cucumbers.

Squash and cucumbers should be kept away from each other, by the way, even though their cross-pollination isn't as severe when it occurs among the longer-season cucurbits.

Cabbage, broccoli, cauliflower, and **brussels sprouts** constitute the *Brassica* group of the *Mustard family*. They are so closely related that it would take an expert grower to tell young plants in these varieties apart. Even growers make sure to label them carefully in their seedling flats, with waterproof ink, to prevent confusion.

Two root crops—**radishes** and **turnips**—and one of the leafy vegetables—**kale**—are also members of the *Mustard family*. Like the brassicas, these vegetables only do well as early-season or late-season crops because of their low tolerance of high temperatures. Botanically, they are grouped with the brassicas because their petals and stamens have certain key resemblances and for some similar reasons.

Such technical kinships have little or no practical import to the home gardener, however. Nor—to account for the rest of the vegetables in our general gardens—is it much help to know the particular botanical traits that put **carrots, parsnip,** and **parsley** in the *Herb family*, and **beets, spinach,** and **Swiss chard** in the *Goosefoot family*.

There are other ways to group these and the other vegetables, and so reduce the apparent chaos in the vegetable kingdom when it comes time to figuring out your own garden plan. These more practical groupings should satisfy your desire for an intellectual order to the garden. More important, they should make you aware that your first big challenge will be not what and when to plant, but how to create the kind of soil that will feed and sustain any and all of the vegetables.

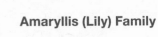

"Families" at a Glance

Amaryllis (Lily) Family

onions

shallots

leeks

garlic

chives

Legume Family

peas

beans

Nightshade Family

tomatoes

eggplants

peppers

Gourd (Cucurbit) Family

squash

cucumbers

Brassica (Mustard) Family

cabbage

broccoli

cauliflower

brussels sprouts

Mustard Family

radishes

turnips

Herb Family

carrots

parsnips

parsley

Goosefoot Family

beets

spinach

Swiss chard

Gilbertie Family

Grace Gilbertie (middle)

Vodola Family

Veronica Vodola (left)

Angela Vodola (right)

Practical Vegetable Groupings

In considering each type of vegetable you want to grow, you'll ask yourself such things as: When can I plant it? How soon can I harvest it? Where in the garden should I plant it?

Let's briefly explore these eminently practical concerns right now and show how they provide the basis for assigning the vegetables within the garden area and favorably scheduling each planting.

Then we'll get down to the crucial question of the soil bed itself.

WHEN CAN I PLANT IT?

Vegetables fall into groupings according to sensitivity to frost and cool weather. In the North it's vital to plant as early as possible, yet without risking the crop, in order to get the most out of the relatively short growing season available. Some vegetables depend on the cooler conditions in spring or fall for their best growth as well, so they must be put in the garden to catch the weather that's right for them.

Most Southern gardeners enjoy a longer growing season but must contend with the realities of frosts and freezes, too—and also with the special demands that a long, hot summer puts on growing certain crops.

Once you pin down your spring and fall frost dates, it is a simple matter to establish when you can plant certain vegetables: merely consult the safe spring and fall planting dates provided for common crops for all parts of the country in the charts in the Appendix.

Ideal spring crops would be those that mature in a relatively short period of time and that perform well in cool weather. These include:

> peas
> radishes
> lettuce
> spinach
> Swiss chard
> brassicas (cabbage, cauliflower, brussels sprouts, and broccoli)
>   if set in the garden as transplants

Ideal fall crops would be those that mature in a short- or medium-length growing season, hold well in frosty weather, and, except in certain cases, also store well over the winter months. These include:

- radishes
- fennel
- lettuce
- chicory
- spinach
- turnips
- brassicas
- beets
- kale
- mustard greens
- endive
- collards
- escarole
- rutabaga

Short-season crops—those that mature in 60 days or less—lend themselves most readily to succession planting. These include:

- peas
- radishes
- beans
- spinach
- mustard greens
- Swiss chard
- mesclun greens
- lettuce
- mini-cabbage
- kohlrabi
- scallions (early onions)

Medium-season crops—those taking 70 to 80 days to mature include:

squash
cucumbers
beets
cabbage
brassicas
beans (some varieties)

Full-season crops take 90 days or more to mature, and in most sections can't be succeeded by anything else. These include:

corn
carrots
potatoes
garlic
shallots
tomatoes
eggplant
Spanish and Bermuda onions
leeks
peppers
celery
parsnips

There are even ideal summer crops. These might be defined as crops that thrive or, at least, do creditably in hot weather and that mature quickly. These include:

cucumbers
okra
beans (bush)
New Zealand spinach

HOW SOON CAN I HARVEST?

There are three reasons for knowing the exact amount of time each vegetable crop requires to mature, all of which become obvious during the first year of gardening.

One, it makes for sensible planning. You won't be tripping all over a late-maturing crop—like leeks, which take four months to mature—to get to the spot in the garden where you placed an early crop like spinach, which is ready in six weeks.

Two, it gives you advance knowledge of where and when you can replace an early crop with a succession crop—an old and worthy trick for increasing productivity.

Third, it informs you of the range of crops from which you can select at any point in the growing season, a range that will be dictated in large part by the number of days remaining in your growing season to the time of your first frost in the fall.

WHERE IN THE GARDEN SHOULD I PLANT?

To locate vegetables effectively within the garden plan requires cognizance of the space each takes; the height to which each grows; the type of support, if any, required; and the soil condition preferred.

These considerations can be analyzed conveniently by grouping the vegetables as follows:

Leafy Crops
  Swiss chard
  endive
  kale
  spinach
  mini-cabbage
  fennel
  celery
  parsley
  basil

Root and Bulb Crops

onions

carrots

turnips

garlic

shallots

radishes

leeks

beets

parsnips

Fruit and Flower Crops

tomatoes

summer squash

zucchini

eggplant

beans

broccoli

cauliflower

peppers

cucumbers (fenced or trellised)

Not Recommended in Limited Space

Leafy Crops

celtuce

cabbage

escarole

Root and Bulb Crops

potatoes

Fruit and Flower Crops ————————————————————————————————

> corn
>
> melon pumpkins
>
> winter squash
>
> pole beans
>
> cucumbers (not fenced or trellised)

Several practical insights are gained by organizing your desired vegetables in these categories.

Root and leafy crops grow to a relatively limited height; fruit and flower crops generally grow bigger and bushier. Thus it makes sense to avoid placing the former where the growth of taller crops would eventually cast them in shadow. In this respect, designing a garden is just like arranging the standard school class picture: you have to make sure you put the short kids in front—or sitting down.

Short-season leafy crops like lettuce may be planted between larger crops like tomatoes, provided they reach maturity before the tomatoes grow to full height. Indeed, such interplanting is another old trick for squeezing the most out of a limited garden area.

But note that you would be making a mistake to plant carrots in between young tomatoes. Your carrots would be only halfway toward maturity before the leafy tomatoes put them in total shade, in effect pulling the plug on their photosynthesis process.

Fruit and flower crops are the most complex organisms among vegetables, consisting of not just root and leaf (like carrots and lettuce), but root, leaf, flower, fruit, and sometimes vine. These crops logically require more elbow room in the garden—and usually, something to rest their elbows on. In limited garden areas, tomatoes need stakes or cages and cucumbers need a fence or a trellis. Peppers, eggplant, and bush beans need staking or *hilling*—a cultivating technique that provides extra support for the plants by throwing up soil around their stems while they're still in adolescence. Peas usually need something to grow on, too, and so do climbing varieties of beans.

Root crops require the best soil tilth of all the vegetables, simply because their edible parts form beneath the soil line. Lettuce may do all right in soil full of rocks and debris, but beets would be misshapen and carrots would grow like corkscrews.

However, as I will now try to make clear, it is not merely the absence of sticks and stones that makes for good soil for vegetables.

"Build Soil"

In what he called a "political pastoral," Robert Frost captured the peculiar stubborn pride in people who grow things for a living:

> Let those possess the land, and only those,
> Who love it with a love so strong and stupid
> That they may be abused and taken advantage of
> And made fun of by business, law, and art;
> They still hang on . . .

And though he was certainly using the idea of soil improvement (he titled the poem "Build Soil") as a metaphor for other things, Frost also put his finger on a theme of importance to big farmers and home gardeners alike:

> . . . plant, breed, produce, [he urged]
> But what you raise or grow, why, feed it out,
> Eat it or plow it under where it stands,
> To build the soil. For what is more accursed
> Than an impoverished soil, pale and metallic?
> What cries more to our kind for sympathy?

"To build the soil" is the first big task facing any newcomer to gardening—and many experienced gardeners, too. For the fate of all the vegetables, no matter how they may be related or when or where or how they're planted, is linked mainly to the life and structure of the soil in which they're put. If that soil happens to be "impoverished," the garden will not produce on the average small farm.

A lot of people have a blind spot for the true function of soil in the life of plants for two reasons.

One is because, though we're often described as a nation of asphalt and cement, it is more accurate to say that we are paved over with grass. The great proliferation of lawns that occurred in the postwar years not only doomed a lot of Victory Gardens, but also obscured the nature and function and the look of soil for many of us.

The other reason is that—at least until the boom in environmental consciousness in recent years—many of us went along with the simple and seemingly flawless reasoning of the fertilizer industry, backed by the USDA, in promoting "N-P-K farming." Exclusively using the three big plant nutrients—nitrogen, phosphorus, and potassium—in synthetic form in agriculture did in fact keep up production for a time, though often at the expense of the land, which in many places literally became "pale and metallic" after a few years of this approach. In any event, the average gardener got the idea that growing vegetables wasn't so complicated after all, and that the secret was in a bag of chemicals, not in the soil.

A *rich* soil does contain a balanced amount of nitrogen, phosphorus, and potassium, for these are the nutrients principally responsible for a plant's leaf, fruit, and root development. A rich soil also contains minute quantities of dozens of other minerals important to the health of the plant—and desirable in human nutrition, too. The calcium in a good head of cabbage doesn't come with the seed packet; it comes from the soil where the cabbage grows.

A soil with *good structure*, or *tilth*, contains the oxygen and water needed for plant growth and to support the life of the thousands of different species of microscopic plant and animal life present in organic matter. Organisms such as fungi, algae, molds, insects, and worms break down such matter. In the process, nitrogen and other nutrients are converted to forms a plant can use. At the same time, these organisms help to keep the soil well conditioned. Earthworms alone turn over tons of earth in their travels. The USDA estimates that one acre of good agricultural land can produce over five tons of worm castings, rich in nitrogen, phosphates, and potash. Earthworms are credited with turning more than 50 tons of soil in the course of a year.

Rich, well-structured, ready-to-garden soil seldom occurs in nature, and when it does, the developer strips it off the land with a bulldozer and sells it to somebody else. If you want a good garden soil, you're going to have to build it yourself, at least to some extent.

Organic Soil Amendments

The liberal use of organic materials builds up your garden soil and adds needed nutrients for plant growth. Organic material is essentially the remains of plants and animals, most often in the form of bird and animal manures, plant (green) manures, cover crops, compost, and life forms of the sea.

Animal manures include horse, cow, pig, rabbit, chicken, and sheep, either as processed, composted products in bags or in somewhat raw form. They vary greatly in the amount of fertilizing nutrient they contain. Raw manures have a 60 to 90 percent moisture content, so they are less useful for building humus in the soil than many plant manures.

Plant (green) manures are derived from plants, either as ground-up plant products, whole plants, or cover crops. With a higher carbon-to-nitrogen ratio than most animal manures, they are excellent for improving soil structure.

Home compost. There are many systems for constructing and managing a compost pile. (My lasagna-style composting method is described in a later chapter.) Good compost comes from a mix of organic materials that decompose over time. A correct balance of air, water, and temperature has to be struck in the compost pile for the materials to break down properly.

Municipal compost. A number of cities are composting tree trunks, leaves, branches, and grass clippings that otherwise would be clogging their landfills. The usual procedure is to first sort out undesirable materials, grind up the acceptable waste, then manage the pile until it is suitably decomposed. The end product may vary from one recycling plant to another, but the best grades are similar to potting soil.

Peat moss is the fibrous, decomposed remains of a family of sphagnum mosses that grow in the wild in very wet areas in North America. Some preservationists argue that, as a nonrenewable resource, peat moss should be used sparingly or not at all. It's an excellent lightening agent for garden soils. Packed in bales, it should be broken apart by hand if hard and dry, then moistened before mixing with soil or compost.

Perlite. White in color, perlite is derived from naturally occurring volcanic glass. It is similar to pumice. Mixed with garden soil, it makes the soil more open to air while still having good water-retention properties.

Wood ash. Ashes from your fireplace or wood stove can be added to soil to improve its tilth and supply trace amounts of phosphorous and potassium.

Kelp meal is suitable for application directly to the garden soil and is easily mixed with other dry fertilizers and amendments.

Dried raw seaweed. Raw seaweeds are prepared by various methods and sold under a number of brand names. They contain about 1 percent nitrogen, a trace of phosphorous, and 2 percent potassium, along with numerous trace elements.

Even our earliest farmers understood that soil needs a helping hand to produce the desired results in a crop. The American Indians fertilized their maize by sticking a dead fish in along with the seed they planted. The nitrogen and phosphorus contained in a decomposing fish happen to be the two elements that corn needs most to do well.

The labor of creating good fertility and tilth in the garden soil is greatly simplified by elevating the garden in the first place. But in any case the job of building the tilth should come first. That's because even a fertile soil won't help plants grow well unless the soil has a structure that permits roots to fan out, develop properly, and feed.

Geologists have identified some 150 different soils in the United States. But don't panic—there are actually just three different major soil conditions to be concerned with in terms of structure.

If you're lucky, your soil will be naturally rich in humus. Humus is an accumulation of mostly vegetative rot over a period of years. Life forms such as grass and weeds, leaves and twigs from nearby trees, and insects and animals die and decompose and gradually form a dark brown or black organic matter that is perfect for garden soils.

Good as it is, a humus-rich soil often needs to be lightened so that more air and moisture can be retained. Sand or light gravel are both cheap lightening agents. Peat moss and perlite are more expensive to purchase but also lighten garden soil.

Then there are soils that are *too* light and sandy. Sandy soils have large soil particles and feel gritty to the touch. They need to be enriched with humus, organic matter such as animal manures, green manure (cover crops or other plant matter), or compost. Compost is nothing more than homemade humus, and there are as many different formulas for making compost as there are recipes for lasagna—which in fact it resembles in one important way. (Again, more on compost and lasagna later.)

Finally, there are soils that are too clayey. Clay soils have small soil particles and feel sticky to the touch. These hardpan or gumbo soils have neither the richness of humus soils nor the lightness of sandy soils, so they need to be amended with some organic matter.

If you're not sure which category your own soil belongs in, take a few spadefuls of earth from different parts of the garden site, drop them into a shoe box or a pail, and take the mixture to show a grower at your garden center, or ask that kindly veteran gardener in your neighborhood to have a look. One of them will be able to help you identify the present tilth of your soil and offer suggestions for improving it.

When a customer brings a sample of garden soil to me to check, I take a handful and make a fist. This test won't work if the soil is too wet or too dry; if it's of average moisture content, the ball should break apart when I release the pressure of my hand. If it remains stuck together, it needs more compost to lighten its tilth.

The ABCs of N, P, and K

You can't judge your soil fertility by feel, the way you can tilth; rather, you must rely on a chemical analysis.

Or you could learn about deficiencies in your soil the hard way—by planting a garden and watching how everything turns out. Then you'd be looking for the following clues:

- Nitrogen promotes healthy stem and leaf development, so if lettuce or your other leafy crops turn out poorly—assuming the garden is getting enough sun to start with—then you can deduce there is a shortage of nitrogen.

- Phosphorus helps plants set their roots down quickly and vigorously and promotes fruit and flower development. If you grow lots of vine but no fruit on your tomato plants, even though they've got all the sun they need, it probably means your soil is short on phosphorus.

- Potassium also aids in the development of fruit and keeps roots healthy and disease-resistant. If your root crops are puny, chances are you're out of potassium.

Obviously, it would be smarter to get your soil tested before you plant your garden. Kits are available for doing it yourself, but the most reliable method is to ship off a soil sample to your own extension service. USDA-based extension services are connected with major land-grant universities and found in every state, with extension agents in virtually every county. For a minimal charge they will test your soil and in most cases send you a computer printout of the results. Be sure to request the standard test, which will identify the all-important pH level in your soil (more on pH in a later chapter) as well as the relative amounts of nitrogen, phosphorous, and potassium. (Many extension services also offer a variety of plant tissue testing, water testing, and compost testing, which usually command higher fees.)

You might as well collect your soil specimen at the same time you gather a pailful for the local expert on tilth, and if you can do both things in the fall, you'll be ahead of the game for next year's growing season.

Make sure the sampling for chemical analysis is representative of your entire garden site. Your extension service will provide you with detailed guidelines they want you to follow in gathering and submitting your soil sample, but here's the basic process: Take a small spade—or a piece of hollow plastic pipe or tubing—and drive it into the area to be gardened to a depth of 6" or so, at six or seven different spots. Mix all the samplings up thoroughly in a bucket, then pack two cupfuls of the results in a secure, waterproof container and mail it to the extension service, along with a note saying what you intend to grow. This will ensure that the report pertains to vegetable gardening in your particular soil conditions.

Research on the uses of commercial fertilizers in large-scale farming operations has dramatically revealed the effects of the three essential nutrients on vegetable growth. As you have gathered by now, I do not recommend the use of commercial fertilizers in the home garden. Nor do I think that the individualized feeding programs for vegetables that large-scale growers apply are desirable or practicable on a small scale.

Nevertheless, studying a sampling of the recommended fertilizer applications for commercial growers who specialize in certain crops may be a good way to understand clearly the different roles these elements play in plant growth.

Consider the leafy crops first. Tests have shown that spinach does best in a soil that has been enriched with fertilizer in proportions of 10 parts nitrogen, 9 parts phosphorus, and 10 parts potassium—or about equal amounts of all three. Compare these "ideal" fertilizing requirements for spinach with those of another leafy crop, cabbage:

	NITROGEN	PHOSPHORUS	POTASSIUM
SPINACH	10	9	10
CABBAGE	13	14	16

As you'll see when we look at fruit and root crops, the proportions for these two leafy crops are pretty similar, but cabbage needs more of everything because it is a bigger, slower-maturing, leafier crop.

Now let's look at three crops whose edible parts grow underground. Radishes, the simplest, require 6 parts nitrogen, 9 parts phosphorus, and 10 parts potassium. Like spinach, they need a little bit of everything—and less nitrogen, because there is less leaf growth. But compare radishes with a bulb crop and an even more complex tuber crop:

	NITROGEN	PHOSPHORUS	POTASSIUM
RADISHES	6	9	10
ONIONS	12	9	10
POTATOES	12	24	26

Onions require twice as much nitrogen as radishes because their stem part is bigger and slower-growing than the equivalent part of the radish—the leafy top. Potato plants require dramatically more phosphorus and potassium than onions because they produce a much bigger root system and, stemming from the roots, the prodigious tuberous growth that we dig up and eat as potatoes.

Finally, consider some of the fruit-producing vegetables. Bush beans require 6 parts nitrogen, 7 parts phosphorus, and 8 parts potassium—like the leafy crops, nearly equal proportions. Compare their needs with those of the heavier fruit-producing plants:

	NITROGEN	PHOSPHORUS	POTASSIUM
BEANS	6	7	8
SUMMER SQUASH	6	24	26
TOMATOES	16	24	26

Organic Fertilizers

When the word *organic* is used to describe fertilizer, it generally means that the nutrients in it are derived solely from the remains or a by-product of an organism. When packaged as fertilizers, organic products have the fertilizer ratio (N-P-K, denoting nitrogen, phosphorous, and potassium) stated on the package label. Composted manures sold as soil conditioners do not usually have a nutrient guarantee on the label, although small amounts of nutrients are present.

Some organic fertilizers are high in one of the three macronutrients; others are low. Some are fortified with ingredients, for example, rock phosphate to increase phosphorous or greensand to increase potassium.

All organic soil fertilizers improve the tilth of soil as well as provide nutrients.

Animal manure is a complete fertilizer but low in the amount of nutrients it supplies. In liquefied form, homemade manure tea (compost or manure plus water) is a useful fertilizer for side-dressing crops. It's a messy, smelly concoction—and it's good for your vegetables.

Blood meal is dried, powdered blood collected from cattle slaughterhouses. It is a rich source of nitrogen (up to 12 percent); so rich, in fact, that it may burn plants if used in excess. Reputedly, its scent keeps deer out of the garden, although the scent is diminished by rainfall or watering.

Liquid fish emulsion, a balanced fertilizer, is a partially decomposed blend of finely pulverized fish. Its strong odor dissipates within a day. In the late spring, when garden plants have sprouted, an application of fish emulsion followed by a deep watering will boost plant growth. Caveat: avoid fish emulsion products touted as containing more than 5 percent nitrogen, as they may have been fortified with chemical fertilizer.

Fish meal, alfalfa meal, and **soybean meal** are all nitrogen-rich fertilizers, useful but fairly expensive as soil additives. (Cottonseed meal, also sold in many garden centers and nurseries, is a by-product of the fiber industry; many organic gardeners frown on its use because cotton crops are heavily sprayed with chemical insecticides.)

Bone meal is a rich source of phosphorous to aid in blossom and fruit development. The powdered form of this by-product of the slaughterhouse may attract animals, but a liquid version is mostly free of scent.

Rock phosphates, derived from ancient marine or volcanic deposits, provide alternative sources of phosphorus.

Greensand (glauconite) is a clay-type mineral rich in potassium that releases into the soil very slowly. Greensand helps to build soil structure.

Natural potassium sulfate (langbeinite), extracted from Utah's Great Salt Lake by means of a slow evaporation process, is another potassium-rich additive used in certified organic agriculture.

Azomite is a material mined from an ancient volcanic site in central Utah and available to gardeners in pelletized form. Containing a broad spectrum of active minerals and trace elements, it has been used to improve livestock and plant growth.

Again, the jump in plant nutrients is reflected in the type of productive growth pattern required. Summer squash is a smaller plant than tomatoes, so it gets no more nitrogen for leaf growth than bush beans do. But its fruit is large in proportion to the rest of the plant, and therefore the plant needs just as much phosphorus and potassium (which help form the roots that spread to find the nutrients that the big fruits need) as does the tomato. Tomatoes need the extra nitrogen to sustain their considerable leafy growth. This would be particularly applicable for commercial tomato growers, by the way, for they don't stake and prune the plants as most space-conscious home gardeners do.

I hope these figures help to impress on you the complexity of the relationship between soil and plant—and also make it clear that an organic gardening venture that fails to address the fact that soil beds need adequate N, P, and K is not going to be a productive venture at all.

The figures also point up the significantly greater nutritional requirements of the fruit-bearing vegetables, especially for phosphorus and potassium. That's why it is necessary to side-dress these plants in midseason, as we'll see later.

Please understand, the reason I don't put commercial fertilizers on our shelves in the garden center is not because I underestimate the role that the N-P-K nutrients play in plant growth. Indeed, I think the data show clearly that all vegetables need all three. I don't promote commercial fertilizers simply because the N-P-K-only chemical approach doesn't add anything of value to soil tilth, and it tends to promote lackadaisical gardening habits.

Feeding Your Garden for 12¢ a Day

One of the few remaining vegetable farmers in my area got me over to his place around 6 A.M. one day in early June. As he led me to his barn to check something or other, we stopped briefly to contemplate his lettuce crop—five acres of crisp head lettuce sparkling in the dawn's early light.

I told him I thought the lettuce looked great, but he snorted.

"The lettuce was even bigger in the old days," he said. Then he added, "You know what's missing, don't you?"

"What's missing?"

"You know."

"What can be missing?" I repeated, puzzled. "It's a beautiful crop."

"Sal, the *manure*," he said. "The manure's what's missing!"

Now, any other time this farmer would have scoffed at the idea that animal manures might play a useful role in his business. Years ago he had converted to commercial fertilizers, because it was cheaper and easier than collecting and spreading animal manures on his 60-odd acres. And I knew that one moment of sentiment before the spectacle of his lettuce was not going to send him back to the methods of the "good old days."

Home gardeners, however, are pretty much unaffected by the financial and productivity pressures that face commercial farmers. That's why I think you can and should, in your limited area, make use of naturally occurring ingredients to improve soil tilth and fertility, and on a continuing basis.

The main objections to farm animal manures are that they're unavailable, or too messy and bulky to handle, or not balanced in terms of the nitrogen, phosphorus, and potassium contained in them. (Dog or cat manure, by the way, should never be used in the vegetable garden—or in the compost pile—particularly because of the potential hazard to human health.)

Let's assume for this discussion you have roughed out a soil bed of approximately 1,000 square feet. The soil's of average quality and condition, and you want to upgrade its suitability for vegetable crops.

If you happen to have access to fresh stable manures, you would have to spread about 18 bushels, or 9 wheelbarrow loads of the stuff, across your garden in the fall, if you were starting then, and again in the spring.

This considerable labor would add much favorable soil-building material to your garden, plus adequate nitrogen and potassium. But as most manures are notoriously short in phosphorus, you would be well advised to supplement your spring feeding with an application of bone meal. Bone meal is 22 percent phosphoric acid, and it sells for $2 to $3 a pound.

You now have fed your garden adequately, but it has been a cumbersome procedure, and an expensive one.

Now suppose you have access to rabbit manure. If you added merely 5 bushels, or 2½ wheelbarrowfuls, to the same area, your actual contribution to the richness of the soil would be 16 parts N, 11 parts P, and 10 parts K.

Thus the work of feeding the garden would be cut by a third, and because rabbit manure is rich in phosphorus already, the extra expense for bone meal during the spring feeding and the summer side-dressing of fruit-producing crops would be eliminated altogether.

A single rabbit produces 5 to 6 bushels of manure a year. After the initial investment—maybe $20 for a suitable cage, and $5 for each rabbit—upkeep is low. I figure it costs me 12¢ per day to feed each of my rabbits, so at the end of a year I will have paid, in effect, $8 or $9 per bushel of manure.

Five bushels of rabbit manure (at an effective cost of $40 to $45) provide about the same amount of N, P, and K as 150 pounds of 5-10-5 fertilizer, which in 2009 was priced at about $150. If you added 5 bushels of peat moss to the soil, it would cost another $15. An application of superphosphate around June would cost about $10. So a typical chemical approach to sustaining 1,000 square feet of soil bed would set you back approximately $175.

Rabbit manure also provides trace elements, besides N, P, and K, and it adds to the tilth of the soil. It also breaks down more slowly than chemical fertilizers, and so will be available to plants more evenly throughout the growing season.

I should add that rabbit manure isn't the only great natural manure in the world. The partially decomposed *guano*, or bat manure, that is collected from caves in the Southwestern United States is also rich in all three major plant nutrients. But clearly it's easier to raise rabbits in your yard than bats in your belfry. (In fact, some companies specializing in organic products carry bat guano; in 2009 Territorial Seed Co. offered a two-pound bag of guano-based fertilizer for $25.95.)

Triggering the Nutrients in Soil

You could truck in topsoil, add sand and manure, and toil from dawn to dusk to create a garden soil that looks and feels like the original Fertile Crescent.

And it still might not work. For if your garden soil is too acid (or "sour") or too alkaline ("sweet"), it won't yield good and plentiful crops. Building a rich, well-structured soil bed does not automatically provide the garden with the slightly acid condition that vegetables like.

Fortunately, the chemical soil analysis you've just sent away for will tell you the exact degree of sourness or sweetness in your garden soil, expressing this as a certain "pH" figure. When your soil is in the correct range, with a pH reading of about 6.0 to 7.0, it means all the nutrients that you've gone to so much trouble to get into the soil will actually break down, in interaction with other things, and become available to your plants.

Below 6.0, the soil might be said to suffer from acid indigestion. The availability of nitrogen, sulfur, calcium, magnesium, and potassium is reduced. And the key plant nutrient of phosphorus is severely blocked. Phosphorus becomes locked up in a too-acid soil and the plants can't get at it.

Above 7.0, the availability of iron, manganese, boron, copper, and zinc tapers off. These are all classified as "minor elements" or "trace elements" in the pattern of plant growth. That may be as misleading as saying that your little finger is a minor part of your hand. You still don't want to lose it. The same goes for trace elements: in a zinc-deficient soil, for instance, spinach develops a kind of marginal burn on its leaves—the leaves blanch and dry all along their borders.

If the soil tests either below or above the desired pH range, it needs to be treated to prevent the uneven growth patterns (and possibly even toxic conditions) that will ensue. Beets will split and scab if the pH is too high, and onions won't form much bigger than marbles if the pH is too low.

The recommended treatment for adjusting pH will be included in the report from your extension service. Soils that are too sweet are acidified by adding small amounts of sulfur. Most Connecticut soils happen to be too sour, so the addition of limestone—land lime, not the lime that masons use to make cement—is usually recommended to sweeten them. Ground limestone mixed into the soil at the rate of 10 pounds per 1,000 square feet would raise a pH reading one full unit—for instance, from 5.5 to 6.5—so the correction of pH doesn't take that much material or effort on your part.

The organic matter that you add to the soil—particularly at the start of your gardening venture, when large amounts of material may be involved—can affect the pH. Peat moss, evergreen needles, and the leaves from trees—particularly oak trees, rhododendron, and mountain laurel in these parts—tend to increase the acidity of soil. Manures tend to make the soil more alkaline.

For this reason, it's a good idea to have your soil retested at the end of your first year of gardening to make sure the pH is still in the range that triggers the availability of all the nutrients your plants need.

Production-Plus Planting Procedures

Each vegetable must be sown, grown, and harvested on its own terms, and later on I will explain in detail the techniques I have used to get maximum productivity out of every crop I plant.

Before that, however, I think it would be helpful for you to know more about my garden procedures for getting the most from the space available to me in the limited growing season in which I have to operate. I think sketching these procedures for you at this point will make it easier for you to appreciate my approach toward such things as watering, cultivating, and pest control later on, and, ultimately, my method for bringing vegetables into the garden in carefully scheduled planting groups.

1. **Start as many crops as possible from healthy transplants.**
   I use transplants to get a jump on the season, to ensure that I get the crop I've sketched in for such-and-such a row on my garden plan, and to minimize waste of seed and space. First-time gardeners must depend on reliable local sources for transplants. More experienced gardeners may be able to grow transplants from seed indoors. There's more later in the book on the subjects of starting seed indoors and the uses of a cold frame—a device for starting and conditioning young plants in a protected outside location.

2. **Plant seeds and seedlings with a "gardener's yardstick."**
   A gardener's yardstick is any straight and manageable light board that you can use as a measuring rod for your particular garden. It's a great aid, because it allows you to plant quickly and efficiently and it makes sure that you keep all your plantings straight and orderly.

   For the model garden at our garden center in Westport, which is divided into two 12' halves, I use a 1" x 3" board that is exactly 12' long, and I mark it at 6", 10", and 12" intervals. This way I can accurately space all seedlings.

   With the yardstick, it's also easier to lay straight furrows. Driving stakes at each end of the desired row and tying a string between them is a bother. Furthermore, when you draw a stick or tool along the string to dig the furrow, the string usually gives a bit, and you tend to create a curved row rather than a straight one. Using a board as a brace for drawing the stick along ensures a straight line. The 3" mark or the 3" width of the board provides a good way to mark the distance between closely planted short rows such as onions.

The gardener's yardstick can also be used as a leveling device after you've turned over the garden and raked it out in the spring.

The exact size of your own yardstick depends on the most common row length that you'll be planting in. Cut off your board to that length (or to half that length), then mark it accurately for a few key spacings, some in inches (for measuring the distance between seed drills, and seedlings) and some in feet (for measuring rows and distances between rows, and for positioning the space-hungry transplants like tomatoes and peppers).

3. **Sow seeds as shallow as possible.** I'm a "high" sower of seed, especially in the wet spring planting period, because it usually leads to quicker and better germination. If you compare my recommendations for depths at which to plant seed (beginning on page 134) with most extension service literature and with the directions on seed packets, and you'll find I'm invariably sowing seed closer to the soil surface.

I sow carefully to eliminate excess thinning in some spots and vacancies in others. In sowing tiny seeds like carrots, I use an inexpensive battery-powered device called a seed vibrator. It's a tapered metal affair that vibrates the seed out into the furrow slowly and evenly. You can make a homemade version with stiff paper in a modification of your basic paper-airplane design. If you do it this way, simply tap the seeds out along your gardener's yardstick, or any handy board, to ensure even distribution of the seeds. (Pelleted carrot or lettuce seed is easier to handle and can be sown by hand.)

4. **Use sand to cover seed in furrows.** The use of clean sand—sharp mason's sand or the sand sold in sacks and used for children's sandboxes—helps in several ways.

First and foremost, it holds seed in place in the furrow. Shallow sowing of seed such as I recommend invites easy displacement by water or other jostling, but sand is heavier than ordinary garden soil and helps the row hold to its pattern as sown. This is especially valuable for keeping in place tiny, lightweight seeds like radishes, carrots, beets, turnips, and lettuce.

The sand itself is a good soil conditioner, and it clearly marks the rows for you to see and remember when you do use it to fill the furrows. It works better than marking your rows with quick-germinating radishes, by the way, as we'll explain under individual crop techniques later on. Also, water filters through the sand more quickly than through ordinary garden soil, so germination of all the seeds may be quicker.

5. **Plan short rows, but close together.** One standard packet of spinach seed is supposed to plant 25 feet of row, with 1 foot of space left to either side so you have room to tend it. Planting spinach this way takes up about 50 to 75 square feet in the garden. Such generous spacing may be all right for farmers, who have acres to spare (and who need a lot of space between rows, anyway, to get their machinery in and out). But gardeners can double up and triple up in shorter rows on most leafy and root crops and use their space more efficiently and without detriment to the growth pattern of the particular crop. I can plant the same packet of spinach in three 8" rows, leaving 6" between the center row and the end rows, get as much spinach out of the crop, but take only 16 to 24 square feet in the garden.

The use of short rows is encouraged by designing the garden in two equal parts in the first place.

6. **Cultivate early to kill weeds when they're small and to expose more soil to the warm sun.** Use a tool like a hoe to cut into the soil at ½" depth along your newly planted rows in spring. Don't cultivate with a tool any closer than about 6" for root crops and 9" for transplants, to prevent damage to new roots. For the occasional weeds close in by the crop, you're going to have to get down and remove them carefully by hand. A good trick for pulling out such a weed without totally disrupting the crop's root system is to put one hand palm down on the soil so that two fingers straddle the weed. Then, while pressing down gently with that hand to keep the soil in place, pull out the weed with the other hand—very much in the manner of a dentist extracting a tooth.

Careless weeding often promotes more vigorous weed growth. That's why it's better to cut into the roots of the weeds with a sharp hoe, for those weeds growing at a distance from the crop, and to extract weeds close to the crop, roots and all. A sharp hoe is a hoe with a cutting edge, and the more you use it, the duller it becomes. People who work in the fields for a living carry files to keep their tools sharp as they cultivate. It's a lot easier to weed with a properly sharpened hoe.

If you cultivate early in the growing season, the weeds will be easy to remove. In addition, the act of cultivating at this time will turn over more soil and dry it out a bit. In a damp spring when the nights are cold, this procedure facilitates more rapid development of the plants.

Cultivate once a week all during spring, starting about two weeks after the ground has been planted, and keep at it until the crops are big enough to shade out weeds on their own.

7. **Establish a "supply garden" to fill gaps in rows as you harvest.** Prepare a small corner of the garden for sowing seed of a favorite lettuce (see the radish bed instructions later on for details). Then, as you harvest lettuce that you originally

planted from transplant, fill in the holes with seedlings from your supply garden. This will give you a perpetual supply of lettuce (or cabbage, or some of the fall crops) and keep your productivity rate high. To really master usage of this tiny territory in your garden, consult the five-stage supply garden; a plan for one is included in our section on plans.

8. **Side-dress in midseason as needed.** Heavy feeders like tomatoes and all the other fruit-bearing crops should be given an extra boost from a sprinkling of bone meal, compost, or aged manure at about the time they are ready to swing into their major production cycle. I throw a spadeful of rabbit manure around the base of each plant, and for faster results cover the manure over with soil. Water plants evenly and gently at the base so that the fertilizer soaks into the ground. Two liquid fertilizers could be used for your side dressing at this time— fish emulsion or manure tea (compost or manure dissolved in water). Such liquid applications penetrate the soil and reach the root systems of your plants more quickly, encouraging more rapid fruit production. (Fish-based side-dressings may attract skunks or raccoons in areas where those animals are present.)

    I also lightly mix in some rabbit manure in soil where short crops like peas or beans have been harvested. This replenishes the soil for the succession crop that I'll put in those spots after giving the area a week's vacation.

9. **Harvest on time.** I'm in the garden every day once a particular crop has started producing, because I know that the more I pick, the more I'm going to get out of the crop before it's finished. If I let lettuce or spinach go to seed, or tomatoes and peppers rot on the vine, I am cutting into my productivity far more deeply than the loss of those particular fruits would indicate. I'm wasting valuable garden space, in the case of the leafy crops that should no longer be there, and I'm short-circuiting the drive to produce in the fruit-producing crops.

10. **Tiptoe through the tomatoes.** Don't go in the garden unless you're there to pick or for other good reasons, and stick to the pathways as much as possible, to minimize soil compaction. If you have worked hard to create a soil of good tilth, you should be acutely sensitive to the consequences of performing unnecessary fandangos on top of it. Use your gardener's yardstick, or any handy piece of lumber, as a kind of board-walk when you have to get to some out-of-the-way spot.

Water

Many gardeners look forward to coming home from work in the summer, turning the sprinkler on in the garden, and sitting down with a martini.

Actually, it would probably be better for your vegetables if you served them the martini and sat under the sprinkler yourself.

Improper watering is one of the most common gardening mistakes I've observed over the years. It runs a close third to locating the garden under insufficient sun and putting plants too close together. The use of an overhead sprinkler in the evening is particularly risky, because it soaks the plants and leaves them damp for the rest of the night. This can cause blossoms on fruit-producing crops to rot and drop off before setting their fruit. The foliage becomes an ideal breeding ground for fungus, which requires a combination of dampness, darkness, and warmth to thrive. And for slugs and snails, the wet garden by night is an irresistible draw.

Another common problem is frequent shallow waterings, rather than occasional prolonged waterings provided only when you have determined, by examining the plants or by probing the soil bed, that water is in fact needed. In my part of the country certainly, too much watering causes more problems than not enough.

Bear in mind that in working toward building a deep, well-conditioned soil bed, you are greatly improving the ability of your ground to retain moisture. A loamy soil holds twice as much water as a sandy soil. A good organically enriched garden loam holds even more.

Rainfall supplies some of the water required for plants to achieve maximum growth and output. But in most regions and in most years, gardeners must supply the rest. The watering questions are *when*, *where*, and *how*?

Let's first look quickly at the problem of irrigation as it presents itself in the course of a typical growing season. Then we'll prescribe some basic guidelines for watering that apply at any time, but particularly during the critical summer period.

EARLY SPRING

Except at transplanting and sowing time, watering is not usually necessary for the first early plantings of spring, during March and April (in most areas), simply because normal precipitation during that period should supply the garden with all the moisture it needs. In fact, you should take care not to tramp around in the spring garden unnecessarily, as you could easily damage the soil structure by making it too compact. If your garden soil has good drainage—and it should in an elevated garden—you ought to be able to walk in it the day after a heavy rain without sinking in up to your ankles.

In any event, after the initial watering at transplanting or sowing time, nature usually takes care of the water needs of your first plantings—the peas, onion sets, radishes, and your first lettuce transplants—so you don't have to untangle the garden hose for a while.

Occasionally, however, a spring comes along that defies this logic. One year in our area we had the warmest April and the coldest May that I can remember. That particular sequence wreaked havoc in many gardens. Early radish, beet, and spinach seed had enough moisture to swell, split, and send out roots, but then cold, dry weather set in and threw a monkey wrench into their growth cycles. The opportunity for steady and vigorous growth was denied them, except where gardeners were lucky enough to have planted on the late side—and alert enough to keep their seedbeds moist.

The point is, *if the soil looks dry on top when there's seed underneath, you'd better water.*

LATE SPRING

By the time you're ready to put in your tender crops, in May (again, depending on your region), weather conditions will have changed and the ground may have begun to dry out. Before putting in seed, you may have to soak the area first, to hasten sprouting, if in your judgment the soil looks and feels too dry. In planting seedlings such as tomatoes or cucumbers, you may have to soak the area where the plants are to go both before and after transplanting, to help them get over the trauma of transplanting and establish their roots more quickly. And be sure to soak the transplants too—a dry seedling will take much longer to recover from the shock of being moved to a new location.

EARLY SUMMER

By the time you have completed your garden planting and things are beginning to look professional out there—in June, say—the irrigation question becomes more important. But don't get nervous if you hear that your garden should be getting 1 inch of water per week at this stage. Let the condition of your soil and plants be your guide, so you don't risk overwatering.

FULL SUMMER

By this time, and all the way through the beginning of harvest—during July, August, and September—the garden needs more water, because summer heat dries up soil faster and the plants themselves will have grown and developed more avid thirsts.

This is a critical period for watering, and it comes just when novice gardeners tend to let down their guards a bit about the matter. They go off on vacation, or drift into a lazy summer mood, or simply fail to notice that the soil bed has dried out.

If you've planted a general garden, you should be visiting it almost daily during this period, so you ought to notice right away when the ground is too much like the Sahara, or if plants have begun to wilt or have taken on an unhealthy complexion. You'll be in the garden simply because there are lettuces and other early crops to harvest, and tomatoes and cucumbers to cultivate and tie to their supports as they climb. There are also succession crops to be planted to replace the row crops you do harvest.

The main things to keep in mind about watering during any period of the growing season may be summed up as follows:

1. **Water in the morning.** If you come home one balmy summer afternoon and find your plants have begun to wilt, don't rush out and water them on the spot. Wait until the following morning. They won't perish overnight, and by keeping the garden dry after dark, you'll discourage fungus and slugs.

2. **Water only when the garden needs it.** Frequent short waterings do plants more harm than good by making the top 2" of soil too wet, by encouraging the formation of a lot of puny roots near the surface, and by discouraging the development of deep tap roots. Shallow-rooted plants are more vulnerable in periods of real drought, and also more susceptible to being blown down in storms.

3. **Wait until plants have just begun to wilt before you water.** If you can't bear that idea, try this to keep yourself from watering prematurely. Probe the soil between rows to a depth of 6" or so. If the soil is dry for the first 2" to 4" but damp at 4" to 6", it means there is still enough moisture in the soil bed for healthy plants to reach and use. It might be a mistake to water now, because it would cause the tap roots on the plants to cease their trip downward. By waiting another day or two, you'll encourage the plants to dig a little deeper and thus enlarge their feeding area.

4. **Water thoroughly when you do water.** This goes hand in hand with the previous rule. A deep watering is one that leaves the soil bed moist to a depth of 8" to 12". This can't be accomplished in one shot in rich soils. If you tried to provide this amount in one watering, you would risk flooding the upper layer of the bed and injuring the soil structure.

   So when you do water, you should go through the garden with the hose once using a gentle water pressure and then start all over again. Watering in two stages in this manner will get the moisture down to the proper depth, and it won't take any more time and effort, in the long run, than doing more frequent but shallower quickies.

5. **Water at soil level.** To keep plants dry and free of fungus problems, it's better to apply the water in gentle doses around the base of the plants, rather than attacking from the air via a lawn sprinkler, as I've already pointed out.

Many of my customers don't understand why I am always running down their lawn sprinklers. They figure sprinkling the garden can't be any different from rain falling on the garden.

Actually, there are two differences. First, summer rain is almost always accompanied by air movement—by winds—and that facilitates the evaporation process after the plants do get wet. Water won't stay on plant foliage after a shower for nearly as long as it stays after sprinkling the garden on some muggy, airless summer day.

Second, tap water or well water is usually much colder than summer rain, which warms up on its plunge through the atmosphere. Warmed soil promotes much more rapid plant growth than cooled-off soil does. In terms of plant physiology, it's the difference between a pat on the back and a slap in the face.

Admittedly, watering by hand is a bit trickier than turning on the sprinkler. This is especially evident in a garden that hasn't been properly designed and planted. If you find yourself knocking down tomatoes and lopping off lettuces as you drag your hose through the garden, you may end up with nothing left to irrigate.

If you've spaced your plants properly and in straight rows—and especially if you've designed your garden in halves from the outset—you should be able to irrigate without any problem.

A few sturdy stakes placed strategically here and there should also help to keep your garden hose from snaking out of control behind you. My Uncle John, who's invented various gadgets for home and garden, devised a pipe that screwed onto the hose at one end and fed water out in a gentle stream at the other; the water came out gently because he had hammered out the end of the pipe. He could go through the garden and water plants at root level without bending over. You could do the same thing by strapping an old broomstick or some other manageable pole to the last 4' of the business end of your hose. Inexpensive watering wands that attach to the hose are now on the market. They make irrigating at soil level easy and convenient. Make sure you pick one with an on/off switch at the point where the wand connects to the hose. This will save you steps going back and forth between garden and faucet as you water different areas, and it will save on water.

Trench irrigation is a method for watering the garden from the sides, through a network of trenches or furrows built into the garden from the start. I don't think it's feasible for a lot of people, not only because it takes up valuable growing space in the garden, but also because it demands a bit more engineering savvy than many of us possess.

I once had a customer who created a system of aqueducts for his garden—just like the ancient Romans—but when it finally came time to irrigate, he discovered that all the water ran out of his garden in the wrong direction.

Much Ado about Mulch

Mulch is any material spread over the soil surface in your garden, and its use has a number of fiery advocates.

"Organic" mulchers use naturally occurring materials like peat moss, hay, grass clippings, chopped-up corncobs, wood chips, and sawdust in their gardens. (Grass clippings, by the way, would be a bad choice as mulch if they came from a lawn treated with herbicides.)

Many commercial vegetable growers use sheets of black plastic or treated paper for mulching.

I don't recommend using any kind of mulch except during a drought in July and August, when it would definitely help conserve moisture in the soil bed.

Except for that one purpose, I think using mulches creates more problems than it solves. This is particularly true for newcomers to gardening who tend to think of mulching as a short-cut or cure-all approach. In fact, it takes an experienced gardener to know how and when to mulch effectively under any circumstances.

Since mulching has been a popular theme in many articles and books about gardening, I think I owe it to readers to be as specific as possible about my objections to its use. Let me launch my argument by listing the main reasons people give for mulching in the first place, and pointing out possible problems in each instance.

It is said that *mulch eliminates the need for weeding.* This is usually the big reason people mulch, and, if I may be blunt, this is the reason that attracts lazy folks and those who don't really have time to garden properly. Unquestionably, synthetic mulches, especially black polyethylene sheeting, will smother all weed growth. Organic mulches will keep down many weeds, too—though hardy perennial weeds tend to break through many of the natural covers.

But mulching itself takes time. You have to acquire and spread the stuff, a fact usually overlooked by mulch advocates.

And cultivating on a regular basis keeps you more aware of what's going on in your garden and gives you a head start on solving any problems that may crop up.

Cultivating once a week early in the growing season not only removes unwanted weeds, but also loosens and aerates the soil around young plants, fostering earlier, stronger growth, especially for tentative sprouters like cucumbers and squash.

Cultivating later in the season actually involves relatively little weeding, as once vegetable plants get established, they tend to shade out other growth. The hilling of beans, peppers, and eggplant—a job done at this time—enlarges the feeding areas and strengthens the plants for supporting the weight of bountiful fruit later on.

It is said that *mulch conserves moisture.* True, as I've said, and in periods of drought mulching may be a good idea.

But in periods of rainy weather, mulch can eliminate proper aeration in the soil and generate problems such as fungus, slugs, and wet rot.

Commercial growers will use mulch in areas where water is in short supply for their large tracts, or where the local water has too much salt, or some other substance harmful to vegetables.

Realistically, a water shortage would rarely affect the small home gardener. If you had to supply a 1,500-square-foot garden with all its water needs all summer long, you would still consume much less water than is used in taking showers and flushing toilets in your home in the same period. And with a good, moisture-retentive soil bed, you wouldn't have to be out there with the hose every day, either. Even on a burning-hot summer day, you'll lose no more than ½" of soil moisture to evaporation and transpiration.

It is said that *mulch adds organic matter to the soil.* True again; if you use an organic mulch, and spade it under every fall, you will improve the tilth of the soil to a degree.

But mulch such as leaves, grass clippings, or wood chips will not rot away in the course of one winter (little decay occurs in cold weather), and you may find that the residue from this material actually impedes efficient planting procedures in the spring.

Also, and perhaps more important, the addition of such material puts an added demand on the soil that may reduce its ability to nourish vegetable plants adequately in the spring. When it is turned under, mulch begins a process of decomposition that requires the cooperation of various microorganisms in the soil, and also various chemical elements, notably nitrogen.

It is said that *mulch protects fruit from soil and so reduces rot.* This would be true if for some reason the plant wasn't staked and it toppled over, or if the fruit became so ripe it dropped off the plant.

But healthy, well-supported plants don't fall down, and in a maximum-production garden, fruit is picked before it gets overripe.

I'm not unalterably opposed to mulching, but I do think many beginners fail to appreciate some of its possible drawbacks, and that, like the chemical approach to fertilizing, mulching can promote bad gardening habits in people with limited experience.

Mulching should be viewed as one possible tool in a multitude of small but valuable tricks and techniques that make up the playbook of any solid, experienced gardener.

I have a good friend who's tried to talk me into mulching for years. Last year he finally resorted to an experiment in hopes of proving how much more productive his mulching method was. He grew potatoes on small plots side by side. One he mulched with hay and the other he cultivated.

At harvest he got exactly the same amount of potatoes from both plots. Just one experiment, but food for thought.

Weather

The one thing you can't really control in the garden is the weather, which is why gardeners always have one eye out for it, and not much good to say for meteorologists generally.

Obviously, you can't turn off the cold or the wind or the wet. But you can take action when there are specific threats by weather to your crops.

Besides the practical advantage in becoming weather-wise and learning to recognize possible threats on the horizon, there's a lot of fun in trying to outwit nature—and some frustration and despair. Moreover, you gain a satisfying deeper awareness of the way the seasons of the year unfold.

There are perhaps a half-dozen key weather or climate factors affecting the life of the garden at different stages, and it's a good idea for gardening novices to acquaint themselves with these. That way, if you get the urge to start collecting rainfall in a calibrated soup can, or begin to betray a more than ordinary curiosity about full moons, you'll know you're not alone.

The frost-free date for your area is the most important fact of life in the first part of the gardening season. You can and should start working in the garden and planting some of the hardy crops before the day of the last expected freeze, but your main schedule is controlled by that frost. You don't really feel comfortable about putting things in the garden until it's time to cut your grass, and then you can be pretty sure the growing season has begun in earnest.

In our area the last frost usually hits in the first week of May. To be on the safe side, I wait until about May 15th to put out our frost-sensitive transplants. I figure there's no sense in risking the whole crop by planting on the early side, because I know I'm not going to get that much growth during the extra week or so that I might gain.

You're never quite sure you've had your last frost date, of course, and sometimes you haven't. Years ago we had a killing frost on June 2nd, and there wasn't a pepper plant left standing in all of Fairfield County. If a late frost is predicted—and when this happens it is usually in conjunction with a high-pressure weather system moving into your area—take steps to protect your tender seedlings with hot caps or old burlap or blankets, as I'll describe in more detail with early frosts in the fall.

Most springs are wet enough so you don't have to worry about watering the garden. Too much wetness is usually the problem—although less so in a fast-draining raised bed. If the garden area is too wet, you shouldn't try to work in it. It's better to wait until the soil dries to a nice, crumbly tilth before you go after it with a spade, or spread your compost or manure on it. If you're not sure the soil is ready to work, pick up a handful and squeeze it. If it's muddy or squishy, it's still too wet to work.

New seedbeds can be protected against driving rains in the spring by covering them with a length of wide-mesh burlap—not the closely woven feedbag type, but the sort interior decorators sometimes put on walls. This sturdy but porous material will permit air, light, and moisture to pass but hold the soil, and the seeds beneath them, in place. You can leave it on right up to sprouting, but you should remove the burlap once the first plants do appear.

Setting your own transplants into the garden can be a tricky business if you don't have a *cold frame* to harden them off in. Basically, it's a protected place where young plants started from seed indoors can gradually adjust to outdoor conditions. A cabbage plant conditioned to temperatures of over 60° F indoors might die if you suddenly exposed it to wind and temperatures under 40° F for a night. (For more on the cold frame, see page 195.)

If you buy your transplants from a good garden center—as you should do in your first year or two of gardening, rather than starting them indoors yourself—you won't have to worry about putting them through a hardening-off process, as they will have already been given that treatment.

In any event, it's usually a good idea to plan your spring plantings to coincide with periods of warmer weather. This can be arranged if you're attentive to normal weather cycles in spring. High-pressure areas bring in three or four days of cold weather from the north, and these are usually succeeded by low-pressure areas bringing in three or four days of warmer air from the south. The idea is to time setting out your transplants to the beginning of a low-pressure-area presence in your region. That way, the plants will get acclimatized by the time the next cold snap blows in from the north.

I've said some nasty things about plastic mulch over the years, so I ought to mention one useful application for this material in early spring. By covering a section of your garden with clear plastic, you can raise the soil temperature underneath it a good 5° to 10° F in a week or two of normal weather conditions.

An advanced gardener might want to try that to get a jump on planting radishes, lettuce, spinach, or carrots.

During the growing season, the main thing about the weather is to keep track of how well the garden soil is holding water, and I've gone into that already. And don't forget to stay out of the garden immediately after rainfall. When plants are wet, they bruise and cut more easily. Beans and cucumbers are especially susceptible to rust or wilt when this happens.

Another thing to watch for is too much rainfall. Nitrogen is the only plant nutrient that leaches out of the soil bed—dissolves and seeps down into lower strata, out of reach of roots. In a very wet summer, then, you should be prepared to replenish the nitrogen supply in your garden by spreading more aged manure, compost, manure tea, fish emulsion, or dried blood.

Toward the end of the growing season, the fall frost date looms in importance. Sometimes there are freak early frosts against which your only defense is covering frost-sensitive plants, like tomatoes, to keep the cold air from penetrating. A woven material such as burlap is ideal, but even paper bags and bushel baskets can do the job. That plastic mulch is ineffective, because the cold goes right through it. My mom used to keep her old blankets and sheets in the basement expressly for this purpose, and they worked fine, too.

Basically, this emergency plant protection is a pain. In a bad year you might have to run in and out of the house a half-dozen times. You're listening to more weather forecasts than you really can stand to hear. You're calling home to get members of your family to help on the project. ("Cover the peppers with the old window curtains. That's what I said—cover the *peppers* with the *curtains*.") But it's got to be done, and it's well worth the effort when a month of glorious weather follows after that freak frost, as sometimes happens. Vegetables don't grow as much in cooler fall weather, but some of them benefit considerably from the extra exposure.

In planning the garden around the fall frost date—the average date of the first *killing* frost, not necessarily that first, premature light frost—the idea is to make sure your succession crops will mature before cold weather sets in permanently, so that you can harvest them, store them, or leave them in the garden if they're storable there in ripe condition.

I would say that you can and probably should gamble a bit more on the fall frost date than the one in the spring, in order to stretch your garden productivity to the max. Unlike the tender seedlings and transplants of the spring garden, the fall garden's plants are already well established at the time cold weather threatens. Some of them, like carrots, aren't hurt by freezes anyway. Others, like brussels sprouts, leeks, and kale, are actually improved quite a bit in taste and texture by a cold spell.

It's the delicate plants—tomatoes, peppers, eggplant, beans, squash, and cucumbers—that you have to worry about. Sometimes you can predict a frost yourself. We always have a frost in the fall if there's a high-pressure system in the area at the time of a full moon. That's when I know we've got to get out the burlap bags and the window curtains.

Bugs & Co.

Toward the end of May and into June, customers begin to report to us on a mysterious development in their gardens. Namely, that something is eating the leaves off their beans or squash, and that it is invisible.

Usually "it" is "they," and they are "invisible" only because they are on the underside of the plant in question. Most garden bugs feed upside down, rather than right side up like the housefly, as many people seem unconsciously to expect. So if you don't look under the leaves, you may not find that you have an insect problem until it's too late.

Or they feed after dark. Slugs, snails, and cutworms always work the night shift. These you won't see except with a flashlight, or by looking under logs, stones, boards, broad-leafed plants, and any other conceivable hiding place in the area.

Or they wear camouflage. From a standing position in the garden, or even closer, the cabbage worm blends into the rib of the leaf, and the green aphid is exactly the color of a nice salad bowl lettuce. The tomato hornworm starts as little more than a speck on the underside of a tomato leaf. Even as it grows, it is hard to see even if you look under that leaf because of the worm's amazing protective coloration. But if it is allowed to grow to its full potential of 5', at which point it resembles a creature out of science fiction, its voracious feeding habits will destroy your plant. And as used to be said of the martini, there is no such thing as one tomato hornworm. Neighboring plants will also be infested.

(One of the best bug-identification guides I've seen is the "Pest Control Library" on the National Garden Association's website, www.garden.org. The "Bug Mugs" section is a photo index of caterpillars, beetles, grasshoppers, borers, and smaller pests such as aphids, mealy bugs, and spider mites, with descriptions of their specific threats to vegetable plants, along with organic techniques for combating them. Insects beneficial to the garden, such as ladybugs, parasitic wasps, and green lacewings are also posted.)

Bear in mind in every case that if some pest is big enough to eat a hole in a leaf, it is big enough to be found and destroyed.

I haven't mentioned bugs until now for two reasons.

First, I think the subject can be needlessly alarming. Much garden literature breeds a kind of paranoia about the insect kingdom, especially in new gardeners, by dwelling at length on the hundreds of different types of creatures and diseases that can invade a garden.

Second, keeping bugs out of the garden should be achieved mainly as a by-product of the various good gardening techniques already discussed, and not by pushing a button on some deadly spray, or using some other highly specialized cure.

The same goes for plant diseases. Sure, fungi, bacteria, viruses, and nematodes—all of which can attack vegetable plants—exist. But a healthy, well-maintained garden is disease-resistant. Here's why:

Building a rich, well-drained soil bed for a garden eliminates dank spots and fosters healthier plant development. Strong, healthy plants resist bugs and fungus or disease problems better than weak plants.

Elevating the garden keeps some pests from crawling in. Border-planting with alliums deters still others.

Proper spacing in the garden encourages good air and light circulation. Proper cultivation keeps the weeds down. Bugs are much less likely to be drawn into a neat, clean garden patch than they are to a thickly planted, weedy patch.

Taken all together, these and other preventive techniques will not eliminate pests and diseases from your garden altogether, but they will certainly minimize the problems. With routine attention to your garden—and the awareness that most bugs eat their breakfast and lay their eggs on the underside of leaves—you should be able to control most of your problems simply by picking them off by hand. And they must be removed. Some of my customers have another false notion about bugs, which is that they'll stop eating when they get full. Actually, they have unlimited appetites and will strip leaves down to the veins. They will also invite their relatives and friends and multiply rapidly if left unchecked.

If you don't have time to hand-pick the bugs yourself, find a young bounty hunter who will. One of my customers gives his nine-year-old son two cents for every Japanese beetle, five cents for every slug, and ten cents for every cabbage moth (butterflies aren't that easy to catch). He winds up with a clean garden, and Alex has plenty of money to spend on baseball cards.

Unless you have permitted a real infestation to develop, I would not even consider resorting to chemical warfare to get rid of insects in the garden. Many of the 500 insects that can do significant damage to crops have built up a resistance to insecticides anyway. If there are too many bugs to destroy by hand, or if you can't find the bugs that are causing the damage, you could use an appropriate organic insecticide like pyrethrin, which is derived from a species of chrysanthemum, or rotenone, an extract of the tropical derris root. Both are biodegradable and not considered hazardous to birds, wildlife, the environment, or the toddler who wanders over from your neighbor's yard.

Also, let natural enemies of harmful bugs do their predatory work in peace. Don't assault any toads or snakes you may find in the garden. And again, stay out of the place when it's wet, not only because your presence could jar plants and abuse the soil, but also because that's when more birds are likely to be attracted to the garden in the first place. Unlike many novice gardeners, birds do look under leaves for bugs.

Ladybugs and praying mantises are often offered through catalogs in packages of battalion strength. I do not recommend buying these to control your pests, simply because a stiff breeze may carry them into your neighbor's yard five minutes after you release them in your garden, or will not remain on sentry duty but will transfer of their own accord as soon as they've finished off the insects you do have.

Those electric bug-zapping units are of dubious value to the home gardener as well. They function effectively only at night, and their special light attracts and electrocutes bugs from all over town, not just in your own yard.

INSECT CONTROL VIA COMPANION PLANTING

Santolina, Santolina,
How I love my Santolina.
Some are green and some are grey,
Rub them each and every day.
It's amazing—you will praise them
As they chase the bugs away.

I wrote this rhyme for a brochure we prepared for our customers a number of years ago. The technique of companion planting has been used against bugs by organic gardeners since ancient times. But the technique of scientific analysis has not yet been used against companion planting—at least not to my knowledge— and so what we have on the subject today amounts to a fascinating mixture of both fact and fancy.

Three things are definitely true:

- With the exception of the Allium family, no herb, flower, or plant is effective as a companion plant against a large number of different bugs.

- Some companion plants attract their own pests.

- No companion plant achieves its desired effect unless it is used in sufficient quantity.

Many gardeners are particularly naive about this last requirement. It is an observable phenomenon, for instance, that marigolds repel many bugs. But one small marigold planted in the center of a 100-square-foot garden (I have seen it done) is not going to protect that garden from anything.

Once you start using companion planting in the quantity required, however, it begins to interfere with your vegetable production.

For example, the herb hyssop repels the cabbage moth. But you would need about one hyssop plant for every head of cabbage for the moths to stay away. Since hyssop always grows much bigger than cabbage, and has little culinary use to recommend it, it would seem to be a waste of both time and space to use it as a companion plant. Hyssop belongs somewhere in your garden if only for its ability to attract bees.

I would suggest as an approach to companion planting in a limited garden area that you use only those companion plants that serve you—and their companions—in more than one way.

Onions are a perimeter defense against bugs, plus a crop in themselves. As I've said a couple of times already, I believe that border-planting of these alliums is the single most effective and practicable form of companion planting for most gardens. That's why all my garden plans include some combination of garlic, garlic chive, onion sets, Bermuda or Spanish onions, and leeks around the borders.

Marigolds naturally deter many bugs, plus they are pretty, so you might use them for their aesthetic effect along one border, where they would not take up a significant amount of your planting space.

Herbs That Repel Insects

COMMON NAME / BOTANICAL NAME	PESTS REPELLED
Holy basil / *Ocimum sanctum*	flies and mosquitoes
Lavender / *Lavendula*	mosquitoes and gnats
Lemon balm / *Melissa officinales*	mosquitoes and gnats
Lemon thyme / *Thymus x citriodorus*	mosquitoes and gnats
Mexican marigold / *Tagetes minuta*	mosquitoes and gnats
Mugwort / *Artemisia vulgaris*	moths
Pennyroyal mint / *Mentha pulegium*	fleas and ticks
Pyrethrum / *Chrysanthemum cineriifolium*	mites, aphids, and leaf hoppers
Santolina / *Santolina chamaecyparussys*	all insects
Scented geranium / *Pelargonium graveolens*	mosquitoes and gnats
Southernwood / *Artemesia abrotanum*	moths
Tansy / *Tanacetum vulgare*	ants

Basil, thyme, rosemary, and sage are all useful culinary herbs, so these can serve a dual role if planted in the garden.

Basil repels white flies and mosquitoes. My mother planted basil among her tomatoes, because when she wanted tomatoes for sauces or salads, she usually wanted some basil as well. Every time you break off a basil leaf, the aroma fills the air, so harvesting some leaves is like spraying that section of the garden with an insect repellent. It can be effective planted near cucumbers and squash as well.

Thyme keeps away the cabbage worm. Rosemary and sage repel the cabbage moth, bean beetle, and carrot fly. These herbs are also popular in many recipes.

Nasturtium can serve three purposes: as a decorative feature in the garden, because it flowers; as a crop, because its leaves and petals can be eaten in salads; and as a companion plant, because it repels the aphid, a particularly pesky insect on such vegetables as squash and lettuce. Unfortunately, nasturtium has no effect on spider mites and sometimes becomes infested with them.

Two herbs that are seldom mentioned as companion plants but are quite effective are the *Santolinas* and the *Artemesias*. The wide variety of these herbs is also quite attractive, but they need too much room to be considered for use in smaller gardens. Be sure to include them, however, if you have room for a small herb garden. An herb garden of any kind should always be put as close as possible to the vegetable garden, for it can be in effect a collection of many different companion plants.

OTHER ANTI-BUG METHODS

Neither regular surveillance of the garden nor careful companion planting, if you have the room, will solve all bug problems. But there is still another way to deal with pests, and it might be described as the Heroic Counterattack Method of Pest Control. Two of my customers resorted to this method and had great results.

One was a young fellow. He came in around mid-June looking for a nonchemical method for dealing with an invasion of cabbage maggots. He was a coleslaw fanatic and had planted two dozen heads of cabbage in the spring, but now they were all beginning to wilt. I told him that wood ashes were good to use against this pest, which eats at the roots of the cabbage, but that it sounded as if the problem was too far advanced to do much about it.

The fellow felt differently. He got his hands on some fireplace ashes, went home, dug up all twenty-four cabbages, washed off all their roots, refilled the planting holes with a mixture of soil and ashes, and put them back in their places. He saved every head.

Another man, a squash-lover, discovered that his six prize plants were starting to wilt just about the time they were supposed to start producing fruit. I told him it sounded like squash borer to me and described how that pest usually operates; it works into the stem of the plant from the ground and then eats its way up, invariably killing the plant. My customer promptly went home, slit each stem on his squash plants with a sharp penknife, fished out the culprit worms, then wrapped gauze around the wounds and watered all the plants well. After a brief postoperative decline, all six plants returned to good health and produced more squash than even he could eat.

These are obviously very special anti-bug methods tried by very special gardeners, but I think they point up a message that really applies to everyone at every stage of insect control: against pests and problems in the home garden, you are your own best defense.

Herbs for the Kitchen, Flowers for the Table

As I mentioned earlier, I like to see vegetable gardeners include some cutting flowers in their gardens—sunflowers at the back of the garden, say, snapdragons and zinnias between rows of lettuce or beans—mainly because making regular visits to collect bouquets for the home encourages the gardener to stay in touch with progress—or problems—in the vegetable patch itself. The flowers make only a slight dent in kitchen garden productivity, and they serve as one more motivating factor to be out and about in the kingdom of plants.

Also, flowers for me represent the beauty of color and fragrance, virtues that are found in herb and vegetable gardens but in more subdued form. Long before my father started growing herb plants, he specialized in raising cut flowers for the New York wholesale market. I recall, as a kid, tramping out to our barn's "packing room" in February, when snow was still on the ground, to help my father and Uncle Angelo bundle up cut flowers and pack them into shipping boxes for a 2:00 A.M. pickup by the truck that would deliver them into Manhattan.

What remains most vivid to me in memory is the startling contrast in colors that the flowers provided at that most colorless time of year—the deep blue of irises, the happy yellow of daffodils, and the rainbow of hues in our tulips. These and other flowers—pansies, freesia, sweet peas, carnations, chrysanthemums, anemones, snapdragons—would be harvested all day long in our greenhouses and placed in buckets of water. After supper, we would go out and tie the flowers into bunches—snaps and mums by the dozen, which my father made a baker's dozen of thirteen; carnations and other varieties in two-dozen amounts—in reality, twenty-five flowers per bunch. (Nowadays, in case you haven't been counting, most commercial bouquets of a "dozen" flowers contain but nine or ten stems.) We were entertained during our evening labors in the packing room by radio broadcasts of favorite shows of that bygone era, including *Life with Luigi, Amos 'n Andy*, and *Fibber McGee and Molly*.

Incidentally, the flower departments that are so common in supermarkets today may have gotten their start back in that time. I remember my father telling me of innovative flower growers from Holland making the rounds of florists' shops, trying to sell the shopkeepers on the idea of buying cut flowers in wholesale bunches from the Dutch every week. But the florists were afraid of getting stuck with too many unsold bouquets—so the Dutch salesmen turned to the grocery chains.

Today, many shoppers go home with almost as many flowers in their grocery bags as peas and carrots. The beauty of a cutting garden, of course, is that you can enjoy fresh bouquets in your house all summer long, for a fraction of the price you pay in the supermarket or at the florist's shop. Not everyone will have room for a full-fledged cutting garden. That is why I suggest making room for at least a few cut flower varieties amid the vegetables. In any case, I have devised a plan for a large cutting garden (see page 229) for those who have the space and inclination to build it or some variation on its design.

As with my vegetable plants, I grow cut flowers in straight rows. This gives me the most production per foot of row. At the same time, the orderly plan makes it easier to take care of, water, and harvest the plants. I have a neighbor who likes to kid me about my "obsession" with neatness and order. Her own flower garden surrounds her house and barn with a sprawling, haphazard mixture of annuals and perennials. It looks beautiful from a distance, but up close it makes me dizzy.

My neighbor's garden is a variation on the informal "cottage garden" that originated in England hundreds of years ago. The earliest of these gardens, often attached to a working-class cottage, was a mixture of vegetables and herbs, with flowers used to fill in any spaces in between, along with some fruit trees and perhaps a beehive and a place for the family pig and a few chickens. A romanticized version of the cottage garden evolved to include rose bowers and old-fashioned favorites such as hollyhocks, pansies, and delphiniums. Add a peacock, a sundial, and pathways covered with creeping thyme, and you have a cottage garden straight out of the pages of Jane Austen.

The less romantic and more practical cutting garden that I recommend achieves a beauty of its own, but I admit it is less likely to inspire any watercolor-artist friends you may have. Here are the main flower varieties I would recommend you consider for inclusion in your own cutting garden.

- **China asters.** Plant as seedlings. A workhorse of the cutting garden, this annual aster has a long blooming season and enjoys exceptional vase life. Growing to about 2', China asters come in numerous colors and bloom shapes. They perform exceptionally well in late summer and early fall. Keep cutting for maximum production.

- **Cosmos.** Sow directly from seed or plant in the garden as seedlings. Cosmos produce daisy-like flowers in a host of colors, on long stems with ferny leaves. Most varieties grow to 2', 3', or 4', so they belong toward the back of the garden. Many are available in mixed colors, which may be desirable if there's room for only one or two rows. Keep cutting for maximum production.

- **Dahlia.** Plant tubers in the spring for steady blooms from summer into fall. Dahlias come in many shapes, sizes, and colors, with the taller-growing varieties generally offering the best choices for cutting. The shorter varieties often used for bedding are less desirable for use in the vase. Keep cutting for maximum production.

- **Gladiola.** Plant bulbs in the spring. Glads grow in spiky profusion to 2' to 3' and, unless staked, may lean like drunken sailors by summer's end. During early growth, florists pinch off the top few buds to force better blooms. For some reason, gladioli bring out the competitive streak in ardent gardeners. Many gladiola clubs hold weekly contests to determine which member has grown the most spectacular specimen. I guess I lost my taste for glads in those early years when I helped my dad grow them for the business—there were always too many to cut in the fields, and it was always too hot when we had to cut them. But, I admit, glads look beautiful in a vase.

- **Cleome.** Sow directly from seed or as seedlings. Known as spider flower for its delicate, spidery blooms, it is most often available in white, pink, and violet and grows to 3' to 5'. The flower develops a sticky, somewhat thorny stem, but handled carefully, it adds an ethereal element to arrangements. Keep cutting for maximum production.

- **Larkspur.** Plant as seedlings. Larkspur comes in a wide range of colors and grows in a productive branching habit to about 3'. The stems of this delphinium-like flower are straight and strong. Larkspur makes a striking vertical element in any flower arrangement.

- **Lisianthus.** Plant in the garden as seedlings. Lisianthus produces elegantly formed blooms similar to roses or ranunculus, in white, lavender, purple, pink, and some bicolors. This flower thrives in cooler weather and well-drained soil—avoid overwatering. The best cutting varieties grow to 2' to 3'.

- **Blue salvia.** Plant as seedlings. This is a tender perennial that must be grown as an annual in most hardiness zones. It comes in other colors but the blue variety is most prized by flower arrangers. Johnny's Selected Seeds offers a lovely blue variety of German origin, Gruppenblau, that grows to almost 3'.

- **Snapdragons.** Plant as seedlings. Snaps grow in elegant, softly puffed spikes in many different colors to 3' to 4' (shorter bedding varieties are not as useful for cutting). Tolerant of the cold, they can be transplanted into the garden before the ground has warmed, allowing a jump on the season. When I'm cleaning up my own flower gardens in the fall, I often leave a row of my frost-tolerant snaps in place in the hope of having the surprise pleasure of picking a bunch of them as late as Thanksgiving. Many varieties have a lingering fragrance. Keep cutting snapdragons for maximum production.

- **Sunflowers.** Sow directly from seed, and then stand back, as the largest varieties will grow as tall as 12' to 14'. Actually, giant sunflowers are grown not for cutting but for their spectacular look at the back of the garden and for their seed heads, which birds will feast on at season's end. The shortest varieties are too short-lived for my money. The best sunflowers for cutting purposes are in the midsize range of 2' to 5' and today come in an astonishing range of colors—electric lemon, sunset orange, deep red, bronze, and mahogany, to name just a few. Johnny's, Harris Seeds, and many other seed dealers offer dozens of variations on the sunflower theme. The listings in their catalogs are great inspiration on a cold winter's day. If space is available, plan several sowings of sunflowers at ten-day intervals to ensure a longer harvest period.

- **Zinnias.** Sow directly from seed or as seedlings. This mainstay of the country bouquet comes in a wide range of sizes, shapes, and colors, but the midsize Cut 'n Come Again varieties yield the best blooms for use in the vase. It is a great provider of color later in the season when other flowers have become less productive. Keep cutting for maximum production.

FLOWERS FOR CUTTING AND FOR DRYING

Gardeners who enjoy making dried bouquets in the fall often include celosia, gomphrena, nigella (Love-in-a-mist), statice, and strawflower in their cutting gardens. Although these flowers all dry well, they also may be selectively harvested in season for use in fresh bouquets.

A STRATEGY FOR KITCHEN HERBS

Many years ago, when I was suddenly thrust into the garden business after the sudden death of my father, many friends of our family and regular customers at our garden center in Westport became, in effect, a support group for me, providing encouragement, advice, and ideas in hopes of improving my odds at making a success of things.

Mary and Ben Brown were one such couple to take me under their wing. One day, because at this time I was determined to expand our farming operation to include growing live herb plants, Mary came to me and said she and her husband wanted to take me to see a retail herb nursery they had come upon across the state line in New York's Westchester County. So I arranged to accompany them on a visit to this location.

When I got there, I must say I wasn't very impressed by the way the place looked. The herb gardens, such as they were, could only be described as unkempt. Anyway, Mary asked one of the owners if she could have a look at a certain herb she was interested in. I can't remember exactly what that herb was, but I'll never forget the way in which the co-proprietor went about trying to find it.

"I know it's in here somewhere," she declared, kicking around in the weedy undergrowth in one of the garden beds with her feet.

As readers undoubtedly know by now, I am not the kind of gardener who searches for plant specimens with his feet. I like clean, neat, weed-free, well-nourished gardens of excellent soil tilth, because I know I am more likely to grow plants successfully in them.

Although herbs are not the heavy feeders that fruit-producing vegetable crops are, they also thrive in the growing conditions that are ideal for them. In devising a strategy for helping novice gardeners or gardeners with little experience to include the most popular and useful culinary herbs in their garden plans, I have in mind, first and foremost, the conditions that will make the herbs happy and healthy.

My basic approach for adding herbs to your mix of vegetables and cut flowers is simple. I recommend planting some herbs in containers near the kitchen and planting others, which require more space to grow successfully, in selected locations in your raised beds.

Containers come in all shapes, sizes, and styles. A container measuring 18" to 24" across and 12" to 18" deep will support the seven kitchen herbs, all compact growers, that I have listed below. The larger the container, the better, because plants will do better if they have plenty of composted soil mix to draw nutrients from, and watering the plants will be less onerous during the growing season. Smaller containers may seem more manageable for moving about, but they will require much more attention on your part for watering and feeding.

Choose the sunniest location for this container that you can find, even if it means it will be less convenient to the kitchen. This location should receive 6 to 8 hours of sun per day. Bear in mind that plants in containers need more fertilization than plants in garden beds, because water bears away the nutrients in the limited soil base. This means side-dressing the kitchen herb container once a month throughout the growing season. A shot of manure or compost tea or liquid fish emulsion fertilizer, once a month (see "Side Dressing," page 90), will do wonders for your potted herbs.

The seven kitchen herbs recommended for our jumbo patio container are widely available as young plants in garden centers and nurseries in the spring, and that's how I think most newcomers to gardening should obtain them.

- **Dwarf basil.** As a culinary herb, basil combines naturally with any tomato dish, and its clove-like flavor enhances both Italian and Asian cookery. There are many varieties of basil, but the two outstanding compact bush basils that I recommend for containers are Minette and Spicy Globe. Famously sensitive to cold, basil succumbs to the first light frosts of fall (although covering plants can prolong the season). For cooks who want basil in quantity, I recommend planting seedlings of any of the large-leafed Genovese strains of basil in the main garden—next to your tomatoes, naturally. Or plant an extra crop of basil in its own patio pot. A pot 14" to 16" wide and 12" deep will accommodate a full-sized basil variety nicely.

- **Sweet marjoram.** This tender perennial grows in bush form to about 12". It is used most often in cooking for its sweet, pungent flavor. Cooks rub roasts with the leaves or add them to soups in the last fifteen minutes of cooking. Flowers on the plant resemble small green knots; the leaves should be harvested just as the blooms begin.

- **Greek oregano.** Another perennial, this herb varies greatly in leaf size, shape, color, and growth habit, as it is grown from seed collected in the wild in the mountains of Greece. I discovered this many years ago. Art's Deli used to be a great source for Mediterranean specialties near our garden center in Westport. Every day at lunchtime the line would be out the door for Art's legendary grinders. When I first got started in business, I would buy packages of dried Greek oregano from Art, complete with stems, flowers, and seeds. I would go back to the garden center, separate out the seed, and sow it in starter pots. Invariably I'd get six or seven different varieties of Greek oregano, from a small, gray-leaf variety to a large, dark green variety, but they all had the same pizza flavor. The same holds true today, so don't be surprised if your neighbor's Greek oregano doesn't look like your Greek oregano. It's the taste that counts. The spiciest of all the oreganos, it is an excellent seasoning for meats, tomato dishes, and sauces.

- **Parsley.** One of the indispensable cooking herbs, parsley is a biennial available in two forms: the Italian flat-leafed kind preferred by chefs because it has more flavor, and curly parsley, which has some flavor but is more valued as a decorative garnish. Like basil, parsley should also be grown in the main garden to ensure its availability to the cook all season long. Or, as with basil, give it a patio pot of its own.

- **Winter savory.** A nearly evergreen shrub with dainty white flowers, this perennial herb has a stronger flavor than summer savory, an annual. Commonly used to season beans, cabbage, and turnips, it is also prescribed as a salt substitute.

- **Sage.** This workhorse perennial herb of the colonial kitchen comes in several colors and growing habits. My recommended variety, Berggarten, originating in West Germany, is a beautiful compact bush with rounded silvery leaves and lilac-blue flowers.

- **Lemon thyme.** This perennial herb has glossy, dark green leaves and upright growth. Cooks cherish its intense lemon scent and flavor. Although its lavender flowers attract bees, lemon thyme is one of the best natural insect repellents in the garden or on the patio. This herb also comes in a variegated golden hue, which will give your container some bright contrasting color.

Other herbs valuable to the gourmet cook, such as bay, rosemary, and mint, also may be grown in their own pots on a sunny kitchen patio. Bay laurel and rosemary, both staples of Mediterranean cuisine, are tender perennials, and need to be brought inside in northern winters to survive. Purchase them as young plants in the spring and transplant to pots at least 12" wide and 10" deep for the first growing season. In subsequent years it will be necessary to "pot up" the plants to larger pots as their root systems develop. If you have space in the garden, bury the pots of bay and rosemary in soil and you won't have to water them as much. Be sure earth covers the rims of buried terra-cotta pots, which otherwise would serve as wicks and evaporate moisture from the plants.

Mints, which are valued as garnishes for drinks and desserts, for making tea, and for a host of other culinary applications, have such invasive root systems that they are best sequestered in their own containers. I recommend planting peppermint and spearmint, the two most popular varieties (widely available as transplants in the spring) side by side in a large wooden planter or window box that has been divided down the middle with material that will serve as a barrier to roots migrating from one side to the other. Mints tolerate shade more than many herbs. They are so hardy that they are likely to survive even a severe winter, but if you like, you can mulch them for added protection in the late fall, or bring them into the garage for the winter months.

Here are some additional culinary herbs worth considering for inclusion in your garden beds on a space-available basis.

- **Basil.** To supplement the dwarf basil growing in your kitchen herb container, consider planting high-production basil alongside tomato plants in the vegetable garden. Recommended varieties: Nufar, a Genovese variety rich in flavor and aroma—developed in 2006, the first basil proven to be resistant to the fusarium wilt disease; and Aussie Sweetie, sometimes called Greek Columnar, an upright variety that grows to 3' if not harvested regularly.

- **Chervil.** This underappreciated culinary herb is most widely known in French cooking, where its anise-tarragon flavor is a substitute for parsley. Chervil combines particularly well with eggs, vegetables, and salads. It prefers a cool season and goes to seed quickly in summer heat—plant in semishade for best results.

- **Chives.** Easy to grow from seedlings in the spring, easy to like in salads and other recipes for its delicate onion flavor, this perennial grows in manageable clumps and produces pretty (and edible) rose or purple blooms. It fits in almost anywhere. Chives would make attractive corner plantings, for example, in a cutting garden, or as a border around any vegetable bed.

- **Coriander/Cilantro.** Sow it in the garden just like dill. Try the variety Delfino, if you can find it. Developed in 2005 in The Netherlands, it has a fernlike appearance, grows to about 18", and is both very aromatic and slow to bolt in hot weather.

- **Dill.** This elegant annual is best sown from seed in short rows in the vegetable garden. It doesn't take up much linear space, but grows quite tall and produces both ferny leaves and seeds that can be put to good use in the kitchen in ways too numerous to mention. Standard varieties can reach heights of 4' to 5'. The two best varieties for the home garden are Fernleaf, which grows to a manageable 24", and Bouquet, which grows to 24" to 30".

- **Lovage.** This perennial needs a corner of the garden all its own, as it grows to 6'. Its leaves taste of celery with an undertone of curry; they are good sprinkled in salads and soups. Roasted chicken stuffed with lovage, garlic, butter, salt, and pepper gets high marks from diners. Vegetarian recipes call for lovage as a meat substitute. Lovage is one of the earliest arrivals in the spring garden.

- **Salad burnet.** This low-growing perennial may be planted along edgings or borders. Its leaves provide a light cucumber flavor in salads. Pinch off flowers to encourage maximum leaf production. Like lovage, salad burnet is a welcome sight early in the growing season.

- **French tarragon.** This perennial herb in the artemesia family grows to about 12" to 18". Spreading by rhizomes, it likes a well-drained soil. The subtle anise flavor of tarragon complements chicken, fish, and omelettes and makes an outstanding vinegar for salads. One plant serves all. (Be sure you purchase *French* tarragon, not the herb sold as Russian tarragon, which has no flavor.)

- **Lemon verbena.** A tender perennial with the strongest lemon flavor of all the herbs, it's a popular ingredient in beverages and potpourris. Start from an established plant in the spring, as it is extremely slow to grow from seed. One plant is all you need. (Lemon verbena can be dug up, potted, and wintered over in a cool location inside the house or garage. It drops its leaves but comes back to life in the spring.)

III. Maximum-Production Techniques

Plant Your Personality

I maintain two vegetable gardens: one at home, about 750 square feet in size; the other at our garden center, a 1,500-square-foot model garden from which several families enjoy the produce. The garden plans contained in this book are based on my experience in gardening in those two basic areas over the years. In all, I have worked out three plans—750, 1,500, and 3,000 square feet—for growing more than fifty of the most popular vegetables.

In addition to the general plans, I've included three plans for specialized gardens of about 400 square feet. One features salad vegetables, another crops and herbs for use in soups. The third small garden shows what you can do if you're starting too late in the spring to plant a lot of the full-season crops. Also included are designs for a small cutting garden (flowers), a patio garden using containers, and a budget raised-bed garden that does without perimeter materials.

For the fun of it, I've also included a 100-square-foot garden plan in case you'd like to convert a sandbox area into an enjoyable learning experience for young children—who will be just about the right age for appreciating the growing of vegetables when they have outgrown the sandbox stage.

There's nothing to prevent you from adapting or combining or interchanging any and all of these plans for your own purposes. My general gardens have a slight Italian accent, what with the peppers and basil and eggplant and such. You may not have the appetite for all those tomatoes—or the desire to preserve them at season's end. My mother used to can 120 quarts from the 1,500-square-foot garden alone.

I have worked out the plans in such detail not to convert you to Neapolitan cuisine but to give you the means to plan the planting of your own favorite vegetables thoughtfully and accurately. To make it easy for you, all the plans are drawn to scale and all of them show—wherever feasible for the particular crop—the precise number of plants that fit in a row of a certain length.

The plans also show where double- and triple-row planting—or close-row planting, as I think of it—can save space, and exactly how interplanting and succession planting techniques can be used to increase productivity. By copying here and there from these garden plans, you'll be able to come up with a garden plan that actually works. I think you'll find these plans more useful than the usual garden plans, and certainly worth more than a lot of pretty pictures of vegetables (which you can get for free in the seed catalogs).

And it will be necessary, at some point, for you to sit down with pad, pencil, and ruler and make a garden plan that suits your individual requirements.

Each of us has a particular kind of space to garden in. There are, I imagine, more shapes and sizes for vegetable gardens than Euclid ever dreamed of, simply because of the infinite variety in terrain.

Everyone has different tastes, too. Today, more and more gardeners include herbs and flowers with a variety of vegetables. On the other hand, I have one good customer who grows nothing but peas and melons every year. It happens to be a happy combination: the peas always finish in time for the long-season melons to take over. I have another customer who loves potatoes. He has the space for a variety of crops, but he sticks to one crop. In fact, he grows a couple of potato plants in a barrel on his patio every year. On Labor Day, he holds a party at which all the guests are expected to bet money on how many potatoes have formed. Then he breaks open the barrel and counts the potatoes. The winner collects the money and the spuds.

Everyone has different needs. Diet-conscious gardeners may want to grow a lot of salad greens and vegetables. Some people may have to grow certain vegetables to suit their health requirements. No-starch Jerusalem artichokes would be perfect for a person on a low-carbohydrate diet.

If you live in a family group, make sure you consult other members about what to put in the garden. Try to make gardening a group activity, not a one-person operation. Don't exclude the lazy or indifferent family members from the easy and enjoyable parts, such as choosing what to grow and harvesting what has grown. This has practical as well as philosophical implications. You never know when you're going to need somebody's cooperation urgently, as when the hose springs a leak in the middle of a delicate irrigation procedure, or when, some frosty day in fall, you can't get home in time to put parkas on the tomatoes yourself.

Finally, when you do plan your garden, feel free to succumb to a certain amount of "gardener's madness," which expresses itself in an unreasonable desire to grow something that nobody likes, or that's unsuited for your climate or garden space, or that otherwise fails to meet any of the requirements of sensible gardening already mentioned. I haven't accounted for this in any of the plans, because every gardener goes crazy in a different way.

Shopping for Seeds and Seedlings

If you're in your first year or two of vegetable gardening, and are still not quite sure of the difference between a cold frame and a frost date, or hilling beans and drilling beets, then there is no point in worrying about what seeds to buy. Start your fruit crops and brassicas from healthy transplants, and your onions from sets or seedlings, as I suggest, and you'll only have a few seed purchases to worry about.

SHOPPING FOR SEEDS
The main crops that should be sown directly from seed are:

peas
beans
radishes

beets

carrots

turnips

parsnips

spinach

Swiss chard

salad herbs

corn

New Zealand spinach

lettuce (earliest crops should be started as seedlings)

Direct sowing means planting seed in the row or furrow where they will remain until harvest—unless removed early in a thinning procedure. Indirect sowing, by contrast, means planting seed indoors for later removal to the garden, possibly in two or even three stages of transplant.

In any case, direct-sown crops are generally packaged to plant a 25' row. Some seed companies are quite generous with their seed, but to be safe you should figure that the contents of any standard packet is designed to occupy the 25 feet, and no more.

Once you know the quantity desired, buy them either through the catalogs or in the seed racks at your local garden center, keeping a few factors in mind.

Note the crop's days to maturity to be sure it fits into your own planting schedule and the dictates of your region's frost dates.

Some varieties of seed have been developed with built-in resistance to one or more problems. There are beans that possess a special tolerance to bean mosaic, for example, and lettuces that resist bolting, or going to seed, in warm weather. The less experienced gardener is always wise to pick the variety that gives him or her an edge, if there is a choice.

If you're buying seed through a catalog, read each crop description, so you don't make the mistake of ordering a variety that isn't suited for your soil and climate conditions. If you're unsure, compare your choice with a list of recommended varieties from your extension service.

Naturally, select the characteristics you want in size, taste, color, and other traits of possible interest. Note, for example, that some varieties are more suitable for home-freezing than others.

SHOPPING FOR SEEDLINGS

Eggplant, pepper, tomatoes, squash, and the various brassicas are usually available from a good garden center in individual peat pots or pellets, which you can plant directly into the soil, or in small fibrous or plastic quantity containers, called market packs, usually holding 6 to 12 plants, from which you remove the root balls to plant.

If you're planting enough of any one of these transplants, you can save money by buying the market packs. In the Victory Garden days, when more people gardened and did so in greater volume, we sold tomatoes in 16" x 24" cedar flats containing 108 seedlings. That was the minimum order, and my father developed tremendous muscles in his forearms from carrying the heavy flats around two at a time. As a ten-year-old, I could carry one flat to a customer's car, and I dreamed of the day I would be strong enough to handle two. Nowadays our "volume" market pack is down to 12 plants—and many gardeners can't find room for that many.

The fewer plants you buy, the more attention you perhaps should pay to their quality. Let me explain.

A good garden center starts a tomato plant from a large flat in the greenhouse, then transfers the seedling to an individual container and tends it until it is just about 8" to 10" tall. At this point the plant is gradually exposed to cooler temperatures so that, over a period of 7 to 10 days, it becomes adjusted to conditions outdoors. During this period, the plant doesn't get any taller, but it develops strength in the stem and roots. If the greenhouse manager has timed things correctly, it will have hardened off and thickened through the stem by the time it is put out for sale.

A quick-buck grower, by contrast, will raise tomato seedlings in half the time, by force-feeding the plants and submitting them to 70° to 80° F temperatures. Without the benefit of the cooling-off or conditioning period, these plants will develop quite a spindly stem. They will not be able to withstand the vagaries of spring planting conditions as well as the properly grown seedling will. A sudden cool night (40° to 45° F) could damage them even without a frost.

In short, as for anything else, it pays to shop for transplants with care.

The first thing to check is the thickness of that stem. This applies particularly to tomatoes and eggplant. Peppers tend to develop thicker stems even when they haven't been properly hardened off. Little hairs around the base of the stem are another sign that the plant's had a chance to get used to life in the great outdoors.

Check the plant's color. Yellow leaves may mean lack of nutrients in the growing pack, or that the plants have already contracted a wilt disease.

Check under the leaves and on the stem for evidence of fungus. A moldy growth would indicate the plant's been in overly humid hothouse conditions, or overcrowded in the pack, or overwatered. Also check for the presence of bugs—aphids or red spider mites in particular. There's no point in bringing someone else's pests into your garden.

Make sure the plant is erect. If it's growing crooked, it may not be a vigorous plant, and you'll have to take more pains in transplanting it.

If you have a choice, avoid buying a plant that already has fruit on it, unless the plant is individually potted, because this means it was started too early or kept in the pack too long. However, some plants, such as patio tomato varieties, are deliberately developed in larger containers for people who want to get those early tomatoes. These will be fairly mature plants, able to support their fruit clusters.

Don't worry if there are flowers on the plant. These might drop off the seedling after it's set in the garden, but that won't affect the normal development of the plant.

Check the leafy growth of all transplants. If bottom leaves are missing, it could mean the seedlings were grown too close together, or that insects have attacked them. You can always plant such a seedling a bit deeper than normal, but again—if you have a choice of other plants—you're better off picking a plant with more consistent leafy growth.

As in shopping for seeds, ascertain the variety of the seedlings you are buying, and find out maturity dates, size of crop expected, and resistances. A tomato with a maturity date of 80 days is a tomato that is expected to bear fruit 80 days from the date of transplant into the garden. Hybrid tomatoes designated F1, for example, are a cross between two inbred parent plants and usually offer more vigorous growth and more uniform production than other varieties. There are tomatoes that resist the plant diseases of verticillium and fusarium wilt and the rootworm problem of nematodes, and are marked for these traits as, respectively, V, F, and N or, if the tomato is resistant in all three departments, as VFN. There are cucumbers that are resistant to mosaic and mildew.

Look for the varieties that will fit your garden plans, and beware of vagueness. If you want small-head cabbages, or early-spring broccoli, make sure the tag that says "CABBAGE" or "BROCCOLI"—whichever you're really after —before carting the plants off to the cash register. It's difficult to identify the differences in cabbage, broccoli, cauliflower, brussels sprouts, and kohlrabi when they're all in seedling form, so beware of unlabeled plants. Any healthy brassica seedling will stand erect, not weak or floppy, and possess strong color. Make sure there are no holes in the leaves of those you select, as young brassicas are often attacked by insects.

Squash and cucumbers are also grown in individual containers but have 2 to 5 seedlings in them, rather than one, the exact number depending on how many seeds actually sprouted from the original sowing. Pick pots with at least 2 to 3 plants in them for your garden. If the plants are not at least 3" to 4" high, they'll be hard to transplant. They should have a strong green color and stand erect. If any of these seedlings have fallen over limply in the pot, it may mean they've been hit by a damping-off fungus, which might spread to all the plants in that particular container.

Gardening in Small Spaces

Plants have been grown in containers since at least the time of the Hanging Gardens of Babylon, one of the seven wonders of the ancient world. Gardeners of today who may be limited in what they can grow in their windows or on their decks and patios may not earn a place in history with their efforts, but they can have the satisfaction of a summer-long supply of vegetable varieties that thrive in small spaces.

Container gardening enjoys certain advantages. It allows the grower to take complete control over the soil medium used, ensuring it is sterile as well as fertile. Soil-borne diseases, insects, and nematodes, a common threat to garden soils, are less likely to afflict plants in containers. Fertilizer applications in containers can also be managed with more precision. And, when properly chosen, arranged, and planted up, containers can add a pleasing esthetic element to a patio, balcony, deck, or terrace.

But I don't want to give the impression that small-space gardening is a cinch. It is more challenging to grow tomatoes or other vegetable crops in a container than in the garden. Containers dry out more quickly; hence they require more frequent watering. This increase in irrigation in turn flushes nutrients from the soil more quickly, so containers require more fertilization.

Speaking of containers, you undoubtedly have seen utterly charming images in magazines and elsewhere of plants growing out of discarded boots and hats, ancient wheelbarrows, plastic milk containers, and sundry other makeshift containers. Caveat emptor: novelty containers and bizarre growing techniques do not a garden make.

Having said that, let me assure you that gardeners can grow vegetables successfully in containers if they know what they are doing and make sensible choices about what to grow and where to grow it. And let's face it, many gardeners have no choice but to use containers. City dwellers with terraces and suburbanites with patios, decks, and window boxes, but no sunny yard locations, can harvest respectable amounts of food for their tables if they employ proven methods for gardening in containers.

For example, here's a small but diverse patio garden that can be created with eight wooden whiskey barrels or square wood planters measuring at least 24" in diameter and 18" in depth—ideal for fruit-producing crops—and two long window box- or trough-type planters measuring 4' long, 12" wide, and 15" deep, ideal for leafy and root crops grown in rows.

Plan to use four of the large barrels or planters for tomatoes—one tomato plant per container. Plant a single bush cucumber and a single zucchini plant in each of two other large containers. Group three pepper plants and three eggplants in the remaining two planters.

The two long planter boxes can be used to grow lettuces, carrots, and beets from seed and onions from sets or seedlings. Incidentally, a handyman of average skills could save money by building these long planters as an easy weekend DIY project:

1. Nail two 1" x 8" cedar planks together for the long sides.

2. Use a 2" x 12" inch cedar plank for the bottom and sides.

3. Drill ¾" drainage holes in the bottom at 12" intervals.

4. Set all containers on wood blocks to further improve drainage.

Compact, Dwarf, and "Mini" Vegetable Varieties

Today, thanks to the development of new varieties by plant breeders and seed companies, many vegetables with compact growth habits and relatively high crop yields lend themselves to planting in containers of limited size. At our own garden center, for example, we offer these varieties in the spring for transplant directly into containers:

- Sugary grape tomato, producing large yields of sweet half-ounce fruit.

- Early Girl Bush tomato, a compact, disease-resistant strain producing 6-ounce fruit in less than 60 days.

- Patio tomato, a popular dwarf that grows only 2' tall but yields large harvests of 4-ounce fruit all season long.

- Red Robin tomato, an ornamental dwarf growing to 12" tall and producing masses of tasty half-ounce fruit.

- Taxi tomato, a lemon yellow compact variety yielding fruit the size of baseballs.

- Windowbox Roma tomato, a dwarf plant producing pear-shaped 2-ounce fruit of excellent flavor.

- Baby Bell eggplant, a plant growing to 24" with 3-inch-long fruit.

- Fairy Tale eggplant, a compact plant producing 4" to 6" purple and white-striped fruit.

- Pickle Bush cucumber, a compact vine yielding 4" fruit that make crisp, whole pickles.

- Salad Bush cucumber, another space-saving plant that produces dark green fruit up to 8" long.

- Tabasco hot pepper, a late-bearing pepper that produces the pepper that made Tabasco sauce famous; 3-inch-long yellow fruit is ready to pick when it turns fiery red.

- Thai Hot pepper, a decorative 8" bush bearing 2" fruit that turns bright red at harvest time; the "firecracker" of Thai and Chinese cooking.

Other recently developed vegetable varieties with compact growth habits can be grown in containers directly from seed, the most popular being lettuces, spinach, peas, radishes, carrots, and beets.

Other containers may be considered for small-space gardening. Terra-cotta and clay pots are attractive, but in large sizes they are expensive and may weigh too much for you to lug them around your terrace and bring inside to forestall cracking during winter freezes. Unless you have a philosophical aversion to plastic, molded polypropylene pots provide a good alternative to clay pots. They have the look of clay without the weight, and the soil in them will not dry out in hot weather as fast as it will in clay, terra-cotta, or thin plastic. They are available in large sizes.

Containers made of wood are preferable to other materials, in my opinion, for growing and maintaining healthy plants. (But avoid growing food crops in wood planters treated with creosote, Penta, or other toxic chemicals, for obvious reasons.)

SOIL MIX

A lightweight, well-drained, and well-aerated planting medium is best for growing vegetables in containers. Garden soil alone will be too heavy for containers and is likely to become compacted. I like to mix my own custom planting mix for my containers by combining in equal amounts:

- Compost (There's a wide range of excellent bagged compost products available today; I like a seaweed-and-shrimp-based compost made by Coast of Maine.)

- Peat moss

- Perlite

To this mixture, I add for its nutrient value pelleted dry chicken manure—I use a commercial variety called, perhaps not surprisingly, Cockadoodle DOO—but other dried manures will work just as well. Add about 1 quart dried manure per bushel of planting mix

Incidentally, the original soil bed in First Lady Michelle Obama's White House vegetable garden was made up of a similar mix: compost, crab meal from Chesapeake Bay, lime, and greensand. So I guess we are in good, organic company!

PLANTING

Plant vegetables in containers as you would in the garden. To avoid damage to maturing root systems, provide stakes or cages for tomatoes, stakes for eggplant and peppers, and trellises for cucumber vines at planting time. These supports will help the plant remain on its feet under the weight of fruit production and during high winds.

WATERING

Years ago, my parents had a house in Vermont that they used for weekend get-aways with other couples. I remember this quite clearly, because my dad would leave me a list of chores to do in the garden and greenhouses that would have kept ten workers busy! Anyway, the Vermont retreat was where my father had hoped to retire and plant gardens full of his beloved delphiniums, and it came with a patio where he grew flowers in containers. He always took his Super 8 film camera with him on these trips and recorded untold amounts of footage showing my mother and the other women visitors, all still in their bathrobes, watering the pots and planters on the patio. I don't know why he found this subject so fascinating, but I do know the governing principle behind the watering itself—always water container plants in the morning! (Never water them at night.) The idea being, give your plants all day to slowly absorb the water and the nutrients in the water.

I can't overstress the importance of finding the right balance between watering container plants too much and watering them too little. If roots remain in soggy soil too long, they rot. If root systems dry out, your plants will be under stress and will not perform as well. They will be an embarrassment when you have guests over for a cookout.

The easiest way to irrigate vegetables in containers is with a watering can or gallon jug. Some plants may need watering every day in the summer, depending on container size and weather conditions. Water your containers one at a time, then repeat the rotation to be sure water reaches the entire soil base. To avoid overwatering, stick your finger into the soil to a depth of 2". If it feels moist, hold back on watering.

Cat Cafeteria

If you have cats, you might set aside one patio container of medium size for their pleasure. Plant catnip seedling at the back of the container. This will grow to 2' to 3' with aromatic, minty foliage that is irresistible to felines. Then sow cat grass in the front of the container. Cat grass is in the wheat family and available in seed packets that invariably feature a picture of a cat. Keep the seed bed moist until germination, which occurs within days. Your cats will eat the grass, pull it up blade by blade, or just roll in it.

FEEDING

The down side of proper watering is that soil in containers loses its nutrients more rapidly than garden soil. This is why vegetable plants in containers need fertilizing more often than vegetables in a garden. I recommend using liquid fertilizers such as fish emulsion or manure tea or compost tea. The rate of application will vary with plants, conditions, and container size, but side dressing plants in containers once every 2 to 3 weeks is a good schedule to strive for.

With an array of large containers for your vegetables, and a few other pots set aside for herbs and flowers, you can have a patio that will be the envy of your neighborhood—and a bright spot in your daily life.

Maximum-Production Techniques for Over Fifty Popular Vegetables

I have not tried to cover the whole vegetable kingdom in the following pages. Some of the vegetables included in my garden plans are not described here because they're not that popular, or I have no particular slant on growing them extra productively, or their culture is similar to that of one of the vegetables I do describe.

Other vegetables are omitted because they don't fit into the scheme of things—as I see it, anyway—for most people gardening in limited areas. I'm talking about the big space-eaters like melons, winter squash, and pumpkins.

I have included cultural information on corn and potatoes because, though these do require a lot of space, they are highly productive food crops—potatoes in particular—and they're favorites of many people. One or both can be fitted into the 3,000-square-foot garden by removing a few rows of tomatoes, peppers, and brassicas. It would take a bit more finagling to fit corn or potatoes into a much smaller garden and still have variety. In every case, corn has to be located carefully, so that as it grows it doesn't put other crops in the shade.

Still other vegetables aren't included because I've never grown them. These include collard greens, sweet potatoes, and Southern peas, all of which are suited to the hot-weather conditions of the South. I believe my general approach to gardening is of interest and relevance to Southerners, so I hope they will not be put off from the main points if I leave out advice on regional favorites I've never been able to try.

Your own extension service or local garden center will steer you clear of those vegetables that have a record of doing poorly in your particular area and will tell you the recommended varieties of the vegetables that do perform well. I should reiterate that the planting sequence presented here is based on the frost dates for *my* area. Your own sequence may start much earlier or later, depending on your local weather and climate conditions. For the sake of clarity, I've listed in parentheses the exact dates of planting in my own garden, but I've reported germination and maturity factors, plus details on spacing and harvesting, so that anyone can apply them for each crop. There will be some variation if extra-fast or extra-slow varieties are selected for planting, or if exceptional weather conditions occur in the growing season. I tend to plant fast-maturing vegetables in spring so there's time for more succession planting and therefore greater overall productivity within the limits of my growing season. Nevertheless, to convert the sequence accurately to your own normal conditions, all you have to do is plug your frost dates into the overall schedules, which appear with each plan, and work from there.

The planting schedule itself is flexible in that it reflects my own desire for the convenience of planting certain things in groups, and not always at the absolute earliest date of planting for each vegetable included. Also, in analyzing my gardening habits over the years, I realize I have mixed both risk and caution in my approach to frost dates—mainly caution.

I think I plant beans a little on the early side, for instance, but I am conservative when it comes to the more substantial investment represented by the fruit-bearing crops. I should probably put the beans in a week or so later, to be sure the seeds do not rot in any bout of cold wet weather. But even if they should fail, I know I'm only out the price of a package or two of beans, and that I still have all spring and summer to plant more beans. If I gambled and lost in putting in my tomatoes too early, I would be out a much larger investment, in terms of both the value of the young seedlings and the extra labor involved in transplanting them correctly.

I have included a number of productivity tips that are unique to certain crops—for instance, broadcast-sowing for radishes. Other techniques have application for more than one crop. For example, close-row planting is sometimes misleadingly referred to as "wide-row planting" even though, by this technique, a limited number of rows are planted closely together (that's what makes the row "wide"). This is a technique that can be successfully applied to bush beans, Swiss chard, turnips, parsnips, onions, leeks, beets, carrots, spinach, and New Zealand spinach. By locating rows of these fairly small root or leafy crops closer together than may be recommended on seed packets or in extension service bulletins, you can save on garden space without hurting crop development or making it inconvenient to cultivate, tend, and harvest. Beans, Swiss chard, and turnips grow big enough so that no more than 3 rows of these crops should be closely planted. The others may be planted in 5 or 6 close rows. I've noted such techniques wherever applicable.

FIRST PLANTING GROUP (APRIL 1ST TO 15TH)
Plant 4 to 6 weeks before frost-free date.

> peas
> garlic
> shallots
> onions
> Spanish onions and Bermuda onions
> leeks
> chive

The first plantings in the vegetable garden are as much an act of faith as anything, especially up North. It's certainly more than just coincidence that Irish gardeners in the Boston area, say, try to get some of their peas in by St. Patrick's Day (March 17th), and that Italians think St. Joseph's Day (March 19th) is the deadline. I know my Uncle Angelo planted peas on St. Joseph's Day even if a blizzard was in progress.

Besides faith, of course, it is also good to possess an idea of your overall garden design before planting the first cool-weather crops of peas and onions, because portions of the rest of the garden are going to be affected by your earliest actions for a good part of the rest of the season.

Locate the peas with a succession crop in mind, or to share space briefly, later on, with young transplants from among the tender crops such as squash and peppers.

Locate the onions along your borders to serve their important secondary role of deterring pests. If you plan more onions than there is space for on the perimeter, simply allocate the rest of them in rows evenly throughout the garden.

As bulb crops, all onions do better in soil that's on the sandy side, where their underground life can evolve without hindrance from rocks or overly heavy soil. We've stipulated the basics of a good soil bed already. If you haven't arrived at the ideal tilth yet, and your soil is definitely on the heavy or clayey side, you'll make life easier on the onions this year simply by mixing some sand with the soil in the onion bed areas. A side dressing of wood ashes or greensand—a rich natural source of potassium—at planting time, if available, will boost bulb formation.

Onions may be started from seed, but it takes so long that in some areas it isn't possible or practical. New gardeners definitely should start them from sets or seedlings.

During a particularly cold and wet spring, you may not get around to turning over your garden and raking it out before it's time to plant both peas and onions. By covering those sites with clear plastic for a week or so prior to the planting time, you can get the soil warm and dry enough to be turned over by hand and ready for planting. That way you can get the early crops on their way and wait until the weather improves before turning over the rest of the garden.

The first planting group serves an important practical purpose that usually goes unnoticed. It simply gets the gardener going.

Peas (April 1st)

- Start from seed.

- Sow in pairs at 4" to 6" intervals, 1" deep, in rows 2' apart.

- Sprouts appear in 10 days.

- Ready to harvest in 65 days.

I always waited until after my Uncle Angelo planted his peas on St. Joseph's Day because if we did get bad weather that last week in March—as is quite probable in our area—peas in the ground would not develop. And though they are a cool-weather crop, peas actually can tolerate only light freezes and may be harmed by a severe freeze or snow.

For most home gardeners, the dwarf varieties are more practical than the tall varieties because they don't require as much space or as elaborate a support system. Wrinkle-seeded varieties are also a must, because if you're going to the trouble to grow your own peas, you might as well grow those that produce the sweet, delicate flavor that these do.

Plant the pea seeds in pairs (to ensure that at least one seed will germinate in that spot—and if both germinate, don't thin them) 1" deep at 4" to 6" intervals. To double productivity, provide some means of support for the small bushes to grow on after sprouting; with such support they will develop more elaborate branch systems and set forth more pods. I cut small, erect 3' saplings from the woods and stick them in a row 6" from the peas. I use enough saplings to create a trellis-like network all along the row, with no voids. Gardeners without access to brush or saplings could use the more traditional method of supporting peas by driving in posts at either end of the row and stretching taut two lengths of string or wire between them, one at ground level and the other 24" to 30" high. Then run more string in a vertical pattern at 6" to 8" intervals between the two main wires. What results is a fence woven out of string or wire to which the vines will cling and climb. Remember that some method of support is necessary because, though pea plants may be described as bushes at times, they are really vines and lack the strong stems to support themselves. That's also why it's so much trouble to grow them in multiple rows as some experts have suggested.

Peas take care of themselves, by and large. They seldom if ever require any more water than early spring naturally brings. But do watch them closely once pods have appeared, which will be 6 to 8 weeks from planting. It's important to pick them before the peas inside have hardened—a sign that the sugar inside has turned to starch and made the crop much less palatable. Also, unseasonably warm weather can change the taste of peas from good to average in a day's time. Once they begin to ripen, pick them almost every day, as you would strawberries.

Garlic (April 1st or Fall)

- Start from cloves.

- Plant at 6" intervals along the border of the bed, 2" to 4" deep.

- Ready to dig out 150 days from sprouting for use and/or replanting for next year.

You can get a reasonably good harvest out of garlic by planting it in the early spring—and many new gardeners will have no choice but to do that.

A fall planting will yield bigger sets of garlic cloves the following year. Soil is warm in the fall and root systems develop quickly. (I put in my garlic on or around Halloween.) Moreover, if garlic is planted along the perimeter in the fall, it will start alienating pests in early spring even before you've set foot in the garden. It may also be inspiring to you to see 4-inch shoots in your garden before the crocuses and daffodils show up. If you do plant in the fall, pick a spot along a perimeter so you stay clear of your spring tilling operations.

There are two basic types of garlic. Softneck garlic is the kind that can be braided into bunches. It is the garlic of choice among commercial growers, because it is easier to machine-harvest. Hardneck garlic is a specialty of many organic growers. It forms a woody stem and develops an edible green shoot called a scape. That itself can be harvested for use in salads and stir-fries. There are many varieties within the hard neck family—German, Spanish, Italian, red, white, and so on—but the essential garlic flavor is a constant.

If fall-planted, as I recommend, hardneck garlic is ready for harvest in midsummer, when the first three sets of leaves have appeared on the stem. Softneck garlic is ready to dig up in late summer.

You can use store-bought organic garlic cloves to plant in your garden, if you like, but garlic sets purchased from a seed company or garden center will give you more cloves per mother bulb. Each clove is a bulb for a new plant; it simply needs to be set in the ground, root end down. The root end is not as pointy as the stem end. Organic hardneck garlic is generally available through catalogs only in the fall.

Plant the cloves at 6-inch intervals. Poke a hole in the ground to a depth of about 2" to 4": bury your first two fingers to the second knuckle for the right depth.

Dig out all the garlic in the fall. Each plant will have produced a full set of cloves. Use a couple of these fresh sets to replant the perimeter of the garden for next spring. If you leave the garlic in the ground for a second year, it will go to seed on you.

Shallots (April 1st or Fall)

- Start from bulbs.

- Plant at 4" intervals along border, 2" deep, or in rows 6" apart.

- Ready to dig out 130 days from sprouting for use and/or replanting for next year.

Shallots can be grown just like garlic and are a good alternative for people who don't use garlic in their cooking.

You can get an extra "crop" out of shallots by clipping the tops of the plants in midsummer with a grass clipper or kitchen shears. Cut the top 3" to 4" and use the clippings in salads or omelets. This will promote more vigorous bulb formation in the plants, so you'll have bigger and firmer shallots when the time comes to dig them up. Shallots form a loose set of bulbs of different sizes, not a tight, uniform cluster like garlic. In a warm spring, shallots will tend to grow tall and leafy too soon. If they fall over limply from the top by midsummer, clip them back whether or not you intend to eat the clippings.

Onions (April 10th)

- Start from sets.

- Plant at 2" intervals, 2" deep, along border or in close rows 4" apart.

- Ready to thin for scallions in 30 to 50 days.
- Ready to harvest/store for winter use in 110 days.

Onion sets are small dried onions grown from seed during the previous year and stored over winter. They're smaller and more strongly flavored than the large sweet varieties. You can buy them through a seed catalog or garden center. Make sure the bulbs you get are ½" to ¾" in diameter—if they are much bigger, they are likely to go to seed on you before the onions are big enough. Also, open the sets as soon as they arrive. Spread them out in a cool, dry area to prevent rotting while awaiting a favorable day for planting. If one onion gets damp, it will spoil the barrel.

Onion sets are sold about 100 to 120 to the pound, depending on the size of the individual sets. That's enough to plant 20' to 25' of row if you put them in the ground 2" apart. Six weeks later, you can harvest every other onion as a fresh green scallion and let the rest of them mature to full size.

Plant the sets at a depth of 2", with the rounded root section on the bottom and the pointy end sticking straight up.

There's a possibility that onions will go to seed during the summer. If you see caps reminiscent of the Kremlin forming atop some of them, they are going to seed. Go down the row and clip the tops, 6" to 8", off all the onions. That will set the stems back but won't hurt bulb development. Or you can break off the seed-pod stem at the base of the plant and leave the remaining foliage.

In the fall, mature onions begin to lose interest in standing tall. When you see that a few of them have fallen over, go down the row and knock down the rest with a rake or hoe. That will effectively end the active role of the onion stem in the life of each plant and encourage the bulbs to form a harder outer skin. Leave them in the ground another two weeks, then pull them out and dry them for storage and for use over the winter.

Some of my customers braid their onions and hang them in the cellar to dry. Another method is to spread them on a screen or slatted crate in a shady, rain-protected spot for about a week. Then clip the stems 1" from the bulb, throw the stems on the compost, and hang the onions in a mesh bag in a cool, dry, shady spot. Make sure you let them dry out in the shade, as too much sunlight will soften them.

Spanish Onions and Bermuda Onions (April 10th)

- Start from seedlings.

- Plant at 6" intervals, 2" deep, along border or in rows 6" apart.

- Ready to clear soil from tops in 70 days.

- Ready to harvest in 110 days.

These are the large, sweet varieties of onion used for enlivening salads or topping hamburgers. They are available as seedlings via mail order or from a reputable local source. They have a hollow stem and, since they grow larger, need more space in the row. They shouldn't be thinned for early onions the way the onion sets are—they simply don't grow fast enough at first. Spanish are bigger and heavier and keep a bit better than the milder and flatter Bermuda, but both types are usually grown for eating right after harvesting, not for storage.

A quick and efficient way to get a lot of onion seedlings in the ground is to lay them out at 4-inch intervals along a straight row. Then poke a hole for each one with your index finger to a depth of about 2". Place each seedling in its hole as you go along, then squeeze the area around the plant with thumb and forefinger to make sure there are no air pockets.

In midsummer, or a little over 2 months after planting, carefully remove the dirt from the top of each bulb so that each is uncovered at about its midpoint, or equator. Exposure to the sun will cause the bulbs to swell and nearly double in size.

Leeks (April 15th)

- Start from seedlings.

- Plant at 6" intervals, 2" deep, in close rows 6" apart.

- Ready for blanching beginning in 90 days.

- Ready to harvest in 115 to 130 days. May be left in the garden through Thanksgiving.

Leeks are the slowest allium of all, particularly in the first part of the growing season, and they require much more patience than actual care. They should be planted in an out-of-the-way place in the garden, so their leisurely methodical growth pattern doesn't get on your nerves.

Plant them exactly as you plant the large onion varieties. The 4" spacing is important to give to leeks so they can develop their heavy stalky bottoms.

In midsummer, or about 12 weeks after planting, begin to throw dirt against the base of the leeks to extend the blanched section of the stem, which is the most useful part in cooking. Do this gradually—maybe a spadeful of soil per foot per week—to prevent smothering the stalk and encouraging rot. The technique is worth trying because it will give you a third more usable neck by harvest.

Leeks have to be dug up with a fork spade, they develop such extensive and tenacious root systems. They should be dug up individually and used as needed, and not removed wholesale, because they don't store well.

If you cover leeks with 6" of leaves or salt hay, you can leave them in the garden all winter.

Chives (April 1st)

- Start from seedlings.

- Plant 2" to 3" deep.

Chives are readily available and inexpensive in many locations, so they're hardly worth starting from seed. Buy in clumps and plant in corners of the garden. Chives can be used as part of your allium border defense against insects.

If you want to grow chives from seed, sow the seed in an unused or out-of-the-way section of the garden sometime in July. If you sow the seed any earlier, the plants will become tall and stringy. But if you sow chives in July, it will develop into a thick and rich crop the following spring and summer. It takes 6 to 8 days to sprout.

Chives will go to flower if you let them, and many people do so for the aesthetic effect, as well as to add the lavender blossoms, which are edible, to salads. But you'll get many more and more tender chives if you keep picking them. Cut your clumps down to the base to ensure new growth. If you cut them midstem, chives will become hollow and tough and no new growth will occur.

If you want to bring chive indoors, wait until January. Give the plant time to go dormant and recoup its energies. Dig it up during a mild spell in the first of the year, put it in a large pot, and bring it indoors, and it will give you what you're after.

SECOND PLANTING GROUP (APRIL 15TH TO 20TH)
Plant 3 to 4 weeks before frost-free date.

> radishes
>
> beets
>
> Swiss chard
>
> lettuce

The garden so far: By this time, the peas should be up and growing, the onion sets and garlic should be poking their shoots out, and the leeks won't have changed a bit. You should have the rest of the garden completely turned over by now, ready for a final raking off and the nitty-gritty planting to begin.

I always go to work on this second planting group as soon as I see that the lawn has grown enough to cut. When the lawns in your neighborhood need mowing, it means the radishes need planting.

Radishes (April 15th)

- Start from seed.

- Scatter-sow in prepared bed, or row-sow ¼" deep. Sprouts appear in 5 days.

- Ready to thin (if row-sown) in 10 days.

- Ready to harvest in 20 to 30 days.

- (Also suitable as fall crop.)

Radishes go into excess leaf production in hot weather and get tough to eat, so they must be grown as a spring or fall crop.

Like onions (and beets, in this same planting group), radishes do better in soil of proper tilth. They sprout quickly, so they are rarely lost in the seed stage. The problem is usually too much germination for the space allowed in planting. The seed is small, but if it is sown carefully at ¾" to 1" intervals, much less thinning will be required and you'll be able to plant more rows. Mix some sand in with the seed before sowing to encourage good spacing. Or buy or improvise a seed vibrator.

Sow the seed ¼" deep; if you can't make a furrow that shallow, simply distribute the seed along the line of your row and cover it with fine sand to hold it in place. A shallow sowing will cause better germination and allow the plants to develop more quickly and thoroughly.

Pick radishes as needed, but if you find yourself with a surplus, store them in the refrigerator rather than leaving them in the ground. Overripe radishes are tough and too hot.

Feed the tops to your rabbits!

Broadcast-sowing of radishes in a properly prepared soil bed of their own will give you a radish for virtually every seed in the packet.

Here's how to do it. Mark off an area of about 3' x 3' in the garden. Spread an inch of sand across the top of it, then turn it under. Use clean, sharp mason's sand—not sand you borrowed from the highway department, which usually has a lot of road salt in it, and not salt-water beach sand. A bushel, or half a wheelbarrowful, will do the job.

Turn the sand under, then pass the first 3" of the resulting mix through a screen, if necessary, to remove any rocks. Use ½" wire mesh for the screening process; anything smaller will create too fine a soil that will tend to pack down after rain. Keep some of the mixture after screening (a two-gallon bucketful is plenty); you'll use it to cover the sown seed.

Now you have the perfect planting medium for your radishes. Instead of planting the seed in rows, scatter it by hand so that it is evenly distributed throughout the planting area. You might practice scatter-sowing with a handful of sand to get the knack of doing it with a flick of the wrist. It's the same technique you would use in sowing grass seed in thin portions of your lawn. If you do spill too much in one spot, use a small rake to gently spread it more thinly.

Done correctly, a standard packet of seed will scatter-sow the entire 9 square feet. After seeding, scatter a light coating of the reserved sand-soil mix to hold the seed down in case of rain. Radish seed will float into low spots if not kept in place before sprouting.

By scatter-sowing the radishes in this manner, you will double your productivity—and also eliminate the job of thinning.

Don't let this excellent soil bed go to waste after your radishes finish, either. Use it as your supply garden. Sow lettuce to replace those you harvest in the regular garden as the season progresses, and to sow fall-crop seedlings. (More later on this other potentially valuable role of your special radish bed.)

Beets (April 20th)

- Start from seed.

- Sow seed 1" apart, ½" deep, in 3 to 6 close rows that are 6" apart.

- Sprouts appear in 6 days.

- Ready to thin to 2" to 3" apart in 20 days, when 4" high.

- Ready to harvest in 50 to 55 days.

- Also suitable as fall crop.

Beets do well in any organic soil of reasonably good tilth. They attract few pests and reach maturity in a short time, so they can be planted at several stages in the growing season.

Beets require relatively little attention if sown correctly. Use a stick or the wrong end of a hoe to make a furrow about ½" deep and place the seed at 1" intervals. Beet seed is small but chunky—each looks like a miniature meteorite and actually contains several seeds in one, so it's easy to sow with precision. If you give each seed proper spacing, you won't have to thin as much three weeks later. More important, you won't disturb neighboring roots when you do thin the weaker sprouts.

A thick stand of beets, as will result from close-row planting, will keep the soil cooler and slow the growth rate of the beets, and thus give you more choice-size beets over a longer period of time. This also helps keep the weeds down, with a minimum of fine-tooth cultivation.

By the way, in thinning you should remove the plant by the root and not clip it with a shears at ground level. If there's a clear danger of disrupting other roots, simply use your free hand to keep the soil intact while you pull the weaker seedling out.

Let the leaves grow to 4" before thinning, then eat the greens as one crop and the roots as another crop a bit later.

Beets should be harvested when they're big enough to putt—when they're about golf-ball size. If you let them get much bigger than 2" across, they may split, get woody, and lose their fine fresh flavor.

Swiss Chard (April 15th)

- Start from seed.

- Sow 4" apart, ½" deep, in 3 rows that are 12" apart.

- Sprouts appear in 6 days.

- Ready to thin to 8" to 10" apart in 15 to 20 days, when 4" high.

- Ready to harvest beginning in 55 days.

- May be harvested throughout summer.

- Also suitable as fall crop.

Swiss chard is a prolific home-garden green that can be left to continue to bear from spring to fall. One standard packet will plant 20' to 25' of row and produce an average of two servings per family per week all summer. It's heat resistant and won't bolt on you if you keep picking it. For a more colorful row, buy the rainbow assortment of chard varieties in hues of red, yellow, orange, white, and purple.

The seed looks just like beet seed and is as manageable. Sow it ½" deep at 4" intervals in three rows 12" apart. You can start harvesting chard when the plants have only a half-dozen leaves. Cut the outer leaves at 2" above ground level and be sure to leave the growing bud intact. Don't let the leaves grow more than a foot tall or they'll get tough.

Some gardeners sow chard more closely together and use the thinnings as their first crop. My own preference is to plant as I've indicated, then harvest the leaves for a period of 3 to 4 weeks. At this point I remove the entire crop and resow with another. This gives me tender, sweet chard at every picking and allows for a strong fall crop, which can be harvested in my area right up through Thanksgiving. Many gardeners think this second sowing is a waste of time and energy, seeing as chard bears so well all season; but we all have our little gardening quirks, and a weakness for growing chard is mine.

Lettuce (April 15th)

- Start from seedlings.

- Plant at 10" to 12" intervals, 2" deep, in rows 12" apart.

- Ready to harvest in 40 days (leaf), 60 days (head).

- Also suitable as summer and fall crop.

The secret of good lettuce production in the home garden is selection of the correct varieties. There are five basic types of lettuce:

> *Head lettuce*, the familiar commercial variety that forms dense heads with crisp leaves, and never fits in the crisper drawer in your refrigerator.
> *Cos* or *romaine lettuce*, the elongated type that forms stiff, upright leaves.
> *Stem lettuce*, or *celtuce*, which is grown for both the stem and the leaves.

These three types require longer growing seasons (from 65 to 80 days) and greater amounts of garden space (from 12" to 18" of space in a row) than the other two varieties.

> *Leaf lettuce*, such as Oak Leaf, Grand Rapids, Ruby Red, and Salad Bowl.
> *Butterhead lettuce*, such as Bibb and Buttercrunch.

These loose-leaf and loose-head varieties are smaller, but high in quality, quick to mature, and low in space requirements, so they're eminently suited to the needs of most gardens.

Start lettuce from transplants as early as possible in the spring so you can begin harvesting early and to avoid the problem of hot-weather bolting, especially head varieties. All leafy plants have delicate roots, so handle these seedlings with even more care than you give other types. Keep soil balled around the roots when you move them from starting tray to garden.

Plant the lettuce seedlings about 10" apart. If you run into a space problem, you can cheat on this spacing—if you're planting loose-leaf or butterhead varieties. Put them in at 6" intervals and harvest every other head early.

You can also save a bit of space by staggering the rows as I've done in some of the garden plans.

When transplanting, drive your first two fingers into the ground down to your second knuckle for a perfect slot for lettuce. After placing the seedling, squeeze the hole to remove air pockets.

Salad Bar on Demand

The advent of packets of lettuce seed mixtures, in response to the growing popularity of mixed salads in our diet, offers home gardeners a chance to compete with three-star restaurants in putting desirable greens on the table. Many seed growers have devised a wide variety of these salad mixes: mild or spicy mesclun blends, heirloom lettuce blends, Provençal and Niçoise blends featuring French lettuces and herbs, Italian salad blends, and more. A recent introduction is a mix of so-called "micro greens," containing the baby seedlings of arugula, beet, mustard, radish, kale, and salad burnet. At our own garden center, we offer Sal's Mesclun Mix, which consists of one part red salad bowl, one part Bull's Blood beet, and one part red Russian kale, plus one-half parts green salad bowl, arugula, mizuna, totsoi, and red komatana.

One of the beauties of gourmet salad mixes is their swift payoff, as the first harvest of tender leaves can begin 3 to 6 weeks from sowing. The blends may be sown in short rows, like spinach, or broadcast-sown, like radish seed, on the 4' x 4' supply garden area designated in the plan for our 750-square-foot garden.

Often, in a tray of a dozen lettuce, one or two seedlings will be quite a bit smaller. I put these small ones in between large ones rather than giving them extra space in the row. That way, when the big ones are harvested, the little ones can take over.

Lettuce can be picked when it's only 6" to 8" across. That happens to be when the leaf and loose-head varieties are at their most flavorful, anyway. Don't pull the lettuce out by the roots to harvest it or you'll get dirt on the leaves. Cut the plant at the base, then remove the root in a separate operation.

Remember, if you want a full head of head lettuce, you should plant as soon as possible in the spring, or plant as a fall crop. Don't attempt it after your first planting date for lettuce in the spring.

PRODUCTIVITY TIP

A lot of people think the way to get the most lettuce for their money is to leave the same heads in the garden all summer and pick from the plants as leaves are needed. Actually, you get much better productivity by picking it all on the early side and *in toto*, then replacing each plant with a new seedling from your supply garden where the radishes grew. You'll get much fresher, tastier lettuce this way, and three times as many usable greens from the same amount of garden space.

THIRD PLANTING GROUP (MAY 1ST TO MAY 10TH)
Plant 1 to 2 weeks before frost-free date.

cabbage

broccoli

cauliflower

carrots

turnips

parsnips

spinach

parsley

beans

celery

New Zealand spinach

You might be tempted to harvest a few radishes or scallions by now, though it's still a bit early. The peas should be climbing the sapling trellises with enthusiasm, the garlic should be up 6" or more, and the leeks should begin to look as if they're going to make it after all. Beets and chard should be up an inch or so.

Some cultivation might be needed throughout these crop areas at this time. Be careful not to disturb roots.

The third group's planting is a solid morning's work. Bring hoe, hose, gardener's yardstick, trays of transplants, seed packages, some sand, burlap, and any volunteer labor you can muster.

The brassicas ought to be planted in the same general section of the garden, if at all possible, to make crop rotation procedures feasible next year.

The root crops need good sandy or well-drained loam to do as well as possible.

Cabbage, Broccoli, and Cauliflower (May 1st)

- Start from seedlings.

- Plant at 24" intervals, 2" deep, in rows 24" to 30" apart.

- Ready to harvest in 70 days (according to variety).

- All suitable as fall crops.

The brassicas can be planted as seedlings even before the spring last frost date, because they're not hurt by cold weather. In fact, the idea in using transplants is to get them started quickly so that they'll mature before the hot weather. If planted to mature in midsummer, they would not be productive except in cooler high-altitude areas in the North.

Even many experienced gardeners make the mistake of planting brassicas too close together. Broccoli, cauliflower, and standard-size cabbage should be put in the garden at least 18" apart, and preferably 24" apart, in rows no closer than 3'. This gives them each an adequate feeding area for their relatively complex growth patterns, and also allows plenty of air circulation, which is especially important for a family of plants as pest-prone as this one is.

Mini-head cabbage may be planted safely at 12" to 15" intervals, because it is a smaller variety, as the name suggests. In fact, I prefer the mini-head for home gardens because there's not nearly so much wasted outer-leaf growth as there is

with the whoppers—the ones you see at grange and county fairs and other cele-
brations of local growers—yet each head still provides three or four servings
at the table. And you can get 20 to 24 mini-heads in the space that 12 standard
heads would need.

Prepare 2" holes for the brassica transplants in the manner you used for the
lettuce. Take even more care to protect the roots of the brassicas, and if you
have wood ashes or greensand, mix some in with the soil at the planting site as a
defense against maggots. Plant the seedlings one at a time and fill in around each
with soil right away. Water the seedlings well after transplanting, as at this point
in the spring the ground is likely to be beginning to dry out. If your garden
catches quite a bit of wind, you might plant your brassicas a little deeper, so that
they don't flop around in the wind and become disturbed as young transplants.

Asian Greens

Asian vegetables, popular in stir-fries and salads and as boiled greens, are commonly available today from seed racks and often as seedlings in garden centers
and nurseries. Snap sugar peas and snow peas are already familiar to American
gardeners. Chinese cabbage combines the crisp, clean texture of lettuce with
the flavor of cabbage. Bok choy (pac choi, pak choi) is a vase-shaped plant in
the brassica family available in numerous varieties and sizes, with white or green
stems and green leaves, both prized for their delicate flavor. Asian greens have
the zesty flavor of mustard greens. Some are grown for their flower-bud stems,
and others, such as the family of mizunas, for their leaves.

Snow peas, snap peas, Chinese cabbage, bok choy, and the greens just
mentioned are cool-weather crops and should be started in the garden at the
same time you plant cabbage, broccoli, and cauliflower. Daikon radish may be
included in this planting group as well, bearing in mind that its large root requires
a well-worked, sandy soil bed to a depth of 8" to 10". Unlike most radishes, it
does not become woody and tasteless if left in the garden; it can be harvested
and enjoyed even in late fall.

All these varieties can be started from seed in midsummer for a fall crop.

Brassicas have sturdy leaves and, like sailboats, tend to catch the wind more than most other crops.

Cauliflower heads have to be tied up in their outer leaves when they reach a width of about 2" to 3". Use a rubber band—or clothespins, as one of my customers insists on using—to wrap the head so the sun won't get at it. As with blanched asparagus and leeks, this is another case of tampering with photosynthesis to get the best eating. The cauliflower is ready to pick when the head is full and compact.

Harvest mini-head cabbage when it has the size and firmness of a softball—don't wait much longer or the head may split open in the sun, and then it will *taste* like a softball, too. If you're not prepared to eat or preserve all the cabbage that reaches harvestable stage, pick it anyway, because it will keep well if stored properly.

Broccoli should be harvested in two steps for maximum productivity. First, cut the large cluster of green flower buds that forms at the top of the main stalk. This will be about 50 days from the date of transplant. Cut this section from two or three of your plants and you'll have more than enough for a family meal. After you cut off the main stalk, side shoots will begin to form flower clusters more energetically. These smaller but more numerous shoots can be cut 1 inch from the main stalk 2 weeks later. If you wait too long, the flowers will mature and bloom yellow, making the parent plant happy but the broccoli not as tender or sweet.

The brassicas are a troublesome lot of crops to grow, especially in a changeable and bug-ridden spring, and especially using strictly organic methods to raise them. Newcomers to gardening would be better off waiting until they have a year or two of experience under their belts before spring-planting these crops. Cauliflower in particular is fussy about weather conditions, and when you do put any of them in for the first time, be ready to give them more than normal vigilance as they grow.

> **PRODUCTIVITY TIP**
>
> This applies equally well to cabbage, broccoli, and cauliflower. If you can get them in early enough, you'll be able to clear them all out by mid-July (in my area) at the latest. That will give you the time and space for planting new seedlings of the same variety for a fall crop. This is probably

the most convenient way to make use of your vacancies, though other fall crops could be planted, too.

When the early brassicas do finish, be sure to pull up the roots and throw them on your compost heap, to reduce their tendency to promote certain soil-borne diseases in the garden.

At the same time, in preparation for your fall planting, scatter a dressing of compost or well-rotted manure to replenish the soil bed in those sites. If you have any wood ashes left, sprinkle them on, too.

Carrots (May 1st)

- Start from seed.
- Sow seeds ½" apart, ⅛" deep, in 3 to 6 close rows that are 6" apart.
- Sprouts appear in 20 days.
- Ready to thin to 1½" to 2" in 35 days, when 2" high.
- Ready to harvest in 85 to 90 days.
- May be left in the ground through Thanksgiving.

Carrots are a tricky crop for consistent success. Their tiny seeds must be sown very near the surface; thus they are exposed to a lot of jostling by the elements. They take nearly 3 weeks to germinate—longer than almost any other vegetable—and so are likely to get more than their fair share of this jostling in the first place.

Carrot seedlings themselves are quite fragile and have an awful time breaking through crusted or clod-filled soil, and once they do emerge, they have their hands full competing with weeds.

A related problem is that by the time you discover that your first crop of carrots may have failed, the season is well under way. In most parts of the country you have time to make another sowing, but if that sowing also fails, you're out of luck for carrots for the year. That's a good reason for buying new seeds every year, and not trying to use up an old package unless you've tested it for germination rate.

Despite all that, most home gardeners understandably insist on growing carrots. Special attention to the crop during the sowing and the long germination period will greatly increase their chances of success.

To keep carrot seed from floating away during its long presprouting time, draw ⅛-inch-deep furrows for the planting, as straight as possible. Sow the seed no closer than 2 per inch. You'll be able to do this much more easily if you have a seed vibrator, or if you mix the seed with a little fine sand beforehand. After sowing, fill the entire furrow with the fine sand rather than with lighter garden soil that's more subject to displacement.

Sow 3 to 6 rows close together—no more than 6" apart—to save on garden space.

I don't agree with the common advice to mix radish seed with carrot seed "to mark the rows," because it's a royal pain to have to weed the radishes out afterward. I don't mind weeding weeds, but weeding potentially good radishes strikes me as a ridiculous situation. Anyway, if you use the fine sand, as I've suggested, your rows will be marked as plain as day.

During the germination period, keep the carrot bed free of weeds, and pay attention to the weather. If thunderstorms are forecast, or if a hard, driving rain actually begins, cover the bed with a length of wide-weave burlap for the duration.

To keep the carrot bed moist during this period, in the event there is no rain of any kind, sprinkle it in the morning every few days.

Thin your carrots—after they finally do sprout—when they're 2" high. Leave 1½" to 2" between those that remain. As in all thinning, remove weaker-looking plants, roots and all. These are not always the short seedlings. Sometimes the taller ones are pale and infirm and should be the first to go.

Once you get to this stage with carrots, you can be pretty sure of reaping a good harvest later on if your soil has good tilth. You can begin picking when the tops of the roots measure ½" to ¾" across—and you deserve to eat the first one you do pull up.

Leave some carrots in the ground for winter, if you like, by covering rows thickly with salt hay or leaves. Or try my father-in-law's trick: replant the carrots thickly in a box of mason's sand for storage in your cellar or cold frame. The carrots will last until spring.

Choose a carrot variety that is neither too long nor too short. Carrots that grow as long as 8" to 9" won't do well unless the soil is extremely well worked and sandy to at least that depth. In your first stab at gardening, you may not have achieved such tilth yet. Moreover, if you do have a good soil bed, extra-long carrot varieties still will have a tendency to snap off in the harvesting process, leaving part of your hard-earned root crop in the ground. On the other hand, short, stubby varieties that grow only 2" to 4" won't take sufficient advantage of an average-to-good soil bed. Medium-size carrots will give most gardeners more pounds of carrot per packet.

Turnips (May 1st)

- Start from seed.

- Sow seeds 1" apart, $1/8$" deep, in 3 close rows that are 8" apart.

- Sprouts appear in 4 days.

- Ready to thin to 2" to 4" apart in 14 days, when 2" high.

- Ready to harvest in 60 days.

- When planted as fall crop, may be left in ground through Thanksgiving.

Turnips can be grown for their greens as well as for their roots, and they do well as spring or fall crops in northern climates. The traditional American turnip is purple on top and white on the bottom.

Turnip seed is small but should be sown about 12 per foot of row, or 1 per inch, to minimize the thinning job, and at $1/8$-inch depth. Sow more thickly only if you intend to harvest the greens for the kitchen; some people like the tangy taste of the leaves, which are rich in minerals and vitamin A, in salads and soul-food stews. Either way, you'll have to do some thinning when the seedlings are 2" high. Thin to 2" to 4" apart. They're ready to harvest from about the time they reach 2" in diameter, and they can be safely left in the ground until they reach 4" across. Don't let them get any bigger, however, or they'll toughen, just as oversized beets and radishes do.

Plant one standard packet in three close rows, 8" apart, to conserve space. Sprinkle wood ashes around to deter maggots and to strengthen growth. Make another sowing for fall as soon as the spring crop is harvested.

Parsnips (May 1st)

- Start from seed.

- Sow seeds ½" apart, ⅛" deep, in 3 to 6 close rows that are 6" apart.

- Sprouts appear in 15 to 20 days.

- Ready to thin to 1½" to 2" in 35 days, when 2" high.

- Ready to harvest in 120 days.

- May be left in the ground through Thanksgiving.

Parsnips are a problem-free crop if you can get them started. They grow from a tiny seed and take their time about it, just like carrots. Be sure the soil bed stays damp for good germination. If you can't check the garden every day, soak a length of burlap and lay that over the seedbed until the sprouts appear. In fact, if you're going to grow parsnips you should follow the sowing and thinning techniques described for carrots. Be sure to thin them. They'll grow 10" to 12" deep if your soil permits them to. They'll taste better after a couple of light freezes in the fall. Some gardeners won't dig them up to eat until the following spring. Because they stick around so long, locate parsnips in a low-traffic area.

Spinach (May 1st)

- Start from seed.

- Sow seed ½" apart, ¼" deep, in 3 to 6 close rows that are 6" apart.

- Sprouts appear in 7 days.

- Ready to harvest in 50 days.

- Also suitable as fall crop.

Having been a great Popeye fan (Bud Sagendorf, the creator of the famous cartoon character, was a longtime customer of mine and a great gardener besides), I have long counted spinach as my single most favorite garden vegetable, and that's why it's in all my garden plans.

I sow my spinach more closely than I have ever seen it recommended anywhere, and most of my good gardening friends think I overdo it a bit. But I like to cut my spinach early and young, 5 to 6 weeks after sowing. That way it's great whether in salads or cooked, and I avoid the thinning process altogether.

Sow spinach seed in a shallow (¼") furrow and use the back of your hand to slap or flick topsoil onto the seed to cover it lightly without burying it alive, or use fine sand as for other crops. Plant in close rows 6" apart. Two packets will give you six 8' rows, all of which can be closely planted, as the crop is short and small and can be reached and harvested from either side of the Popeye section.

When the plants have about six leaves on them, I harvest every other row for a delicious crop of early spinach. I harvest the remaining rows 1 to 2 weeks later, before the center stem on each plant shoots to seed. Then I pull up all the roots and start all over again.

Parsley (May 1st)

- Start from seed.

- Sow seed ½" apart, ⅛" deep, in rows that are 12" apart.

- Sprouts appear in 20 days.

- Ready to harvest beginning in 60 days.

There are two kinds of parsley: Italian or flat-leaf parsley, and curly parsley. The flat-leaf variety is the universal favorite of cooks because of its more concentrated flavor, and it's what I prefer for seasoning many dishes. Curly parsley is primarily used as a garnish.

Most people insist on growing parsley from seed in their gardens rather than buying transplants. We sell fewer parsley seedlings than any other vegetable transplant simply because a tray of tiny parsley doesn't look as if it's worth the price—$3 per tray at our garden center—compared to what you can get in the grocery store, harvested, at $2.50 or $3 a bunch. In reality, our tray contains some 60 to 80 individual plants, and so would produce enough parsley to start a supermarket of your own. But I've given up promoting it.

Anyway, sow parsley in a shallow furrow (⅛" deep) and cover it with fine sand—play sand as opposed to the grittier mason's sand—to help it hold its place during its long germination period—it takes almost as long to get started as carrot seed. Use a seed vibrator, or mix the seed with some sand, to space the seed thinly in the row—at ½" intervals if you can do it. Keep the soil bed moist during the presprouting period if there's no rain. If there's the possibility of too much rain or of a driving rain, cover the seedbed with burlap for the duration.

Many people try to bring their parsley plants into the house in the fall, hoping to use them in the kitchen all winter long. But, like most biennial herbs, parsley requires a dormant period to survive for another season of growth. They'll peter out by December if they are brought inside.

If you want parsley in the house in winter, you'll have to start a fresh crop from seed sown in September—or come in and buy a pot from us.

Beans (May 1st)

- Grow from seed.

- Sow in pairs at 6" intervals, 1½" deep, in 3 close rows that are 18" apart.

- Sprouts appear in 7 to 10 days.

- Ready to hill in 20 to 10 days, when 12" high.

- Ready to harvest in 50 to 60 days.

- Also suitable as summer and fall crop.

Bush beans are one of the most sensible crops for any home garden. They're easy to sow, productive, and ready in less than two months. You can grow several crops in succession, green or yellow (wax), before calling it a season. The soil must be on the warm side for beans to start well, so the crop shouldn't be tried much earlier than a week or so before your spring frost date.

Plant beans in three rows 15" to 18" apart; then, if you're going to plant additional rows, skip 2' to make an aisle or walkway, and plant three more rows.

This will give you room to cultivate and harvest the crop without taking up unnecessary space.

The seeds are large and easy to handle. Draw a slight furrow with the wrong end of a hoe, no deeper than 1½". I try to sow beans at 1½" to ensure maximum

Pole Beans

Pole beans are one of the architectural wonders of the gardening world. I have seen them trained to grow on discarded swing sets and on mini-cabins made of PVC. By midseason, these vine-covered structures provide excellent hideouts for kids in the neighborhood, meanwhile producing beans hand over fist for the gardener.

Pole beans were one of the "three sisters" of Native American farmers, along with corn and squash. These were the staple crops that made up an important part of the daily diet of pre-Columbian North America. In those times, pole beans were trained to grow up cornstalks while squash was planted between the rows of corn. Dead fish were buried with all the plantings for fertilizer.

Today, gardeners still appreciate pole beans for their dramatic presence, their productivity and variety, and their taste. Basically, they are vines extending up to 10' vertically by the end of the growing season, so some kind of support is essential to cultivating them. If you have access to a woods, simply cut down four to six 8' saplings and drive them into the ground, to a depth of 1¹/₂", at even intervals around a 4-foot-diameter circle. Bamboo poles from a garden center or nursery will also do the trick. Tie off the tops of the poles or saplings with durable twine, teepee-style, and you have your pole-bean planting structure.

Pole beans are as frost-sensitive as bush beans, so when the time is right, sow 5 to 6 beans around each pole, then thin out the weakest-looking sprouts after germination. Rampant growth will begin to occur in midsummer. In fact, plan on harvesting pole beans two or three times a week to make sure the vines keep on producing. Don't pick beans if they're still wet from rain, and when you do harvest pole beans, pinch them off in a way that doesn't endanger the stability of your teepee.

early germination. Make sure your rows are board-straight so you can hill the beans quickly and efficiently when the time comes.

Here is a crucial early step. Plant the beans in *pairs* (as you did the peas) at 6" intervals along your row, pushing each one down a bit to seat it well. The idea of this staggered double-sowing is to make sure that at least one plant will come up from each drill. Should both sprout, your spacing can accommodate the extra growth. This trick eliminates the need for thinning—and also the chance of unproductive gaps developing where two or three consecutive beans happened to go kaput.

Plants should emerge in about a week and will need no particular attention until they're about 12" high—or have begun to lean to either side in the row like drunken sailors. At this stage you should go down each row with your hoe and scrape a thin layer of soil up to bank their stems. Take the soil from a spot 6" to 8" away from the row to make sure you don't injure young bean roots that will be quite near the surface under each fledgling plant.

Hilling provides extra support for the plant when the time comes for it to put forth its crop of pods, three weeks later. It also increases the effective feeding area for each plant, for roots will now develop in the additional soil piled around the stems. And it protects the plants from being knocked over by rain or wind.

In all candor, I should note that beans in a garden soil plied with a commercial fertilizer would not usually need hilling. The extra dose of synthetic potassium and phosphorus in the mixture would make the beans strong enough through the stem to support the crop on its own. Farmers depend on this effect because they don't have the manpower to hill large tracts of bush beans. In a small garden, though, it takes only a few minutes.

Small blossoms will appear on the bushes shortly after hilling, and 7 to 10 days later the beans will be ready for harvest.

Harvest beans while they're still pencil-thin and as soon as you can see the seeds bump into view in the pods. Another test is to take a pod and break it in two. If it snaps crisply, it's ready to pick. In fact, that's how "snap beans" got their name.

There's a stringlike growth holding pod to stem. When harvesting, separate the bean at the *pod end* of this connector, rather than at the stem end, to avoid risking damage to the plant itself.

Harvest the beans in two to four stages. Pick anything over 4" long within a few days of the emergence of pods generally. Then wait every other day to harvest the remainder. You'll get more beans in more usable quantities this way than by picking either too soon or too late, or by picking continuously over the relatively short harvest period for the crop.

Celery (May 10th)

- Start from seedlings.

- Plant at 8" intervals in rows 15" apart.

- Ready to begin blanching in 60 days.

- Ready to harvest in 120 days.

- May be left in the ground through Thanksgiving.

Celery is a worthwhile crop to grow if you have a rich, organic soil, but it must be put in the garden as a transplant in most areas to accommodate its slow maturation rate. At the same time, it must be planted late enough to be able to reach maturity during the cooler fall months, when, I find, conditions help it to acquire its real flavor and succulence. If the crop matures in August, by contrast, the summer heat will cause it to develop side stalks and become tough and bitter.

Celery must be blanched to ensure tender, sweet stalks, and this can be easily accomplished provided they are planted in straight rows in the first place. So use your gardener's yardstick or a mason's line to plant the seedlings. When plants are well along—about 12" high—begin banking soil around them on either side of the row. Many home gardeners use two thin boards for the same purpose. That's probably the more effective method, but unless you have access to cheap lumber, banking the young celery with soil is more practical. Be careful not to bank the soil too high, lest you cover the leaves and cause them to rot.

Celery is perhaps a little more difficult to grow than the average garden vegetable, but it is such a convenient fall-storage crop that I think it's worth the extra effort.

The base of a celery plant is oval-shaped, not round. You can get two rows out of little more than the area normally required for one if you take advantage of this characteristic shape and plant the celery with its oval-shaped bases arranged sideways in your rows.

New Zealand Spinach (May 10th)

- Start from seed.

- Sow seeds 1" apart, ¼" deep, in rows 12" apart.

- Sprouts appear in 15 days.

- Ready to thin to 3" to 4" apart in 30 days.

- Ready to harvest beginning in 55 days.

New Zealand spinach is not a true spinach, being in the Carpetweed family and not the Goosefoot family, and its distinctiveness shows up in its nutlike seed, in its sprawling rather than erect-type leafy growth, and in its near-bitter taste. Yet it may be sown and used almost exactly like spinach—as a potherb and salad green—and, unlike true spinach, it does well in hot weather, thus making an excellent summer crop. Clip 2" to 3" off each stem when you harvest. It seems to be catching on as a staple leafy crop, at least among my customers.

It should be sown in shallow furrows, like spinach, but space the rows at 12" rather than 6" intervals to accommodate the sprawling and long-season growth pattern. It keeps nice and crisp in the refrigerator after harvest if washed and stored properly. It's slow to germinate, but once it is established you'll be able to cut leaves from it throughout and to the end of summer.

FOURTH PLANTING GROUP (MAY 15TH TO MAY 20TH)
Plant after all danger of frost is past.

eggplant

peppers

tomatoes

cucumbers

squash

basil

By this time some of your early planted crops will be well along in their development, so you'll feel as if you're in a real garden when you go out there to work. You'll be picking radishes, scallions, and lettuce for your salads. All the seeds you have sown, except perhaps for the slow-footed carrot and parsnip crops, will have germinated. The brassicas will be showing signs of definite growth patterns by now, and your neighbors will begin thinking you're some kind of gardening expert.

The ultrasensitive fruit-bearing crops shouldn't be put out in the garden until all danger of frost is past. Our hardest selling job in the garden center in spring is convincing novice gardeners that it is still too early to plant tomatoes even though the April day they stop by happens to be exceptionally warm and sunny. It's obvious from their expressions, both facial and verbal, that they don't believe a word I'm saying. They are convinced that I simply don't have the transplants ready for sale and that I'm just trying to stall them until May 10th, the frost-free date in our area.

Less-experienced gardeners are better off starting all their hot-weather crops as healthy seedlings acquired from reliable local sources, rather than trying to start them from seed indoors or in the garden itself. Many veteran gardeners are also better off buying transplants, simply for the convenience, or because the number of plants they require is too few to make the job of starting them from seed worth the effort, or simply to get a selection among the varieties available in the popular crops.

Resist the temptation to space any of these fruit-bearing crops too closely. Stick to the space guidelines indicated. If you have to get in one or two extra plants, don't cheat on the distance *between rows* or you won't be able to work properly in and around the plants later on. If you insist on cheating, cheat on the distance *between plants* in the row. If you're planning to intercrop these slow-maturing crops with a quick-maturing crop such as beans (as we show in our own garden plans), add 12" more space between rows.

With some minor exceptions, fruit-crop transplants should all be handled the same way. First of all, pick a cloudy day to put them in the ground. Or, if you have to do it on a hot, sunny day, be sure to plant in the early morning or evening hours, to protect exposed roots from drying out and to minimize the wilting effect of the operation on the young plants.

In normal spring conditions in most parts of the country, the soil should be moist enough to receive your seedlings. If you happen to be late in putting in these crops, or if you're in a particularly dry region or period of time, then you'll have to water the planting site before as well as after transplanting.

Minimize exposure of the root systems of young plants, in any case, by hoeing out all your planting sites beforehand, using a board or gardener's yardstick to keep everything straight and accurately spaced. Then move the seedlings to the holes one at a time, setting each plant slightly deeper than the level of the ground around it (tomatoes are planted more than slightly deeper, and squash is set in hills, as explained shortly), filling the hole, pressing down slightly, and squeezing the soil firmly around the transplant to eliminate air pockets. If you're planting from a tray pack, be sure to moisten the pack first, and leave as much soil around the roots as possible. Remove any plastic pots, bands, or nylon nettings from root balls before setting in the ground, as these will greatly hamper root development. Peat pots can remain, but be sure to cover the pot with soil. Exposed portions act like wicks, drawing moisture up from the soil to be evaporated and causing a root ball to dry out completely.

After planting, water all seedlings gently but thoroughly, directly around the base of each plant.

You will treat the fruit-bearing crops similarly after you set them out.

Fruit-bearing crops all require extra support—hilling, staking, or fencing. Hilling also helps the soil warm up more quickly and enables new root systems to form above the seedling's original ground line.

They all require careful cultivation at regular intervals. Use your sharp hoe to chop away any weeds growing 6" or more from the plant, but don't cut into the soil deeply, and remove those weeds closer in by hand.

Fruit-bearing crops require extra nourishment when they are half grown, or about midseason. You can feed them all at the same time. Each plant should get a shovelful of phosphorus-rich manure (rabbit manure is ideal) or compost, or a handful of bone meal, or a dose of liquid fish emulsion or manure tea or compost tea. Simply apply the side-dressing around the base of each plant.

Watch the plants for the presence of pests, because they tend to attract a lot of feeders to their rich growth. Eggplant and squash should be checked more closely than the others.

Finally, the fruit-bearing crops all should be harvested to maximize each plant's output. That means picking the fruit before it fully matures, 2 to 3 times a week during harvest period, which begins in about 8 weeks from the time they are set in the garden. The more you pick, the more there will be to pick.

Remember, all these fruit-producing crops will be killed by the first frost in the fall. On marginally cold days, protect them as best you can with burlap or other materials. This will pay off particularly when you're struck by a freakishly early cold spell in the fall. When the first solid freeze is anticipated, bring in all the fruit that's on the vines, whether it's ripe or not. Peppers and tomatoes will ripen when wrapped in newspaper and stored in a cool place inside the house for a few days. Or you may want to preserve the unripe fruit in a variety of ways. End-of-season productivity measures such as these often push your garden operation well into the black.

Eggplant (May 15th)

- Start from seedlings.

- Plant at 24" intervals in rows 30" apart.

- Side-dress in 8 weeks.

- Ready to harvest beginning in 10 weeks.

- Finish the harvest before first fall frost.

- Follow the general procedures for transplants of fruit-producing crops as outlined in the previous pages.

Suckers or shoots are new leafy stems that often form, in eggplant, in the crotch between the main stem of the plant and existing branches. These can be readily identified as such in the early stages of a plant's development. They begin to appear in eggplant approximately 4 weeks from the date of transplant, when the plant is about 15" high. (However, in relatively poor soils these may not appear on eggplant at all.) The bottom 3 to 4 suckers should be removed while they are still small. This will encourage formation of earlier fruit, higher up on the plant, as energy is diverted from these would-be branches to the business of fruit production. Also, this bit of surgery will make it much less likely, later in the season, that wind or rain will cause a branch that's overladen with fruit to collapse. The branches that usually crack under such pressure are those at the bottom of the plant, for they are the ones with the least amount of support from the main stem. Removal of the bottom suckers eliminates this problem.

To get rid of the young shoots, gently pinch, pull, or twist them until they're severed from the stem.

Build up the soil around the base of the growing eggplant. This can be done in the course of normal weekly cultivation simply by throwing up a hoeful or two of soil around the stem. The procedure is similar to that used in hilling bush beans, as described earlier, except that it's done in two or three stages as the plants increase in size.

This gradually creates a larger feeding area for the plant. It also props up the stem for the later job of supporting the considerable weight of the ripening fruit—an eggplant weighs up to 2 pounds, and toward the end of the season a typical bush will bear at least 6 eggplants on it at a time.

Be careful not to scrape soil from too near the plant or you might damage some roots near the surface.

Eggplant puts forth lavender blossoms, preparatory to setting fruit, about 4 weeks after being transplanted into the garden. This may vary depending upon weather conditions in your area. When you spot the fruit beginning to form, you should side-dress each bush with a spadeful of phosphorus-rich manure, compost, or bone meal.

Asian Vegetables

Three warm-season vegetable crops from the Orient are Chinese long bean, Asian eggplant, and Asian "burpless" cucumbers. Long beans grow on a long trailing vine, similar to our black-eyed peas, and need a trellis or other means of support. The beans grow up to 3' long and are cut into 2" pieces for stir-fries. Asian eggplant comes in round or slender shapes and in purple, brown, or green skin colors. Like long bean, it should be placed in the garden after all danger of frost is past. It is best grown from transplants. Japanese and Chinese varieties of cukes produce crisp, sweet-tasting fruit 10" to 15" long; for straight-formed, rather than curved fruits, train the vines to grow on a trellis.

Watch for bugs, beginning in June. Remember, eggplant is more susceptible to beetle attack than peppers and tomatoes, so check under its leaves more often when you think of it.

Harvest eggplant when the fruit is 4" to 6" in diameter. Some varieties of eggplant, like Stokes's Long Tom, produce an elongated fruit 3" in diameter and 8" long when ready for picking. You'll need a sharp knife or a pair of kitchen shears to cut the stem when you do go out to pick an eggplant. If you try to rip them off by hand, you may break part of the plant because the stems are so woody and strong. If you've waited too long, you'll cut into an eggplant and discover that the seeds have turned brown. But you'll soon get the knack of knowing just when to pick them.

If your soil is rich enough, and you have hilled properly, it shouldn't be necessary to stake your eggplant. People who cover their gardens with mulch are forced to stake because they can't hill and the plant can't hold itself up without outside help, especially during inclement weather.

Peppers (May 15th)

- Start from seedlings.

- Plant at 24" intervals in rows 24" apart.

- Side-dress in 8 weeks.

- Ready to harvest beginning in 10 weeks.

- Finish the harvest before first fall frost.

Peppers take up a bit less space than eggplant, and the fruit, though prolific in number, does not equal the eggplant for sheer avoirdupois. Nevertheless, you should employ exactly the same soil build-up procedure around the base of your pepper plants as you do for eggplant.

Pepper blossoms about a month from the time it's transplanted into the garden, but the flowering parts are somewhat more sensitive than those of eggplant. If early in the growing season there are either extremely high temperatures or unseasonably cool nights, pepper will drop its blossoms; the flowers will fall from the plant, and the fruit-making process will have to start all over again.

Tex-Mex Garden Specialties

The increased interest in Tex-Mex and Southwest cooking has led many gardeners to include chile peppers, tomatillos, cilantro, and other Spanish-speaking vegetables and herbs in their home gardens or in patio containers. Many varieties are available that will do well in northern areas. But be advised: If you decide to grow hot chile peppers, keep them at least 20' away from your sweet bell peppers. If you don't, cross-pollination by the bees will ensure that *all* your peppers come out hot.

Apart from that consideration, chile peppers and bell peppers require similar care. It's best to start them from seedlings to get a jump on the growing season. Garden centers in most areas today offer a good selection of young starter plants ready for transplant. Among the varieties we carry:

- *Anaheim.* These 6" to 8" peppers have a crisp, thick green flesh and are only mildly hot. They are a favorite for grilling, roasting, and stuffing (chile rellenos).

- *Serranos.* Only 3" long, but very hot, especially after their color changes from dark green to scarlet. Use fresh when ripe or grill and add to salsas, guacamole, and tacos.

- *Anchos/Poblanos.* When it's green, this chile pepper is called poblano. It's big enough to stuff. When it turns brick-red and dries out, it is called an ancho; these are used to make powder for spicing up dishes and sauces, including the famous mole sauce.

- *Jalapeños.* These peppers can be mild or hot, depending on the variety. When roasted and chopped, they're added to cheese dishes and corn bread for piquancy. When grilled, they're added to tacos or burritos. They also make delicious stuffed appetizers, pickles, and jams. Smoke dry to make chipotles.

- *Tomatillos.* Although unrelated to tomatoes, this staple of Mexican cookery can be grown in similar fashion, without, however, the need to stake. It should be started indoors from seed and transplanted to the garden. Fruits ripen early. Harvest when the fruit is plump and its papery husk splits. Tomatillos are the base for such Mexican treats as salsa verde, chili verde, and the sauce called *sofrito*.

Don't be alarmed; the plants will produce more blossoms as soon as favorable weather conditions return.

The first peppers will appear about 2 weeks after blossom-set, or 6 to 8 weeks from the date of transplant. They'll mature rapidly and should be picked while young and firm. Green bell peppers turn red when left on the bush extra long. Some people enjoy the slightly milder, sweeter taste of these fully ripe peppers. But allowing them to redden on the plant will cut the plant's total productivity—unless you're growing a special variety that is naturally red.

Try green frying peppers if you can find them. They're more productive per bush than bell peppers. Their thin skins make for tasty side dishes when fried lightly in olive oil. We always grow our frying peppers from seed I get from my godmother in New Jersey. She saves the best from her harvest every year to make sure we have enough frying pepper plants to satisfy our customers.

Tomatoes (May 15th)

- Start from seedlings.

- Plant at 36" intervals in rows 36" apart; plant deeper in soil than they were in the pot.

- Ready to stake in 3 to 5 weeks.

- Side-dress in 8 to 10 weeks.

- Ready to harvest beginning in 10 weeks.

- Finish the harvest before first fall frost.

The tomato is far and away the most popular vegetable in America. It is also one of the easiest to grow—partly because it is so popular. In response to demand, seed companies have developed strains of tomatoes that are so sturdy, trouble-free, and productive that the most harried home gardener ought to be able to make a success out of his or her crop.

Yet untold numbers of gardeners have trouble with tomatoes. One reason may be a failure to recognize the crop's great need for sun—but I've already talked about that.

The other reason, which I want to deal with here, is failure to control the growth of the tomato to favor the development of the plant for maximum-fruit production in a limited space.

My method for controlling tomatoes is to remove young leafy stems—the suckers or shoots—in order to develop a strong two-stem plant, and to keep the plant on its feet with a special but easy to construct Y-shaped stake.

Selective trimming of budding new suckers keeps a tomato plant from bursting into unmanageable and wasteful vine production, and instead channels its energies into development of fruit. This also tends to keep your tomato patch neat—and therefore easier to care for properly—and gives plants the air circulation and sunlight they need throughout their parts.

There are two different kinds of tomato plant. The early or "determinate" type grows only 4' tall, topping itself off with a cluster of blossoms, then puts forth early fruit, generally small in size. This type merely needs to be staked at the time of transplant, then tied to the stake once or twice before it finishes.

The main-season or "indeterminate" type grows just about as high as you like (up to 8' if you have both the means to support it and the extra-long growing season to justify the bother), and it produces fruit a bit later but in bigger sizes and greater quantity. This is the mainstay of most tomato patches. It requires the pruning and staking procedures I've just outlined.

Most gardeners include a small number of the early type and a couple of varieties of the main-season type, which are more productive, longer-lasting, and generally better-tasting. And almost every gardener wants one or two cherry tomatoes. They're productive, but their vines are leggy and likely to roam, so they are much more difficult to stake and manage. Still, they're worth it.

Depending on the size of the transplant, selective trimming or pruning may begin as soon as you've chosen the transplants. Remove the bottom three or four shoots—those tiny leafy stems that may have already formed in the crotch between an existing leaf and the stem of the plant. This will prevent a lot of early growth near the base of the plant, which would weaken the stem throughout. We do exactly the same thing for the young eggplant. This will also make it easier to move in to cultivate and feed each plant in later stages.

Wait until shoots are 2" long before removing them, however; if you pinch them off much before, they might grow back on you.

Set tomato transplants deeper than they were planted in the pot—to foster maximum root growth for a plant that will need all it can get below ground level to support and nourish its eventual 5-foot-high growth. All those fuzzy little hairs around the base of the original stem will turn into roots after you've planted.

The exact depth in inches to bury the stem depends on its height (excluding root ball). It should be at least equal to one fourth the height of the seedling. If your plant is 12" high, make sure the stem is buried 3" deep.

Sometimes an otherwise healthy transplant will have a slight curve in its stem. Arrange so that the curve is beneath ground level, and the seedling will straighten of its own accord in short order. Don't worry about burying a couple

Grape and Cherry Tomatoes

Tomatoes have essentially the same growing requirements as standard hybrids and heirloom varieties. Grape varieties, prized for their sugary flavor, are semi-determinate (see page 167) and should be staked in the same way used for full-sized tomatoes to obtain maximum productivity. Cherry tomatoes have a sprawling habit that lends itself to growing in wooden half-barrels. They can also be trained to climb up tripods or allowed to find their own way within the confines of metal tomato cages.

The demand for these smaller tomatoes has been so great in recent years that numerous varieties have been developed. The Sweet 100 was one of the earliest cherry types, and it is still going strong today, despite competition from imitators such as Sweet One Million and many others. Two seed companies that specialize in tomatoes, Totally Tomatoes of Randolph, Wisconsin, and Tomato Growers Supply Company of Fort Myers, Florida, offer literally hundreds of varieties between them. If you get their catalogs in December, you'll have a couple of months to mull over your choices! The good news is, with tomatoes you can't go wrong no matter what kinds you pick.

If you include both a cherry and a grape variety in your garden, you'll get more than enough sweet fruits for your summer salads.

of leaves in the process. In fact, it's better not to remove the leaves, because fresh scars on the buried stem might invite disease.

In 4 weeks, the original 12" plant should be about 2' high. If yellow blossoms weren't on the plant when you bought it, there should be a cluster of them now. These signal the beginning of the fruit-making process in the plant. In anticipation of future growth, you should hill the plant now.

At the same time, you will also note that a number of additional shoots or suckers have formed on the plant. Pinch off all of these would-be stems except the one immediately below the flower cluster. This sucker will look bigger and stronger than any of the others, owing to its proximity to the flowers. Just because it is so vigorous, it makes the best choice from among the fledgling leaf growth on the plant to nurture as a second main stem for your plant. In effect, it's the pick of the litter.

The hilling of the plant and the selection of the second main stem sets the stage for the installation of the main support system for the tomatoes.

At this point I drive a pair of 6'1" x 1" redwood stakes side by side into the ground at a distance of about 6" from each plant. Then I force these pliable stakes 12" apart into a Y shape. At 3' from ground level, I tack a crossbar, about 15" long and made of the same material, into the two stakes. This creates a kind of mini-trellis. It's neat and attractive, and it gives me the means to control the future growth of both the main stem and the new second stem of the plant, simply tying them to the two stakes at about 12" intervals.

As you may be aware, there is more than one way to prune and stake a tomato plant. Indeed, there are dozens of methods, many of them quite effective and sensible for specific uses.

Some people use only one stake and trim away all sucker shoots, to develop only the main stem, and not two stems. This method requires less space per plant in the garden, but results in fewer total tomatoes, as there is only one stem producing fruit.

Other people have turned to growing unpruned tomatoes within the confines of a 3-foot-high ring of sturdy mesh wire. This results in more tomatoes—though they come a bit later in the season than those growing on pruned vines—and demands correspondingly more space. Also, the unchecked growth of vines under this method makes it harder to control insects and diseases and to harvest fruit on time.

Still other gardeners have designed trellis-type structures in a wide variety of forms, using poles, saplings, wire, string, and anything else that's handy to train their tomatoes.

Proportionate to the space required, a two-stem tomato plant is, I believe, at least as productive as any, plus it is more likely to get all the air, light, and attention it needs at every stage of growth. I should add that my use of a trellis is partly for its pleasing aesthetic effect. Other staking methods would support a two-stem tomato plant almost as well. Old-timers use lengths of discarded pipe, small saplings, and even old tires to support their plants, and so may you.

In about two weeks from the first flowering, under normal conditions, a cluster of baby tomatoes will have formed on the main stem. This first-flower-then-fruit sequence will repeat itself progressively all the way up the main stem and, starting a bit later, up the second stem, too.

Once the first cluster of fruit appears, it's time to give the plants a shot of phosphorus-rich manure, compost, or bone meal, and to perform some additional pruning. On the main stem, you should remove all new shoots that have appeared above the fruit cluster, and retain the one immediately below each new flower cluster. On the second stem, you should do the same. Those shoots that you permit to survive the pruning operation will produce additional flower clusters for you later on.

At this point we are well into the summer and the tomato plant is embarking on its most productive period of growth. Check tomatoes twice a week from now on, with three main jobs in mind:

1. Prune new shoots on both stems. Pinch off all suckers that form between the fruit cluster and the flower cluster higher up, except the one immediately below the flower cluster. If the plant becomes too viney, however, start removing all new shoots, including the one below the flower cluster.

2. Tie both main and second stems to the stake at about 12" intervals. Train the main stem to one arm of the Y and the second stem to the other arm.

3. Begin the harvest. Pick tomatoes promptly as they ripen. Individual taste dictates exactly the right time to pick; some people like their fruit on the hard side, others quite soft. But

keep on picking to spur maximum growth elsewhere on the plant. Pluck ripe tomatoes off, rather than pulling them, so as not to disturb others on the same cluster or perhaps injure the main plant. Use two hands.

Cucumbers (May 20th)

- Start from potted seedlings.

- Plant at 24" intervals along fence or trellis.

- Train to fence beginning in 4 weeks.

- Side-dress in 8 weeks.

- Ready to harvest beginning in 10 weeks.

Note that I put both cucumber and squash in my garden about a week later than I plant the tomatoes, eggplant, and pepper. This is because these two vegetables—both members of the Gourd or Cucurbit family—are not only killed outright by frosty weather, but also severely set back by cool weather.

Unless the nights are consistently in the 55° to 60° F range—so that it's balmy enough to go out for a walk without your sweater on after supper—young cucumber transplants will shrink instead of grow, and they'll take several weeks to catch up again. I've frequently planted some early and others late, to test what would happen, and invariably the late ones have turned out to be the early and better producers in the long run.

Setting cucumber or squash out prematurely could also saddle them with fungus problems in a wet spring. There's really no need to rush them into the garden, anyway, for once the ground does warm up thoroughly, you'll find that they develop faster than just about anything else in the garden.

In order to keep cucumbers from spreading through portions of the rest of your garden like an octopus, they should be trained to grow up a 6-foot-high galvanized wire fence or trellis. Put it in the northern end of the garden so it doesn't shade other crops. (Compact-growing bush varieties now available from seed companies and garden centers eliminate the need for this support.)

Wire fence made in a very small mesh—say, 1" x 1"—won't work well, because some young cucumbers may form within the mesh and become misshapen. If the mesh is as big as 4" x 4", it will still provide plenty of wire for the cucumbers to climb on, yet won't interfere with their fruit formation.

Actually, the cukes will train themselves if you plant them properly. Set the transplants at 2' intervals, about 6" from the fence. In 4 weeks, each vine will begin climbing the fence by putting out little tendrils that wrap around the wire as if there were no tomorrow.

During this period, check that all the vines are climbing straight up. There'll be a couple going along the ground or at an angle up the fence. You won't hurt the plant if you break or unwind a couple of the tendrils in repositioning each vine. When they are about 2' high, use some nonabrasive tie to connect each vine loosely to the fence. That should ensure that they all reach the top of the fence and begin down the other side. Around about mid-July, you may have to tie up a couple of errant vines once more, but that's about all.

A side-dressing of rabbit manure or of bone meal combined with wood ashes, applied in midseason, has always helped our cucumber production—to the point where we've almost regretted giving the crop the extra feeding.

There are two basic cucumber types. One is the short, spiny cucumber used for pickling, the other a long, dark green "slicing" variety used for salads and such. All should be picked as immature fruit—no bigger than 6" to 8" for slicing cucumbers and 3" to 4" for pickling types. Once you start harvesting, plan on picking every 2 to 3 days, to keep the vines producing more new fruit. If a fruit has acquired a yellow complexion, it means you're too late in picking. Take it off the vine and throw it on the compost pile.

Cucumbers do poorly if there is too much wetness, which is why, of all the vegetables, mulching them or lawn-sprinkling them in the evening could be especially disastrous, a veritable welcome mat for fungus and disease. Cucumber mosaic causes vines to wilt before they've produced half their quota.

Cukes are the only big fruit-producing crop that doesn't stay in the garden all summer. They're quick enough to be replaced with a bean crop, or a crop for fall, so keep that in mind when you do set them out in the garden.

Note: Cucumbers may be started directly from seed if the soil was warmed up in your area and no further threat of frost is likely. If the ground is cold and wet, however, cucumber seed will rot. But that isn't the end of the world, either. If your sowing fails, you can still use transplants.

Squash (May 20th)

- Start from potted seedlings.

- Plant in hills at 48" intervals, in rows 48" apart.

- Side-dress in 6 weeks.

- Ready to harvest beginning in 8 weeks.

- Finish the harvest before first fall frost.

Squash, like cucumber, is usually planted from containers of 2 to 4 young seedlings that have been sown indoors and then hardened off for the trip to the garden. Sets of seedlings should not be separated but planted together in one spot, and in hills rather than at garden level, as are the other fruit-producing crops. Hills will help the squash plants develop more uniformly and provide greater air circulation within their eventually quite dense, low, bushy growth.

Build the hills at transplanting time by hoeing up soil around your planting site until you have a volcano-like pile about 8" high. Center the transplant in that pile.

Remember to leave more room for squash than any other garden vegetable: 4' to 6' between each plant. This would apply for all summer squash: the yellow crookneck or straightneck varieties, the long green zucchini varieties, and those pattypan types that produce small fruit shaped like scalloped flying saucers.

Squash requires the cooperation of insects, mostly bees, or air movement for the pollination that ensures the development of fruit. The blossoms appear about 6 to 7 weeks after the date of transplant into the garden. Initially, you can tell male blossoms from female blossoms by the fact that the female is shorter in length and more compact. Three days later the female blossom will become even more recognizable for the small fruit that begins to form between the blossom and the stem; that fruit will now form so rapidly that it will be ready for picking 3 to 6 days after the female flower first opened.

Incidentally, the male flowers, of which there are always a great excess on squash, may be picked and fried in omelets, or in a recipe that my family likes for breakfast: dip the blossoms in a flour-and-water batter, then fry them in deep fat until they're light brown—and delicious.

Squash will produce in great numbers if you harvest all fruit as soon as it's ready—while the skin is soft enough to pierce with your fingernail. If you let squash get too big, its seeds harden, it becomes tough and stringy, and the plant will no longer produce well. Pick yellow varieties when they're about 2" in diameter, zucchini when they're 6" to 8" long, and pattypan types when they are 3" to 4" across.

Watch for bugs on squash and remove them as you find them, to keep the insect population from soaring.

Note: Squash, like cucumbers, may be started directly from seed if your soil has warmed up and the threat of frost is past. Also, squash plants that grow compactly are now on the market and can be productive in small spaces or containers.

Basil (June 1st)

- Start from seedlings.
- Plant at 12" intervals.

Basil, the most tender of all the herbs and vegetables, must be introduced to the garden last, and fully harvested from the garden first in the fall.

This king of culinary herbs has come a long way since my mother planted it between our tomatoes when I was just a kid. The number of basil varieties available for today's home gardeners is staggering. Whichever basil bush you choose to plant is likely to satisfy, but here are a couple of guidelines.

Genovese basil varieties have the strongest basil aroma and taste. In addition, these small-leafed basil varieties are less susceptible to Japanese beetles than the large- or lettuce-leafed types, a factor to keep in mind if you are in an area where this persistent scourge is active. (Italian growers have become so proprietary about their Genoa-based basils that they have branded the varieties in much the same way that Chianti has branded its Classico red wine.)

My preferred basil variety is Aussie Sweetie. It grows to 3' in a columnar fashion—never much wider than 12"—so it does not take much space yet provides fragrant leaves all summer, and without going to seed. It too is not a favorite of Japanese beetles.

The purple basils are fun to grow if you have room. They are not as flavorful but make attractive garnishes in salads. I've tried making pesto with purple basil, but the murky color and bland flavor left me unimpressed.

To start a main crop of basil, sow indoors at the end of April, but treat thereafter just as sensitively as you would cucumber seedlings. Don't put young basil out on nights under 50° F, or you will discover that the plants are smaller in the morning than when you left them the night before.

Transplant basil at 12" to 15" intervals, depending on the growth pattern of the variety you have chosen. Dwarf basils can be planted closer together. To make the plant grow in a bush, pinch the center stem 1" from the top when the plants are 6" high. If you don't keep pinching out the center stem, basil will go to seed, especially in warm weather. Check it every 2 weeks.

To bring basil indoors, sow a fresh crop of seed beginning in August or September, then bring it in as seedlings. You should harvest the more mature crops just prior to the first fall frost, and pack them away in the freezer, in plastic bags.

Potatoes and Corn

Plant 1 to 2 weeks before frost-free date.

These crops are cultural mavericks, impossible to treat within the framework of ordinary vegetable gardening.

They require so much extra space to survive and produce that it would be uneconomical to surround a decent planting of either of them with an elevated barrier, as we do with other vegetables.

Both are long, full-season crops, so there's no convenient way to practice interplanting or succession planting to increase productivity for the space being used. Planting pumpkins or cucumbers between rows of corn and training pole beans to go up the stalks are ideas that work better in theory than in practice, as you would discover the first time you put your foot through a young pumpkin or tripped over a bean vine and crashed through a couple of rows of the corn.

They are also both susceptible to a wide variety of insects and diseases, and so require much more preventive attention from the organic gardener.

Finally, both crops demand meticulous attention and judgment to harvest properly. A couple of mistakes at this time and you could spoil the whole crop.

However, corn and potatoes do not require a concentrated effort toward improving soil tilth. You can have fair success planting them in virgin ground, so long as it's well drained and slightly composted or manured. Potatoes definitely take shape better in a reasonably sandy or light soil, but corn will grow well in stony soils, as New England farmers know full well.

For this reason, if you are going to grow corn or potatoes, it might be a good idea to pick a marginal area to plant in, or one that you would like to convert into a first-rate soil bed eventually but don't have time to now.

Potatoes (May 1st)

- Start from seed potatoes.

- Plant 12" apart, 4" to 6" deep, in rows 30" apart.

- Sprouts appear in 15 days.

- Side-dress lightly in 50 to 60 days, when 12" to 15" high.

- Ready to harvest in 120 to 135 days.

- Finish the harvest before first fall frost.

Buy certified seed stock, either from a local garden center or one of the relatively few seed companies that carry potatoes in their catalog pages. "Certified" simply means that the potatoes you will get have not been sprayed with any chemical to inhibit sprouting. Supermarket potatoes usually get sprayed for this purpose, so if used for planting, very little production would result.

Cut your seed potatoes into sections containing at least two eyes—three eyes if you have enough potatoes to plant the desired space. You'll get more planting pieces out of some potatoes than others, because eyes do not develop uniformly. Use a clean knife—one that's been sterilized in your dishwasher—for this operation, and don't leave the seed pieces exposed to sun and wind once they're ready for planting.

Plant each seed piece 4" to 6" deep at 12" intervals. To get early, erect sprouting, make sure at least one eye of the potato is looking you in the eye when you set the piece in the ground; that's the spot from which the new plant will sprout. Keep rows 30" apart.

Usually, seed potatoes are sold in quantities of pounds. Figure that 3 pounds will plant 25 feet of row.

Plants should emerge from the ground in about 2 weeks from planting. Cultivate on a weekly basis, cutting down the weeds with your hoe and at the same time gradually hilling each plant by throwing up dirt from the walkways between rows. One reason hilling is so important is that it protects the tubers forming beneath the ground from sunlight, which would give them a green cast and a bitter taste.

When the plant stands 12" to 15" high, its first blossoms should appear. Now's the time to spread some manure, compost, or bone meal all around each hill. Large amounts of raw organic matter are not recommended in potato beds, because such matter may stimulate a soil-borne disease called common scab. Yet the potatoes need some plant food. If you limit your feeding to about 1 bushel of aged manure per 100 square feet, you'll enrich the soil without endangering the crop.

After side-dressing the potatoes in this manner, the main thing to keep in mind until the fall is the crop's demand for adequate moisture. Water the patch thoroughly once a week in dry periods, especially if you see plants wilting. Water in the morning; with potatoes it is impossible to irrigate without getting some of their dense foliage wet, and it's better to give them the day to dry out.

Though the potato crop accumulates underground, out of sight, it's easy to tell when it's time to harvest. The plants will start to dry out and fall over. This will be in early fall, about four months from planting—depending, as always, on the exact variety grown. About 2 weeks later, pull up all the plants and start digging.

There's a knack to digging for the potatoes effectively. Most of the crop will be located in a 6" to 8" layer, but if you go after it carelessly, you're likely to bring up half the potatoes impaled on the blades of your spade fork. So start from the outside edge of the garden, dig straight down, and then bring the group up in sections and pick the crop out of the soil you've turned over.

If you want to impress the rest of the family with your first potato harvest, fill a basket with potatoes, then use an old roadside-stand trick called "rolling the bushel." Pick up the basket and shake it around to force the potatoes literally to "roll" inside. Fresh potatoes are sturdy, so they won't get bruised or cut by such treatment. More important, all the small potatoes will filter to the bottom, so when you bring your bushel into the house, everyone will look in amazement at the layer of the biggest potatoes on top. They'll think you're Irish.

Corn (May 1st)

- Start from seed.

- Plant at 12" intervals, 2" deep, in rows 30" apart.

- Sprouts appear in 15 to 20 days.

- Side-dress in 50 days, when 2½' to 3' high.

- Ready to harvest in 80 to 100 days.

Corn is probably the most difficult crop for the home gardener to grow using strictly organic methods—harder, even, than the brassicas. Not only does it have a persistent natural enemy in the form of the corn earworm, but the crop is also susceptible to heavy damage from such large pests as crows and raccoons.

Thus one of my neighbors, who must grow corn to feed his dairy cattle, uses just about every chemical known to man to make his crop a success. First thing in the spring, he sprays his fields with an herbicide that kills all the grass and weeds. Then he uses corn seed treated with other chemicals to make it unpalatable to birds and rodents, and also a fungicide to prevent it from rotting in the soil. When he plants the seeds, each drill gets a shot of high-phosphorus corn-starter fertilizer. Then, when the corn is 1" high, he sprays the whole field with liquid nitrogen. A little later, the bugs arrive and he sprays with insecticides. And so on . . .

My neighbor grows corn this way for his animals, but most commercially grown corn for human consumption is also grown this way. That's another reason, in addition to getting the special taste of fresh corn, that a lot of people accept the challenge of growing their own corn, hard as it is.

Another corn farmer I know lives quite a distance from me, but I think of him as a neighbor during the month of May, because that's when he sets up a miniature cannon in his fields to scare the crows away. The cannon fires loud blank charges—once every 90 seconds—and when the wind is right, the sound does carry.

Corn doesn't need as well-worked a soil bed as potatoes, but it should have some compost or manure under each hill or drill—as the Indian farmers realized when they buried dead fish in with the crop.

Plan to plant corn at intervals of 2 to 3 weeks in the spring, if you have the room, so that you can stretch your eating period in the fall. Or do all your planting on one day in the spring, but sow varieties of corn that mature at different rates. Corn seed is available in these basic maturity rates:

1. *Early corn*, maturing in 60 to 70 days, ears 6" to 7" long, stalks 5' to 6' high.

2. *Midseason corn*, maturing in 70 to 80 days, ears 7" to 8" long, stalks 6' to 7' tall.

3. *Late corn*, maturing in 80 to 100 days, ears 7" to 9" long, stalks 7' to 9' tall.

Thus, if you had six 25' rows available, you could plant three rows in a midseason variety and three rows in a late variety, all on the same day, yet achieve the desired extended harvest period in the fall.

Early-corn varieties, by the way, are usually not as productive or tasty as later varieties.

Block-planting of corn is necessary to ensure adequate pollination of the corn by the wind. If you planted corn in one long row, most of it would be poorly pollinated and would produce ears with many missing kernels. A minimum block of corn would be about 7' x 25', or 3 rows with 24 hills or drills per row. Anything smaller invites poor pollination, and is hardly worth the effort, anyway, for what you'll get out of it. Three ears of corn per stalk is the most production you can expect to get out of this crop even when it is properly block-planted and subject to ideal growing conditions.

I plant corn 2" deep at 1' intervals, with rows 2½' apart. Put 4 seeds in each drill and, when the seedlings sprout 2 to 3 weeks later, thin down to 3 strong plants where 4 have come up.

Start cultivating when the plants are 6" to 8" high, and for hilling follow the same procedure as for the potatoes. When the corn is about knee high (corn is supposed to be "knee high by the Fourth of July," but that depends on when you sow it), I side-dress with rabbit manure. If I have wood ashes left over from use in my main garden, I work that in with the manure, too.

Corn needs water like any other crop. In a fairly rich organic soil, corn will strike deep taproots quickly. It will hold up for several weeks of dry weather, then, when a good rainfall does occur, burst into new growth again. It is vital to irrigate the corn crop if and when its leaves curl in toward their midribs; no other vegetable reveals its thirst in quite this manner. If you see this happen, water promptly.

Corn is ready to harvest when the ear feels firm and well filled with kernels and the silk tassel on top has begun to turn brown and dry. This should be about 3 weeks after the time the silk tassel first appears. (This is the most critical period for water, too.) A good way to check ripeness is to peel back an ear while it's still on the stalk and puncture one of the kernels with your fingernail. If it squirts a milk-white runny liquid, it's time to pick it and eat it. If the kernel is still watery, the corn is underripe. If the kernel is large and doesn't squirt at all, it's overripe; the sugar has turned to starch and the corn will be tough and relatively tasteless, hardly better than store-bought corn.

The ears lowest on the stalk ripen first. Once corn does mature, you have to be ready to pick it. An ear can remain in a ripe state for several days if the weather's on the cool side with temperatures in the low 60s. But if temperatures are in the 80s, the corn will go from ripe to overripe in the space of an afternoon.

The best time to pick corn is in the cool part of morning or evening. Hold the stalk, then twist the tip of the ear toward the ground until it breaks off.

Lettuce from the Supply Garden (beginning May 15th)

The "supply garden" is nothing more than the scatter-sown radish bed converted to midsummer and fall planting usages, after the original radish crop is finished.

The best way to sow lettuce in the supply garden is in rows about 4" apart. Sow the seeds loosely—at about ½" intervals—and no deeper than ¼" of a fine sand, then cover the entire sown section with a piece of loose-woven burlap. This will protect the bed from drying out in the sun or being uprooted by a sudden driving rainstorm. As soon as the lettuces sprout, which will be in 3 to 4 days, remove the burlap and water the seedlings sparingly but as needed.

Within three weeks, they'll be ready for transplanting to your main garden, and should be used to fill gaps as they occur.

I sow a slow-bolting variety of lettuce in the supply garden all summer long, usually at intervals of 3 to 4 weeks. If the supply garden becomes overcrowded with young plants nearing maturity or transplant time, I just rip up the largest row for a noontime salad, then start all over again with a new sowing right after lunch. By midsummer, plan to refertilize the area, with either liquid fish emulsion or a light sprinkling of aged manure or compost.

FALL PLANTING GROUP (JUNE 15TH TO AUGUST 1ST)
Plant 80 to 90 days before the first heavy frost.

The fall or winter garden is probably the single most neglected source of extra productivity for home growers.

Planted anywhere from July to September, depending on your section of the country, crops that perform well in cool weather keep your garden full and extend your growing season to the maximum. And there's no better advertisement for the Thanksgiving spirit than going out and harvesting your own vegetables for the big meal on that day.

The fall garden is easier to plan and plant than the spring garden. The soil bed in both the supply garden (crucial to fall planting) and the main garden is already prepared. The fruit-bearing crops that require the most attention can't be planted anyway; they wouldn't mature in time or stand up to chilly nights and frosts. The many root and leafy crops from which to choose don't take up much space, and most of them can be harvested within two months. Many can be sown directly in the garden from seed. Germination rate is always better than in the spring, at least in Northern gardens, because the soil is thoroughly warmed up and there is no excess-moisture problem. And there is not the rush of things in daily life that always seems to ensnare us in the spring. With tax returns and lawn problems and Little League behind us, there's time to think.

In fact, if it were possible to talk first-time gardeners into it, I might recommend that the maiden voyage into gardening begin with planting vegetables for fall. I wouldn't count on many people bitten by spring planting fever to follow that advice, of course. Nevertheless, take a look at my 400-square-foot plan for the winter garden on page 232. It demonstrates that the gardener who was out of the country or in bed with the flu from April 15th to June 15th, say, could still grow a broad range of crops. More important, it shows the need for planning from the outset to exploit the potential in sowing the later crops promptly.

Actually, "the fall garden" may be a misleading term, as the planting is done in summer. And it's easy to slip into a kind of torpor during July and August, when it just will not *feel* like planting weather. You may have to push yourself to get the crops in so they'll mature in time.

This is a good time to use up the rest of any seed you have left over from your spring planting. Ideal storage temperature for such seed, by the way, is 65° F, so find a cool, dry place in your basement or garage. If seed is stored in a hot, humid place, it will not hold. And you can't put it in your refrigerator or freezer, either—as can be done safely with many flowering perennial and herb seeds— because the excess cold will kill most vegetable seeds.

Fall Planting—Direct Sowing

- Sow directly in the main garden where and when space is available:

Fruit Crops

- beans
- cucumbers
- squash
- turnips
- rutabaga
- radishes

Root Crops

- beets
- carrots
- parsnips

- spinach

- Swiss chard

- mustard greens

Revitalize the soil area for fall crops, especially if a crop has just grown there, by spreading a light layer of compost or aged manure and turning it under. It isn't necessary to work the soil deeply or intensively at this time, as it is quite dry by now and its structure should be already established. Merely mix in your compost lightly.

The three fruit-bearing crops mentioned—beans, cucumbers, and squash—may be planted for fall because they grow fairly quickly, whereas tomatoes, pepper, and eggplant do not. You may not want to grow these three, however, if you're in the process of trying to give away the excess harvest of these prolific crops from earlier plantings. In other words, your family may be sick of them.

Nevertheless, they should be considered for the late garden if you have the space for them and the time left for them to mature in the last of the warm fall weather in your region.

Maturity dates for vegetables are usually given for the main growing season, but in late summer and early fall the days have begun to get shorter and the nights cooler. For this reason, I always increase the maturity time by 10 to 15 percent when I'm planting for fall. If I put in a late crop of beans that is supposed to reach maturity in 60 days, I figure it will take 70 days. Then, because beans are a fruit-bearing crop, I count backward in the calendar to be sure I sow the crop so that it has a full 70-day season before the first frost in the fall.

Otherwise, beans are grown exactly as they are grown in the spring and summer. Cucumbers and squash are grown similarly as well, except that now they may be sown directly in the warm ground.

Sow cucumbers, once more along a fence or trellis, in drills at 24" intervals, with 4 seeds per drill to ensure ample seedlings.

Sow squash in hills at 48" intervals, with 4 to 6 seeds per hill.

Remember, timing is most critical with these crops, for if you sow on the late side and get hit by an unexpected early frost, you can scratch all hopes of fruit production. The tender crops will be killed outright. With the rest of the recommended fall crops, however, you can still get a lot of growth during a long Indian-summer period following such a freak early frost.

The root crops indicated for fall planting are sown and grown exactly as described earlier. Timing may be a critical issue only with the long-season carrots.

Rutabaga is a turnip variety that does well in the North. It's grown like a turnip, and stored and prepared for the table similarly as well.

Mustard greens are grown like spinach. Harvest them on the early side for the best taste. Cook them in the same pot with a few turnips for a sample of some good Southern country cuisine.

Fall Planting—Indirect Sowing

- Sow in the supply garden for later transplanting to the main garden where and when space is available:

Brassicas

- cabbage
- cauliflower
- brussels sprouts
- broccoli
- kohlrabi
- kale

Leafy Crops

- endive
- escarole
- fennel
- leaf lettuce
- collards

The supply garden—that specially prepared bed used for scatter-sowing radishes in early spring and for starting your own lettuce transplants a bit later—now assumes still another important role in the life of the garden.

Use it to sow fall crops that cannot be directly sown into the main garden, for later transplanting when and where spots do open up. The plan on page 233 shows that a broad range of fall crops can be started even in a relatively small 3' x 3' sandbox garden.

Sow the fall crops in this area exactly as you did the lettuce. Sow the seed in shallow ¼-inch-deep furrows at ½" intervals, in rows that are about 4" apart. If you're sowing a variety of fall crops, make sure, by marking or staking, that you can keep track of what's growing where. After sowing, cover the furrows with fine sand, moisten the bed, then protect the entire planted area with a section of loose-woven burlap. The burlap will keep the seedbed from drying out in the hot sun that will be prevalent at the time you start your fall planting operations. As soon as the crops begin to sprout, remove the burlap. Keep them moist, by lightly watering in early morning, until it's time to transplant to the main garden in 3 to 4 weeks.

When you move their seedlings to the main garden, brussels sprouts, kohlrabi, and kale should be spaced and tended thereafter like the other brassicas. Somebody once described kale as "industrial-strength broccoli," but actually this large leafy plant acquires a good flavor after you've left it out for a couple of frosts.

Brussels sprouts also do particularly well when they mature in the colder weather, at least in my experience. That's why I don't include them in my spring planting plans. Sprouts grow in clusters around a tall stem, with the ones on the bottom maturing earliest. Harvest them when they reach 1" in diameter. Pinch out the center on the main stem about a month prior to your fall frost date, to encourage quicker development of the sprouts around the top.

Kohlrabi looks like a stereo headset worn by a Martian. It's grown for the bulblike formation that develops above the soil line, from which stems sprout like so many antennas. It can be planted at closer intervals than the other brassicas, 10" to 12" between plants. Harvest it when it is baseball size.

Collards are a large leafy crop, like kale, and can be harvested similarly—leaf by leaf or in whole heads.

Endive and escarole are grown like lettuce but require about 3 months from sowing to reach maturity. Their varied and unique tastes and textures enliven fall salads.

The fennel included here is not the sweet fennel grown as an herb for its seed, which people use in cooking, but Florence fennel (*finocchio a testa di Firenze*), an Italian favorite that is grown like celery and produces large hollow stems. As children, we were always treated to a glass of wine on Thanksgiving Day, and we would use the hollow fennel stem as a straw to drink it. It gave a pleasant sweet taste to the wine, so I've grown it in our gardens ever since, and my family enjoys it every Thanksgiving.

You'll have to cultivate your fall crops more frequently than you did in the spring, because wild grasses and weeds grow much faster in late summer. You also may have to irrigate more frequently if there's no rainfall. Check the fall crops every 2 to 3 days for these various services you may have to perform. You'll be in the garden harvesting your spring and main season crops anyway, so it shouldn't be a chore. Remember to step lightly and only on the pathways.

Fall Finale

- Scatter-sow radishes in the supply garden after fall transplants have been moved to the main garden.

- Harvest, preserve, and store.

- Remove dead roots and stalks.

- Spread compost or manure on those parts of the garden that are finished for the year.

- Plant or replant perennials for next spring: garlic, shallots, chives.

The wind-up operations in the fall garden are many and varied but not particularly complex or onerous. I do think it's important to get rid of all the dead crops so the rotting material doesn't attract unnecessary problems for crops still standing or for your soil next spring.

Most of the root and leafy crops that were fall-planted may be left in the ground through Thanksgiving and almost up to Christmas, at least in our region.

A good trick for keeping the garlic and shallots from being displaced by alternate freezing and thawing of the ground is to blanket them with salt hay—an effective natural insulator that grows near marshes—after the ground has frozen solid to an inch or two; say, as when the temperature has dropped to 20° F three nights in a row. The salt hay will prevent the ground from ever freezing to a depth of more than the inch or two it froze in that initial cold period.

When I was a kid, we always used salt hay to cover the mammoth "root cellar" my family maintained to store some of the harvest from our fall plantings. A trench 2' deep, 2' wide, and almost 100' long was dug out in the fall, bedded down with leaves, then filled with carrots, celery, turnips, cabbage, kale, escarole, and parsnips, and on top of the vegetables was a layer of salt hay.

My main winter chore as a kid was to brush the snow and salt hay aside and get vegetables out of this trench every couple of days. The crops were arranged in an alternating fashion, so that as I worked my way along the trench, I came up with something different for the dinner table each time.

Maybe the most satisfying aspect of a successful fall garden is eating high-quality vegetables at a time when they're not generally available, or are priced out of sight. The summer harvest gives you fine fresh tomatoes and peppers and all, but you can get produce elsewhere at the peak of the summer harvest, too. Farm stands don't usually stay open just to sell you brussels sprouts or endive in November, however.

I suppose that's why I didn't mind digging in the snow and competing with the field mice to find vegetables for the family all winter. I got to eat them, too.

IV. For Next Year

Make Compost as You Make Good Lasagna

I can still remember how amazed I was the first time I saw the results of the composting process. When I was a kid, my family used to construct huge compost piles in the fall to develop soil for use in our greenhouses the following year. We actually went out and raked tons of leaves for people gratis, to get the material we needed to put in the pile, and everyone who worked in the greenhouses came in with their grass clippings and donated them to the cause. Then my father trucked in loads of fresh cow manure, and we began to put it all together, along with some topsoil and various other waste materials and occasional sprinklings of limestone, until finally we had a pile that measured 6' high, 15' wide, and 60' long. You could have hidden three station wagons in it.

Anyway, the following year it was ready to be brought into the greenhouses, and I would look through it in vain for the leaves, for the small sticks and stalks, for the grass clippings and weeds. Nothing was left except dark, loose, sweet-smelling earth. From a small boy's vantage point, this seemed like pure magic—surely a conjuring trick that my grandfather had learned when gardening in his native Naples and brought with him when he settled in this country in 1902 and started the family business.

Composting is subject to a lot of personal interpretation, and different compost piles can have different make-ups and still be successful. The poet Robert Graves seems to have recognized this subtle truth by naming his compost piles after various good friends.

If there is one concept underlying all successful compost piles, it is that materials are layered in the piles thinly and uniformly. My mother built her signature great lasagna the same way—always in many thin layers of pasta, cheese, sauce, and meat, never overdoing any single ingredient, and never skipping a layer in the sequence.

Incorporating compost-making into your routine is the best way to keep your garden soil perpetually enriched and well conditioned, and it costs nothing. My rabbit manure alone might not effectively maintain the tilth in our gardens, so I add compost every year. The process isn't complicated, but it must be understood clearly before it can be achieved.

Autumn is the time when a lot of people turn their thoughts to composting, especially those with big leaf-shedding trees in their yards. But they don't realize that a giant pile of leaves remains a giant pile of leaves almost indefinitely. When a customer tells me his onions have turned out puny "even though I put on plenty of compost," I can guess what's happened. His onions, which prefer soil on the sweet side, have been fed old leaves, not compost. And leaf mold makes soil low in pH—sour—and severely hampers bulb formation in onions.

Some of the various formulas for making compost are unrealistic for the home gardener with limited time to devote to the job. Ironically, it is the formulas that promise to deliver compost in a few short months or even weeks that seem to require more time and drudgery; they usually involve turning the pile over a couple of times, or cramming the material into a small container, and they send you scrambling for adequate quantities of all the ingredients you need.

Some variation of my long-term composting formula may better fit into the typical home-gardening schedule, in that it allows you to make use of waste materials as they naturally occur and keeps the spadework to a minimum.

Let me explain what I mean by "long-term composting" and then suggest an exact procedure for you to consider in building your own heaps.

I suggest that you take your time and build your compost heap during the July to October months in your first year of gardening. That's when most of the raw materials for your compost area are readily available: waste and weeds from garden and yard throughout that period, lawn clippings all summer and leaves in the fall, and kitchen scraps, which families seem to generate in greater quantities in the warm months.

Properly constructed, your first heap will transform its contents into compost ready for spreading on your soil in the fall of your second year of gardening.

Begin your next compost heap immediately and it will be ready the following spring.

Two questions may occur to you at this point.

First, what is used for compost in the first year?

You probably won't be able to compost; instead, you should improve your soil for the vegetable garden according to one of the soil-building methods (see pages 72–77). Rushing to introduce unfinished compost or other partially decomposed material into your soil would make sowing and planting more difficult, and the material would compete with your plants for nitrogen. So you are much better off bringing in humus, composted manure, or peat moss from outside sources in the first year.

Second, what do you do with waste materials after you've finished your compost heap in the fall?

There won't be as much to dispose of by this time, as a rule. It can be used as the base layer for the second compost heap that you will begin to build in earnest next spring and summer. If you do have a ton of fresh leaves left over, keep them to one side and gradually incorporate them the following year.

HOW TO BUILD THE COMPOST PILE

There are three main ingredients to collect and add to the compost pile in the style of a layer cake, or Nana's lasagna:

- **Vegetative waste**, such as grass clippings, plant roots and stalks, weeds, kitchen scraps, and tree leaves.

- **Topsoil** or **humus**, small quantities of which contain the microorganisms that will act on the vegetative waste and break it down.

- **Animal manures,** or fertilizer, as nutrients for the microorganisms. Gardeners who don't have access to animal manures and don't particularly want to use commercial fertilizers could grow the herb comfrey in some out-of-the-way place, and harvest its large leaves for use as a catalyst in the compost process—and for making a cup of comfrey tea after the work is completed.

Three additional ingredients are also essential to the compost pile:

- **Air,** which will enter from the sides and tend to be present in a layer-cake structure.

- **Water,** which during dry periods may have to be added to the pile with a garden hose.

- **Lime,** to keep the pH level at a point that allows maximum decay action—an especially important additive when a lot of leaves are used as the vegetative ingredient.

To actually build the compost pile out of these various ingredients, here's what to do.

First, mark out an area no smaller than 4' x 4' on which to build the pile to a height of 6'. When this 4' x 4' x 6' area (about equal in volume to that of three quarters of a cord of firewood) is filled, it will yield about enough compost for you to top-dress a 750-square-foot garden to a depth of 1½'.

The pile can be freestanding or fenced in if raccoons, skunks, or other pests are likely to dig in it. Either way, install 4' x 4' posts at each corner, or some similar device to control the shape of the pile as it grows.

Break up the sod in the base area with a shovel or pickaxe, then add your first layer of vegetative waste no more than 6" deep. On top of that add a layer of soil—just dig out some of the topsoil in the area near where you've located the pile.

The vegetative layers should be about 3" to 6" in depth. If it's only 3" deep at some point in the building process, you might just sprinkle it with soil. If it's a full 6", you would add perhaps 2" of soil across the entire layer.

For every 12" of vegetative layer, add about 6" of animal manures. In other words, it takes one part animal waste to compost two or three parts vegetable waste. After top-dressing each vegetative layer with soil, add the layer of animal manure. The manure layers should range in depth from 2" to 4", depending on the depth of the vegetative layer they're covering. If you're raising a couple of rabbits, you'll have no shortage of manure for these critical layers.

Keep building the pile until it is 6' tall—or about the maximum height you can reach, anyway. Once the pile is finished, shape the top so that all four sides tilt slightly toward the middle. That will help the pile retain a lot of water after a rain or irrigation.

Kitchen scraps can go in the pile. Spread them thinly and cover with a few more spadefuls of soil to keep the odors down. Keep meat scraps and bones out of the pile, as they could attract pests or neighborhood dogs and cause more problems than they're worth. Other food wastes to keep out of your compost include dairy products and fatty substances of any kind.

Add a sprinkling of lime from time to time even if you don't include many leaves in your vegetative layers.

Once you've finished building your first pile, clear a site for the next one and begin to add to it as your waste material becomes available. If you have the space, and the ingredients are available for building two or even three piles in one summer, don't hesitate to do so, as you'll always be able to find a use for good compost.

Garden Plants That Keep On Giving

Asparagus, horseradish, Jerusalem artichoke, rhubarb, and sorrel are stalwart garden perennials that produce year after year, and, except for asparagus, they are easy to establish. Not every gardener will have the space or inclination to include all of these bonanza providers, but I encourage you to give them consideration.

- **Asparagus**. This is the classic spring harvest edible. Easily grown from roots, or crowns, it will produce tender asparagus spears every spring for 15 years or more. Because it is such a heavy feeder, a rich soil bed in full sun must be established for asparagus at the outset. Two 100-foot trenches, 18" wide and 12" deep, will serve the needs of a family of four. Fill the trenches with 6" of compost or well-rotted manure. In early spring, place asparagus crowns with roots spread evenly, star-burst style, on hills at 12" to 15" intervals. Cover and tamp down with 2" to 3" of soil. As spears emerge from the ground, gradually fill the trench with additional soil, then mound soil slightly around the spears to prevent standing water. Keep the beds free of weeds and irrigate as needed. Asparagus ferns will appear in summer; do not cut these tall ferns until they die back in the fall. Feed asparagus with compost or aged manure each fall or early spring. Begin to harvest asparagus sparingly in the second year, and harvest fully every mid- to late spring thereafter. Harvest by bending each spear until it snaps, or cut 1" below the soil surface.

- **Horseradish**—without which veteran New Yorkers will not eat their beef brisket, and some baseball fans will not eat their hot dogs—is started from root cuttings, available through seed catalogs and some nurseries. It grows best in well-drained, well-composted soil and in full sun. Lift established plants after a hard frost in the fall or in early spring. Wash and peel the roots, grate into a bowl, and mix in white vinegar and salt for a hot and sweet horseradish. Leave some roots in the ground for next year's crop.

- **Jerusalem artichoke.** This native American sunflower is grown for its potato-like tubers, comparable in taste and texture to water chestnuts, that can be eaten raw or cooked. Start the plants from tubers, available through seed catalogs or nurseries. Plants grow to 6' to 8' with bright yellow flowers and make an excellent windbreak.

- **Rhubarb.** The classic companion to strawberries in pie, rhubarb is also used in compotes and other desserts and in glazes for meat and game dishes. Plant crowns in early spring in rich, well-drained soil with full sun. Nurseries catering to vegetable gardeners carry rhubarb crowns and plants in the spring. Set the crowns 1" deep and 3" apart. (Two or three plants will be plenty for most families.)

Water in the crowns to eliminate air pockets. Do not harvest in the first year, to give plants more time to develop. Rhubarb is a heavy feeder and produces best when given annual spring doses of compost. Harvest the stems for culinary use; the leaves are inedible.

- **Sorrel.** Dear to the hearts of French *jardiniers*, sorrel is prized for the intense, lemony, slightly sour flavor of its leaves. It is used in soups, salads, and sauces and considered an excellent accompaniment for fish dishes. It is easily started in the spring from transplants, available in the perennials section at garden centers, and will tolerate light shade. If in full sun, it may bolt in the summer, but if seed stalks are cut back, another crop will come along for the fall. Place three or four sorrel plants 8" to 10" apart for a season-long supply.

Uses of a Cold Frame

A cold frame allows the Northern gardener in particular to stretch the effective growing season at both ends. It can be used in early spring as a holding station for seedlings, and in late fall to hatch small leafy crops once it is too late to sow them directly in the garden. In mild winters you can harvest from a cold frame right through until spring.

Physically, a cold frame is a half-sunken plot with retaining walls of brick or lumber or such, and a translucent top of glass or plastic. For most gardeners, it doesn't have to be bigger than 10 to 20 square feet in area. This area must be dug out to some degree to create the desired frost-protected zone below ground level. My Uncle Angelo's cold frame was deep enough to be a grave—because he wanted a cool place to grow his *broccoli di rapa* (broccoli rabe) all summer—but you really only have to dig down 12" to 18" to make a small one good for most purposes. Then surround the area with your retaining material and attach the top. A discarded storm window or sash makes an excellent top. I prefer glass to plastic, because it insulates better against the cold. If you do use plastic, double-layer it on a wood frame to create a 1" air pocket between the two layers.

You don't have to be an engineer to throw one of these things together. I've devised numerous detailed plans for cold frames to satisfy customer requests, but I doubt if any of them has ever followed my instructions to the letter, simply because each gardener has a special site to contend with, different scrap material available, and varying degrees of skill with a hammer and saw.

It's more important to pick the right place for the cold frame than it is to put it together in a certain way. It must be situated with a clear southern exposure, so that it receives maximum sunlight in spring and fall when the sun is lower in the sky. You may be able to locate it directly against the foundation of your house or garage and save the trouble of building a back wall for it. In any case, attach your cover at a 30° to 45° angle, if you can, and you'll catch more of the available light.

The cold-frame site must also have good drainage. If you must locate it in a generally wet area, dig it extra deep, and add more gravel on the bottom to raise it to the desired elevation.

The cold frame is of greatest value in hardening off or conditioning young seedlings started indoors, such as eggplant, pepper, tomatoes, squash, and cucumbers, and as a nursery itself, for starting lettuces and brassicas directly in the soil in the cold frame (which would have to be prepared from your good garden soil or compost). Thus it gives you the capability of growing all your own crops from seed instead of relying on garden centers. This saves you money if you're gardening on a large scale, and it also greatly broadens your choice of varieties of different crops. Even a first-rate garden center is limited in the variety of transplants it can offer the public.

Starting seed indoors—a technique to be described in detail in the next chapter—requires more expertise than most newcomers will have time to acquire at first, so, as already mentioned, the cold frame itself may not enter into your plans until the second or third year of gardening. Even then, if your garden is no bigger than our 750-square-footer, you may not need a cold frame, for it will still be reasonably cheap for you to buy the limited number of transplants you require.

If you were going to raise all your own transplants, the exact size of the cold frame would depend on the size of the garden it is to serve, approximately as follows:

GARDEN SIZE	SIZE OF COLD FRAME
400 square feet	3' x 4'
750 square feet	4' x 5'
1,500 square feet	4' x 10'
3,000 square feet	5' x 15'

On pages 236–237 are designs for a cold-frame planting for each of the main gardens. You'll note that the cold frames are actually generously sized. In addition to starting all the seedlings you'll require for each of the main gardens, you'll be able to sow a crop or two directly in the cold frame specified. You'll have room to start 10 to 15 percent more than the actual number of transplants you'll use— to be able to choose the strongest and healthiest-looking seedlings for use in the main garden—and also to experiment with an extra variety or two that you're not quite sure you want to plant in the main garden at all.

Once you become a confirmed year-in, year-out gardener, I'm willing to bet you'll want your own cold frame even if you have just a little patch to tend. It can become quite a versatile annex to the garden, and, in its own way, can also contribute in a large degree to maximum productivity.

Here's how to use the cold frame virtually year-round.

EARLY SPRING

The cold frame serves its primary function of conditioning seedlings to outdoor life at this time. Tender, warm-season vegetables started from seed indoors in February to March become acclimatized by gradually spending more and more time in the cold frame. At first put your seedlings out in their flats or peat pots only on sunny days, and bring them back inside at night if the temperature is expected to drop below 30° F. Always keep the top down on the cold frame to protect the plants from the wind, which can be almost as damaging as the frost. As the days get longer and warmer, you can start leaving the top open so the plants get the extra air circulation. Little or no watering is required during this period. If you must water, be sure it is only in the early morning hours.

Tender plants like tomatoes and peppers harden off in about 1 to 2 weeks. This factor must be taken into consideration in coordinating your seed-starting efforts indoors with your schedule for setting transplants in the garden outdoors. If I want to set my tomatoes in the garden on May 15th, for example, I have to have them ready to begin their conditioning process in the cold frame during the last week of April. However, there's margin for error because of the cold frame's unique ability to keep plants in a kind of physiological holding pattern for a time. So you can hold them until the right kind of weather comes along for setting them out.

You can start cool-weather plants like cabbage and lettuce directly in the cold-frame soil bed, or in a flat placed in the cold frame. They'll take a bit longer to germinate than if you started them indoors, but it will be easier to produce sturdy transplants in that environment.

LATE SPRING

Once you've transplanted all your tender vegetables into the main garden, remove the top and use the cold frame to plant a short crop of greens: lettuce, spinach, mustard, or—a favorite among many older Italian gardeners—broccoli rabe. These smaller leafy crops will get along fine in there and produce extra fresh salad fixings for the household.

SUMMER AND LATE SUMMER

Throughout the warm months, the cooler cold-frame soil bed makes an excellent spot for sowing more greens, for harvest directly from the cold frame, or for transplanting to vacancies in the main garden. In other words, it can be used in lieu of or to supplement the supply-garden area. Many gardeners use this space to sow and grow lettuce all summer long. They cover the cold frame with ½" to 1" wire mesh to protect it from excess sun and pests. They call it their "lettuce box."

EARLY FALL

By the time you're starting to harvest the last of your fruit-bearing crops in the main garden, you can sow another crop of short-season leafy crops in the cold frame. Put the top down on extra-cold days and during heavy rains. If you sow these last crops so they get most of their growing completed by the time winter descends for keeps, you'll be able to pick from the cold frame well into the new year.

LATE FALL AND WINTER

For those gardeners who don't get any particular kick out of harvesting fresh Bibb lettuce on Christmas Day, the cold frame can be entirely converted from a sowing area to a storage area. Rather than leaving winter crops like carrots, turnips, parsnips, leeks, and such in different spots in the main garden, you could dig them all up and lay them out in the cold frame under a blanket of sand and salt hay. That way you'll centralize your source of supplies over winter and eliminate the job of trying to extract crops from ground that may be frozen solid.

Starting from Seed

Vegetable seed is much easier to sow indoors than flower seed. Peppers, eggplant, and tomatoes are a bit tricky, but lettuce and cucumbers and the others are a cinch if you know what you're doing. Basically, you have to give them a lot of light, good air circulation, and as little water as possible. In this chapter, I'd like to share some of the techniques we use at our greenhouses for developing finished, healthy vegetable transplants and show how they may be successfully adapted for home use.

Starting vegetables indoors becomes practicable once you have a cold frame in the yard and a year or so of gardening experience under your belt. The bigger your garden and the more individualistic your choice of vegetable varieties, the quicker you'll want to master these techniques. The investment in time and money is relatively small, too. Even if you make mistakes in your first efforts, you'll learn quite a bit and you'll still have time to acquire good transplants from your usual source, so the garden's productivity won't suffer.

Let's look at the various general conditions required for successfully starting seed indoors. Then I'll explain techniques appropriate for each variety.

PLANTING SCHEDULE

One of the biggest mistakes indoor gardeners make is starting their seeds too early. Backtrack from your outdoor spring planting schedule to determine when to start seed indoors, so that each variety becomes ready for transplant about the time you want to set it in the garden. A timely transfer into the cold frame and garden assures the best possible growth pattern in young crops.

Check the starting-from-seed schedule shown in the table to see at a glance how germination rates and other factors will affect your timing. Many people make the mistake of starting peppers, eggplant, and tomatoes at the same time indoors, because they know they always set them out in the garden on the same day. But peppers take a week longer to germinate from seed than eggplant, and eggplant takes a week longer than tomatoes. If you don't stagger starting them

From Transplants First Sown Indoors (Spring Frost Date May 10)

	SOW INDOORS	SET OUT
Spanish and Bermuda onions	February 15	April 10
Leeks	February 15	April 15
Celery	February 15	May 10
Lettuce	March 1–15	April 15–May 1
Peppers	March 15	May 15
Broccoli	March 25	May 1
Cabbage	March 25	May 1
Eggplant	March 20–25	May 15
Tomato	March 30	May 15
Basil	April 15	June 1
Cucumber	May 1	May 20
Squash	May 7	May 20

from seed at one-week intervals, beginning at the appropriate time in winter, they won't be ready for transplant at the same time in the spring.

This should also remind you of the importance of ordering seed early. To have celery and peppers ready to transplant into the garden by before May 15th, for our area, you will have to have your packets of seed on hand sometime in February.

PLANTING LOCATION

Location is just as important indoors as it is outdoors. Adequate sunlight and proper temperature are the main requirements to grow seed successfully in the house. A picture window with a clear southern exposure is the perfect spot. Unfortunately, this is usually in the middle of your living room, and other family members may object if you set up a botany lab there.

The window you do select should receive a minimum of 8 hours of bright light a day. For every hour of bright light that it misses, you should arrange to contribute 2 hours of fluorescent light, or "grow light," to the cause. In other words, if your vegetable plant setup gets only 4 hours of direct sunlight, add 8 hours of fluorescent light and you will be meeting the minimum light requirements of the plants. Rotate young plants every few days to give them even exposure to this light. Don't place directly on hot-water radiators (if your house happens to be heated with these venerable fixtures), as seedlings will dry out from the bottom up, to their detriment.

Room temperature also must be considered in selecting your spot for sowing indoors. Vegetables need 65° to 70° F temperatures to germinate, but after germination anything over 70° F is likely to result in weak, spindly seedlings. Until recently, a lot of U.S. households tended to be too warm. One bright spot in the face of soaring energy prices and the threat of global climate change is that we're turning our thermostats down—into a range that's healthier for vegetable seedlings.

A third consideration in location is how much space you'll need for your various trays and pots. If you're starting just one batch of lettuce, there'll be no problem. However, if you are trying to sow seed for all the transplants you need for the 750-square-foot plan, say, you'll need about 4 to 6 square feet of table or counter space. If you're growing the 3,000-square-footer, you'll need about 16 to 20 square feet.

Note that the actual sowing of seed creates very few space problems. In a 5" x 7" market pack, you can grow up to 48 tomato seedlings. But you'll need 10 times the space when the time comes to transplant those seedlings—as is necessary for tomatoes—into 3-inch-square peat pots.

The 5" x 7" seed starter pack was once the standard for starting seed for the home gardener and, though less common today, it is still available from suppliers. Burpee and The Cook's Garden, for example, offer a market pack, called a "fiber pack," made from recycled cardboard that fills the bill perfectly.

PLANTING MEDIUM

It's advisable to start seed in a soil mix or planting medium that is completely free of bacteria, fungus, weed seed, or soil insects. Young sprouts don't have the resources to cope with disease or to compete with vigorous weeds.

We sterilize our garden-center soil with a steam boiler that pumps steam into the soil, which we cover with polyethylene to keep the steam in for a period. You can achieve the same result by baking small quantities of your own soil in the kitchen oven at 200° F for 1 hour, but this process tends to make the atmosphere in the house a bit ripe for a day or two. If you don't want to mix your own, there are various sterile seed-starting media available commercially, such as Jiffy Mix, Burpee Planting Formula, Cornell Mix, and many others.

Probably the simplest method is to mix some commercially available sterile soil with one third peat moss and one third perlite. This will give you a lightweight, easy-to-handle, and moisture-retentive planting medium. Both vermiculite, which is expanded mica, and perlite, which is crushed volcanic rock, are already free of organic matter. I prefer perlite to vermiculite because it doesn't retain the moisture quite so long, so I think it helps avoid more of the fungus problems that are likely to strike in an indoor sowing project. This one-third soil, one-third peat, one-third perlite mix is fine for starting all seeds except onions and leeks, for which I recommend a mixture of one quarter soil, one quarter peat, one quarter perlite, and one quarter sand—to accommodate the allium family's love of sandy soils.

PLANTING CONTAINERS

Individual pots or tray-type flats made of peat, plastic, clay, or wood are all suitable for starting seed. Clay pots used previously should be sterilized in the dishwasher or oven. Other containers should be cleaned out (washed in hot, sudsy water) to make sure there are no harmful organisms present.

Don't plant more than one type of seed per container, to avoid confusion and the problem of varying germination rates.

Cucumbers and squash are the only vegetables that should be started from seed in their own private containers—4 to 5 seeds per 3" biodegradable container—because their delicate root systems, typical of the cucurbits, don't like transplanting or subterranean disturbances of any kind.

Except for these two crops, I recommend row-sowing in trays for all the other seeds you would start indoors, for several reasons. Careful row-sowing provides all the seedlings with ample light and air circulation. It makes it easier to water the medium without getting the seedlings wet. It would be impossible to keep all the young seedlings dry if you had broadcast-sown the tray, as some old-time gardeners do. Also you get a much broader choice of seedlings than you would in spot-sowing, and so can promote the growth of the healthiest transplants for your garden.

You can later transplant them to individual pots if necessary. This permits growing seedlings in volume without taking up undue space. It also allows selection of the sturdiest and healthiest seedlings for grooming for garden use.

Some gardeners like to spot-sow their tomato, eggplant, and pepper seeds directly into little peat pots and let them grow in these containers until they're ready to set out. I prefer to sow them in rows in a small seedling tray and then transfer them into the individual pots when the plants are 2" to 3" tall. I've found that this intermediate transplanting procedure helps to strengthen the seedlings and gets them off to a much better start once they are set in the garden. Spot-sowing in peat pellets—silver-dollar-sized pellets that expand when moistened—is convenient for germinating seed, but there are usually no nutrients contained in the material, so seedlings must be fertilized in 3 to 4 weeks. Sowing 3 to 5 cucumber or squash seeds in these tiny peat pellets isn't a good idea, because the seedlings come up too close together and lack sufficient air circulation and room to grow.

Most advanced gardeners will want to create their own planting medium for indoor sowing, and do their own sowing—and for the little extra effort involved, they'll be better off.

Fill trays or pots with your planting medium to within ½" of the top edge of the container. The night before sowing, soak the medium with water and allow it to stand and drain. Now you're ready for sowing.

SOWING

It takes longer to open the package and mark the tray for identification purposes than it does to actually sow the seed indoors. Still, it must be done carefully. People tend to sow seed too deeply indoors, just as they do outdoors. To create furrows in trays of soil, lay an ordinary lead pencil on the planting medium and press it down. Then remove the pencil and sow the seed in the straight and shallow furrow left behind. In tray sowing, space rows 1" to 2" apart. Within each row, the individual seeds should not be sown so close together that they touch their neighbors, nor so far apart that you don't get a full stand of seedlings. It's better to allow more space than to crowd the seeds, because when they're crowded it's almost impossible to thin them without disturbing the whole batch, and with more space it's so much easier to water the rows without getting the leaves wet.

You can make sowing the smaller seeds in trays much easier by using a seed vibrator or contriving a homemade version of this device out of stiff paper, as mentioned on page 87.

Once you've sown the seed, cover the furrows with a sprinkling of fine sand or the same mix in which the seed has been planted. Don't use peat moss, as it may be too light to cover the seed properly.

WATERING BEFORE GERMINATION

Use a quality hand-mister that produces a fine spray to keep your medium moist. Watering with a spouted watering produces a shower that can easily displace a lightweight planting medium and the seeds themselves.

Keep the planting medium moist during the germination period, without, however, making it soggy. A good way to ensure effective moisture early on is to cover the container with clear plastic, in effect creating a miniature hothouse. As soon as the first sprouts appear, remove the plastic.

WATERING AFTER GERMINATION

The single biggest hazard to indoor sowing is fungus, and excess moisture at any time is an open invitation to this problem. When in doubt, do not water.

Once sprouting does take place, let the soil mix go almost dry before watering. Exposed to 8 hours of sunlight in a 70° F room, the tray should reach this condition in about 2 days.

In watering the sprouted plants, you should no longer use the mister, as this would get the young seedlings wet. Instead, place the tray in a container with some water in it, so that the planting medium can soak up the water it needs from the bottom. Then remove the tray from the water and allow it to drain and dry off. Don't leave a tray sitting in water, or the root system on the seedlings will not develop properly.

Another way to water young seedlings in the tray is from the top, using a watering can with a tiny spout so that you can water between the rows without getting the seedlings wet. You can also set your kitchen faucet to release water in a slow, narrow stream and move the tray under the faucet to accomplish the same results.

Check the seedlings every morning, and when they are thirsty, water them at that time and not in the evening. Just keep in mind that the seedlings can tolerate drying out a lot more easily than they can overwatering.

FEEDING SEEDLINGS

You need to fertilize seedlings started indoors only if you keep the plants in the same container more than 3 to 4 weeks. If you have timed your indoor operation correctly, you won't have to worry about feeding most of the seedlings. However, if the seedlings begin to yellow under normal conditions—when you're supplying them with adequate sunlight and the right amount of moisture—it's a sign that they're not getting enough nutrients from their soil bed. You should feed them with a liquid fertilizer such as fish emulsion.

COOLING OFF

This is the stage that introduces your seedlings to the real world. Generally speaking, when the seedlings are 1" to 1½" tall, you should move them to a cool, well-lit area, otherwise they'll stretch up too quickly and become weak and scraggly. If you don't have a porch or cool, well-lit room, set them outside on mild spring days so they can enjoy these conditions, but remember to bring them back in before the cooler evening hours. Never put them outside on cold, windy days. This conditioning process helps the young seedlings to develop into stronger, more compact plants with sturdy root systems, and helps ensure successful transplanting.

On the following pages are the key steps to take in sowing vegetable seed indoors for each of the dozen or so crops that can be profitably started in this way.

Spanish Onions, Bermuda Onions, and Leeks

- Sow indoors 8 weeks before the date of transplanting into the garden (sow February 15th; ready for the garden April 10th to 15th).

- For 75 to 100 plants, use a 5" x 7" market pack.

- Sow ¼" deep in 3 rows, 25 to 35 seeds per row. After sowing, cover furrows with sand.

- Use a mister to keep moist until germination, 5 to 7 days later. After germination, keep on the dry side, and water as needed only in the early morning.

- Fertilize with fish emulsion 4 weeks after sowing.

- Begin conditioning in the cold frame 3 weeks prior to the date of transplanting into the garden.

- *Special Conditions*: Remember to mix some fine sand in with the soil mix for starting these alliums.

Celery

- Sow indoors 10 weeks before the date of transplanting into the garden (sow February 15th; ready for the garden May 10th).

- For 30 to 36 plants use a 5" x 7" market pack.

- Sow ⅛" deep in 3 rows, 10 to 12 seeds per row.

- After sowing, cover furrows with fine sand.

- Use a mister to keep moist until germination, 15 to 20 days later.

- After germination, keep on the dry side, and water as needed only in the early morning.

- Transplant to small peat pots or cell packs 6 weeks after the date of sowing, or when seedlings are 1" high. Set plants 1" apart in rows that are 1" to 2" apart.

- Fertilize with fish emulsion 2 weeks after transplanting.

- Begin conditioning in the cold frame 1 week prior to the date of transplanting into the garden.

- *Special Conditions*: Celery is the slowest of all the vegetable seeds to germinate and develop, so be patient.

Lettuce

- Sow indoors 4 to 5 weeks before the date of transplanting into the garden (sow March 1st to 15th; ready for the garden April 15th to May 1st).

- For 30 to 36 plants, use a 5" x 7" market pack.

- Sow ⅛" deep in 3 rows, 10 to 12 seeds per row.

- After sowing, cover furrows with fine sand.

- Use a mister to keep moist until germination, 3 to 5 days later.

- After germination, keep on the dry side, and water as needed only in the early morning.

- Begin conditioning in the cold frame 1 to 2 weeks before the date of transplanting into the garden.

- *Special Conditions*: Lettuce seedlings are like the brassicas in their tendency to stretch and grow faster than is good for them. To prevent this, give them maximum sunlight and cool temperatures. The more sun they get, the less they'll have to stretch for it.

Peppers

- Sow indoors 8 weeks before the date of transplanting into the garden (sow March 15th; ready for the garden May 15th).

- For 30 to 36 plants use a 5" x 7" market pack.

- Sow ¼" deep in 3 rows, 10 to 12 seeds per row.

- After sowing, cover furrows with fine sand.

- Use a mister to keep moist until germination, 16 to 21 days later.

- After germination, keep on the dry side, and water as needed only in the early morning.

- Four weeks after sowing, when the seedlings are about 1" tall, begin conditioning the fiber-pack seedlings for transplanting into individual pots by exposing them to cooler temperatures (between 50° and 60° F) for periods up to 8 hours long. This will encourage them to set stronger roots.

- Five weeks after sowing, when the seedlings are about 2" tall, transplant to individual peat pots, water them well, and thereafter keep them on the dry side to continue to foster strong root development.

- A week after transplanting, fertilize with fish emulsion or any liquid organic fertilizer.

- Begin conditioning in the cold frame 2 to 3 weeks before the date of transplanting into the garden.

- *Special Conditions*: Once sprouted, peppers need lots of sunlight and good air circulation to develop properly.

Eggplant

- Sow indoors 7 weeks before the date of transplanting into the garden (sow March 20th to 25th; ready for the garden May 15th).

- For 30 to 36 plants, use a 5" x 7" market pack.

- Sow ¼" deep in 3 rows, 10 to 12 seeds per row.

- After sowing, cover furrows with fine sand.

- Use a mister to keep moist until germination, 12 to 14 days later.

- After germination, keep on the dry side, and water as needed only in the early morning.

- Three weeks after sowing, when the seedlings are 1" tall, begin conditioning the fiber-pack eggplant for transplanting into individual pots by exposing them to cooler temperatures (between 50° and 60° F) for periods up to 8 hours long. This will encourage stronger root development.

- Four weeks after sowing, when the seedlings are about 2" high, transplant to individual peat pots. Water well, then keep on the dry side to promote the root growth.

- A week after transplanting, fertilize with fish emulsion or comparable liquid organic fertilizer.

- Begin conditioning in the cold frame 2 to 3 weeks before date of transplant into the garden.

- *Special Conditions*: Like peppers, eggplant must have proper light and air circulation to grow into healthy transplants.

Brassicas: Cabbage, Cauliflower, Broccoli, Brussels Sprouts

- Sow indoors 4 to 5 weeks before the date of transplanting into the garden (sow March 25th; ready for the garden May 1st).

- For 30 to 36 plants, use a 5" x 7" market pack.

- Sow ⅛" deep in 3 rows, 10 to 12 seeds per row.

- After sowing, cover furrows with fine sand.

- Use a mister to keep moist until germination, 2 to 3 days later.

- After germination, keep on the dry side, in plenty of sunlight, in temperatures under 60° F.

- Begin conditioning in the cold frame 2 weeks before the date of transplanting into the garden.

- *Special Conditions*: Remember to keep brassicas properly short and compact, and give them lots of light and cool temperatures immediately upon sprouting. Otherwise they will stretch up too quickly and become weak and scraggly.

Tomatoes

- Sow indoors 6 weeks before the date of transplanting into the garden (sow March 30th; ready for the garden May 15th).

- For 30 to 36 plants, use a 5" x 7" market pack.

- Sow ¼" deep in 3 rows, 10 to 12 seeds per row.

- After sowing, cover furrows with fine sand.

- Use a mister to keep moist until germination, 5 to 7 days later.

- After germination, keep on the dry side, and water as needed only in the early morning.

- Two weeks after sowing, when seedlings are 1" tall, begin conditioning young tomatoes for transplanting into individual containers by exposing them to 50° to 60° F temperatures for periods up to 8 hours long.

- Three weeks after sowing, when seedlings are 2" high, transplant into peat pots. Water each seedling well, then keep them on the dry side to promote vigorous root development.

- A week after transplanting, feed the tomatoes with a liquid fertilizer such as fish emulsion.

- Begin conditioning in the cold frame 2 to 3 weeks before date of transplant into the garden.

- *Special Conditions*: Like peppers and eggplant, tomatoes must have proper light and air circulation to grow into compact and healthy plants.

Cucumbers

- Sow indoors 3 weeks before the date of transplanting into the garden (sow May 1st; ready for the garden May 20th).

- Sow seed in 3" x 3" peat pots, 5 seeds per pot—1 seed in each corner and 1 seed in the center. Sow seed at ½" depth. Cover sown seed with planting mix.

- After sowing, keep moist until germination, 6 to 7 days later.

- After germination, keep on the dry side and expose to plenty of sunlight.

- Begin conditioning in the cold frame 2 weeks before the date of transplanting into the garden, when weather begins to warm. Bring them in any time temperatures fall below 45° F.

- *Special Conditions*: Cucumber seedlings are highly susceptible to damping-off fungus and must not be overwatered. Cukes are tender vegetables that can't tolerate cool conditions as seedlings—the way the brassicas and lettuce can—so take extra care to keep them on the warmer side. Keep out of cold wind, which will bleach leaves and impede growth—if not kill the seedlings outright.

Squash

- Sow indoors 2 weeks before the date of transplanting into the garden (sow May 7th; ready for the garden May 20th).

- Sow seed in 3" x 3" peat pots, 5 seeds per pot—one in each corner and one in the center. Sow at ½" depth. Cover sown seed with some planting mix.

- After sowing, keep moist until germination, 3 to 5 days later.

- After germination, keep on the dry side and expose to plenty of sunlight.

- Begin conditioning in the cold frame 2 weeks before the date of transplanting into the garden, when weather begins to warm.

- Bring them in any time temperatures fall below 45° F.

- *Special Conditions*: Like cucumbers, squash seedlings are susceptible to damping-off fungus when overwatered. Also, like cukes, baby squash can't stand very cool conditions. Keep them on the warm side and protect them from cold wind.

"Did I Plant That?"

No gardening venture comes without its disappointments and mistakes. Experienced gardeners know that better than anyone. That's why they have learned to put their feelings into protective custody during the growing season.

If an early bean crop rots even before sprouting because of monsoon-like rains in the spring, experienced gardeners don't sit down and contemplate all the effort of planning and planting that has gone to waste. They quickly sow another crop and forget the first one ever existed. Gardeners are optimists. They practice the power of positive thinking with every seed they sow, every weed they pull, and every tomato they harvest.

And when things come out well, experienced gardeners tend to act as though they had nothing to do with it. My mother would see some Egyptian onions come up, or some broccoli rabe, and she'd declare,

"Where'd that come from?"

"You planted it," I'd remind her.

"No! I never did!"

"But I saw you plant it," I'd say, though I know it was no use arguing.

It's important to watch over your garden—as I hope I've made clear by now. But perhaps newcomers should also be aware of this trick of occasionally turning your back on the garden, in a mental or emotional sense, at times.

Why develop *agita*—Italian ulcers—because of an unexpected frost? Or why spend three weeks standing guard over your carrots, trying to worry them into life? Instead, why not follow all your good gardening practices, then relax and let nature take its course? In a broader sense, that is what you have to do anyway—let nature take its course.

In fact, that's what is more nearly at the heart of the Gilbertie family's gardening outlook than any simple "sow-it-and-forget-it" philosophy. We are not surprised when broccoli rabe springs from nowhere in the garden, so much as thankful that the miracle of plant growth occurs at all. That is what our garden is every year—a miracle in our own backyard. That is what everybody's garden can be.

APPENDIX

Crop and Dollar Yield, 3,000-Square-Foot Garden

This is an estimate of the seed requirements, potential harvest, and dollar value of the 3,000-square-foot garden illustrated on page 225. Seed costs are based on the Johnny's Selected Seeds 2009 catalog. Crop yields given are conservative. Dollar yield is based on the average retail value of crops in season in the New York–Connecticut area.

CROP	ROW FOOTAGE	SPACING	SEEDS NEEDED	SEED COST	CROP YIELD	DOLLAR YIELD
			FALL/APRIL			
Garlic	88	4 per ft.	25 heads	39.00	20 lb.	130.00
Shallots	50	4 per ft.	2 qt.	31.00	20 lb.	159.00
			APRIL			
Peas	75	6"	¾ lb.	7.60	12 lb.	70.00
Onion Sets	100	2"	6 lb.	14.00	40 lb.	60.00
Spanish or Bermuda Onions	100	4"	1/2 oz.	8.75	300 onions	180.00
Radishes	22	broadcast	1 oz.	4.30	35 bunches	80.00
Swiss Chard	75	8"	1 oz.	2.75	45 lb.	70.00
Celtuce	25	15"	1 pk.	2.75	20 heads	60.00
Lettuce	50	12"	1 pk.	2.75	24 heads	72.00
		15"	1 pk.	2.75	20 loose-leaf	60.00
Endive	25	15"	1 pk.	2.75	20	50.00
Chicory	50	6"	1 pk.	2.75	30 lb.	60.00
Leeks	50	4"	½ oz.	4.50	150 leeks	70.00
Beets	75	3"	1 oz.	3.75	300 beets	200.00

CROP	ROW FOOTAGE	SPACING	SEEDS NEEDED	SEED COST	CROP YIELD	DOLLAR YIELD
			MAY			
Beans	100	6"	1 lb.	5.90	60 lb.	180.00
Spinach	75	2"	1 oz.	2.95	24 lb.	70.00
Turnips	75	4"	2 pks.	7.90	200 turnips	82.00
Salsify	75	4"	1 oz.	7.75	75 lb.	150.00
Broccoli	50	24"	1 pk.	2.75	24 broccoli	75.00
Cabbage (Babyhead)	50	18"	1 pk.	2.75	32 heads	40.00
		12"	1 pk.	2.75	32 heads	40.00
Cauliflower	25	24"	1 pk.	2.75	12 heads	36.00
Parsley	25	1"	1 pk.	2.95	30 bunches	75.00
Carrots	100	2"	½ oz.	3.95	80 lb.	120.00
Parsnips	50	4"	2 pks.	5.90	50 lb.	110.00
Celery	50	6"	1 pk.	2.75	100 celery	140.00
New Zealand Spinach	25	4"	1 pk.	2.75	16 lb.	48.00
Lettuce	75	12"	1 pk.	2.75	75 heads	225.00
	50	15"			40 loose-leaf	120.00
Eggplant	75	30"	1 pk.	3.95	540 lb.	800.00
Peppers	100	24"	2 pks.	5.50	240 lb.	450.00
Tomatoes	125	36"	4 pks.	13.00	20 bushels	1,000.00
Cucumbers	25	24" along fence	2 pks.	7.90	50 lb.	75.00
Squash	75	60"	2 pks.	7.90	120 lb.	180.00
			JUNE			
Basil	44	12"	1 pk.	2.75	50 bunches	75.00
Beans	75	6"	½ lb.	11.20	48 lb.	140.00
Spinach	50	2"	1 oz.	2.75	16 lb.	48.00
Lettuce	125	12"	1 pk.	2.75	125 heads Bibb	185.00

CROP AND DOLLAR YIELD, 3,000-SQUARE-FOOT GARDEN, *continued*

CROP	ROW FOOTAGE	SPACING	SEEDS NEEDED	SEED COST	CROP YIELD	DOLLAR YIELD
JULY						
Beans	50	6"			32 lb.	95.00
Spinach	75	2"			24 lb.	70.00
Beets	50	3"	1 oz.	3.75	200 beets	140.00
Swiss Chard	75	2"	1 oz.	2.95	45 lb.	70.00
Turnips	75	4"	2 pks.	7.90	200 turnips	80.00
Brussels Sprouts	25	18"	1 pk.	2.95	48 pints	145.00
Cabbage	25	15"			20 heads	30.00
Cauliflower	25	24"			12 heads	36.00
AUGUST						
Beans	75	6"	½ lb.	5.90	48 lb.	145.00
Spinach	50	2"	1 oz.	2.75	16 lb.	45.00
Broccoli	50	24"	1 pk.	2.95	24 broccoli	75.00
Kale	75	15"	1 pk.	3.95	60 kale	150.00
Fennel	50	6"	2 pk.	5.90	100 heads	100.00
Endive	25	15"			20	50.00
Escarole	25	15"	1 pk.	2.95	20	50.00
Chicory	100	6"	½ oz.	2.95	60 lbs.	150.00
Lettuce	50	12"	1 pk.	2.75	50 heads	150.00
SEPTEMBER						
Radishes	22	broadcast	1 oz.	4.30	35 bunches	80.00
Total				**$295.60**		**$7,486.00**

Seed and Plant Companies

This is a representative list (in alphabetical order according to state) of firms in the United States and Canada that do business via mail order and furnish vegetable, herb, and flower seed catalogs to home gardeners on request. Most seed and plant producers now list their products on line; in fact, some companies have discontinued print catalogs altogether. Google the company by name and in most cases you will find access to the company's website if in fact it has one. Also listed are selected growers of roses and other perennials and fruit-bearing bushes and trees. Make sure that at least some of the seeds and plants you order originate with seed dealers and growers in your region of the country, so that you have a choice of varieties that have been developed to thrive in the climate conditions of that region.

Native Seeds/SEARCH
526 N. 4th Ave.
Tucson, AZ 85705

**Terroir Seeds/
Underwood Gardens**
P.O. Box 4995
Chino Valley, AZ 86323

Bountiful Gardens
18001 Shafer Ranch Rd.
Willits, CA 95490

J. L. Hudson, Seedsman
P.O. Box 337
La Honda, CA 94020-0337

**Laurel's Heirloom
Tomato Plants**
1725 257th St.
Lomita, CA 90717

Mountain Valley Growers
38325 Pepperweed Rd.
Squaw Valley, CA 93675

Natural Gardening Co.
P.O. Box 750776
Petaluma, CA 94975-0776

**Peaceful Valley Farm
& Garden Supply**
P.O. Box 2209
Grass Valley, CA 95945

Redwood City Seed Co.
P.O. Box 361
Redwood City, CA 94064

Renee's Garden
6116 Highway 9
Felton, CA 95018

Roger's Gardens
2301 San Joaquin Hills Rd.
Corona del Mar, CA 92625

Rose Story Farm
Carpenteria, CA 93013

The Kitazawa Seed Co.
P.O. Box 13220
Oakland, CA 94661-3220

Chas. C. Hart Seed Co.
P.O. Box 9169
Wethersfield, CT 06109

Comstock, Ferre & Co.
263 Main St.
Wethersfield, CT 06109

John Scheepers
Kitchen Garden Seeds
23 Tulip Dr.
Bantam, CT 06750-0638

New England Seed Co.
3580 Main St.
Bldg. #10
Hartford, CT 06120

Shepherds Garden Seeds
30 Irene St.
Torrington, CT 06790

White Flower Farm
P.O. Box 56
Litchfield, CT 06759

Golden Harvest Organics
404 N. Impala Dr.
Fort Collins, CO 80521

**Eden Organic Nursery
Services**
P.O. Box 4604
Hallandale, FL 33008

Kilgore Seed Co.
1400 W. First St.
Sanford, FL 32711

Tomato Growers Supply Co.
P.O. Box 60015
Ft. Myers, FL 33906

The Gourmet Gardener
12287 117th Dr.
Live Oak, FL 33008

Burgess Seed & Plant Co.
905 Four Seasons Rd.
Bloomington, IL 61701

Vaughn Seed Co.
5300 Katrine Ave.
Downers Grove, IL 60515

Gurney's Seed &
Nursery Co.
P.O. Box 4178
Greendale, IN 47025-4178

Henry Field's Seed
& Nursery Co.
P.O. Box 397
Aurora, IN 47001-0397

Earl May Seed & Nursery
208 N. Elm St.
Shenandoah, IA 51603

Seed Savers Exchange
3094 N. Winn Rd.
Decorah, IA 52101

Skyfire Garden Seeds
1313 23rd Rd.
Kanopolis, KS 67454-9225

Ferry-Morse Seed Co.
601 Stephen Beale Dr.
Fulton, KY 42041

Fedco Seeds
P.O. Box 520
Waterville, ME 04903

Johnny's Selected Seeds
955 Benton Ave.
Winslow, ME 04901-2601

Farmer Seed & Nursery
818 NW 4th St.
Faribault, MN 55021

Seeds of Change
P.O. Box 152
Spicer, MN 56288

Baker Creek
Heirloom Seeds
2278 Baker Creek Rd.
Mansfield, MO 65704

Stark Bro's Nurseries
& Orchards
11523 Highway NN
Louisiana, MO 63353

Thompson & Morgan
Seedsmen
220 Faraday Ave.
Jackson, NJ 08527-5073

Burnett Brothers
107 Ruland Rd.
Melville, NY 11747

Harris Seeds
355 Paul Rd.
Rochester, NY 14624

Miller Nurseries
5060 W. Lake Rd.
Canandaigua, NY
14424-8904

Stokes Seeds
P.O. Box 548
Buffalo, NY 14240-0548

Appalachia Seeds
99 Treehouse La.
Burnsville, NC 28714

Abundant Life Seeds
P.O. Box 279
Cottage Grove,
OR 97424-0010

Nichols Garden Nursery
1190 Old Salem Rd. NE
Albany, OR 97321-4580

Territorial Seed Co.
P.O. Box 158
Cottage Grove,
OR 97424-0061

Victory Seed Co.
P.O. Box 192
Molalla, OR 97038

Amishland Heirloom Seeds
P.O. Box 365
Reamstown, PA
17567-0365

Container Seeds
64 Greenwood St.
Wellsboro, PA 16901

D. Landreth Seed Co.
60 E. High St., Bldg. #4
New Freedom, PA 17349

Heirloom Seeds
287 E. Finley Dr.
W. Finley, PA 15377

Seedway
1225 Zeager Rd.
Elizabethtown, PA 17022

The Cook's Garden
P.O. Box C5030
Warminster, PA 18974

Burpee & Co.
300 Park Ave.
Warminster, PA 18974

Park Seed Co.
1 Parkton Ave.
Greenwood, SC 29647

Seeds for the South
Vegetable Seed Warehouse
410 Whaley Pond Rd.
Granitesville, SC 29829

Jackson & Perkins
2 Floral Ave.
Hodges, SC 29653

Wayside Gardens
1 Garden La.
Hodges, SC 29695-0001

Gurney's Seed & Nursery
144 Page St.
Yankton, SD 57078

Antique Rose Emporium
9300 Lueckemeyer Rd.
Brenham, TX 77833

Heirloom Tomatoes of Texas
215 W. Bandera Rd.,
Ste. 114 PMB #455
Boerne, TX 78006

Willhite Seed
P.O. Box 23
Poolville, TX 76487-0023

Southern Exposure
Seed Exchange
P.O. Box 460
Mineral, VA 23117

Wetsel Seed Co.
P.O. Box 791
Harrisonburg, VA 22803

High Mowing Organic Seeds
76 Quarry Rd.
Wolcott, VT 05680

J. W. Jung Seed Co.
335 S. High St.
Randolph, WI 53957-0001

L. L. Olds Seed Co.
2901 Packers Ave.
Madison, WI 53704

R.H. Shumway's
334 W. Stroud St., Ste. 1
Randolph, WI 53956-1274

Totally Tomatoes
334 W. Stroud St.
Randolph, WI 53956

Vermont Bean Seed Co.
334 W. Stroud St.
Randolph, WI 53956

Richters Herbs
357 Hwy. 47
Goodwood
Ontario LOC 1A0
Canada

Vesey's Seeds, Ltd.
P.O. Box 9000
Charlottetown
Prince Edward
Island C1A 8K6
Canada

U.S. Cooperative Extension Service

The Cooperative Extension Service is a nationwide, noncredit educational network. Each U.S. state and territory has a state office at its land-grant university and a network of local or regional offices. These offices are staffed by one or more experts who provide useful, practical, and research-based information for farmers and gardeners, small business owners, youth groups, consumers, and others in rural areas and communities of all sizes. Call or write to the main office in your state (addresses and telephone numbers follow) for information and guidelines on home vegetable gardening in your area and for the location of the county agent nearest to you. County agents are also listed under "Cooperative Extension Service" in the phone book.

Alabama
Auburn University
109-D Duncan Hall
Auburn, AL 36849
(334) 844-4444

Alaska
University of Alaska
308 Tanana Loop,
Room 101
P.O. Box 756180
Fairbanks, AL 99775-6180
(907) 474-5211

Arizona
University of Arizona
Forbes 301
P.O. Box 210036
Tucson, AZ 85721-0036
(520) 621-7205

Arkansas
University of Arkansas
2301 S. University Ave.
Little Rock, AR 72204
(501) 671-2000

California
University of
California-Davis
1 Shields Ave.
Davis, CA 95616
(530) 752-1011

Colorado
Colorado State University
Campus Delivery 4040
Fort Collins, CO
80523-4040
(970) 491-6281

Connecticut
University of Connecticut
W. B. Young Building,
Room 231
1738 Storrs Rd., Unit 4134
Storrs, CT 06269-4134

(860) 486-9228 **Delaware**
University of Delaware
Newark, DE 19716
(302) 831-2792

District Of Columbia
University of the
District of Columbia
4200 Connecticut
Ave. NW
Washington, D.C. 20008
(202) 274-5000

Florida
Institute of Food and
Agricultural Sciences
University of Florida
P.O. Box 110180
Gainesville, FL
32611-0180
(352) 392-1971

Georgia
College of Agricultural &
Environmental Sciences
University of Georgia
111 Conner Hall
Athens, GA 30602
(706) 542-3824

Hawaii
University of Hawaii
3050 Maile Way,
Gilmore 203
Honolulu, HI 96822
(808) 956-8139

Idaho
University of Idaho
at Twin Falls
P.O. Box 1827
Twin Falls, ID 83303-1827
(208) 736-3603

Illinois
University of Illinois at
Urbana-Champaign
214 Mumford Hall
1301 W. Gregory Dr.
Urbana, IL 61801
(217) 333-5900

Indiana
Purdue University
Agricultural
Administration Building
615 W. State St.
West Lafayette, IN
47907-2053
(765) 494-8491

Iowa
Iowa State University
2150 Beardshear Hall
Ames, IA 50011-2046
(515) 294-4603

Kansas
Kansas State
Research & Extension
115 Waters Hall
Manhattan, KS 66502
(785) 532-6147

Kentucky
College of Agriculture
University of Kentucky
5-107 Ag Science Bldg.
Lexington, KY
40546-0091
(859) 257-4302

Louisiana
LSU Ag Center
101 Efferson Hall
P.O. Box 25203
Baton Rouge, LA 70803
(225) 578-4161

Maine
University of Maine
5741 Libby Hall
Orono, ME 04489-5741
(207) 581-3188

Maryland
College of Agriculture
& Natural Resources
University of Maryland
1116 Symons Hall
College Park, MD 20742
(301) 405-1316

Massachusetts
University of
Massachusetts
101 University Dr., Suite 1
Amherst, MA 01002-2376
(413) 545-4500

Michigan
Michigan State University
Agriculture Hall,
Room 108
East Lansing, MI
48824-1039
(517) 355-2308

Minnesota
University of Minnesota
240 Coffey Hall
1420 Eckles Ave.
St. Paul, MN 55108-6068
(612) 624-1222

Mississippi
Mississippi State
University
Mississippi State,
MS 39762
(662) 325-2323

Missouri
College of Agriculture,
Food and Natural
Resources
University of Missouri
2-64 Agriculture Bldg.
Columbia, MO 65211
(573) 882-8301

Montana
Montana State University
P.O. Box 172230
Bozeman, MT 69717-2230
(406) 994-1750

Nebraska
University of Nebraska
Lincoln Extension
211 Agriculture Hall
Lincoln, NE 68583-0703
(402) 472-2966

Nevada
University of Nevada
Mail Stop 404
Reno, NV 89557-0404
(775) 784-7070

New Hampshire
Family Home & Garden
Education Center
University of New
Hampshire
200 Bedford St.
Manchester, NH 03101
(877) 398-4769

New Jersey
Rutgers Cooperative
Extension
310 Milltown Rd.
Bridgewater, NJ 08807
(201) 915-1399

New Mexico
NMSU Extension/
Outreach
Gerald Thomas
Hall, Room 220
Box 30003 3AE
Las Cruces, NM 88003
(575) 646-3015

New York
Cornell Extension
College of Agriculture
& Life Sciences
Cornell University
Ithaca, NY 14853
(607) 254-4795

North Carolina
North Carolina
State University
Raleigh, NC 27695
(919) 515-2011

North Dakota
North Dakota State
University
315 Morrill Hall
Fargo, ND 58108-6050
(701) 231-8944

Ohio
OSU Extension
Ohio State University
2120 Fyffe Rd.
Room 3 Ag Admin
Columbus, OH 43210
(614) 292-6181

Oklahoma
Division of Agricultural
Sciences & Natural
Resources
Oklahoma State University
136 Ag Hall
Stillwater, OK 74078
(405) 744-5398

Oregon
101 Ballard Extension Hall
Oregon State University
Corvallis, OR 97331-3606
(541) 737-2713

Pennsylvania
323 Ag Admin Bldg.
College of Agricultural
Sciences
Penn State University
University Park, PA 16802
(814) 865-4028

Rhode Island
College of the
Environment
& Life Sciences
University of Rhode Island
Kingston, RI 02881
(401) 874-2900

South Carolina
Clemson University
Clemson, SC 29634
(864) 656-3311

South Dakota
South Dakota State
University
AGH 154 Box 2207D
Brookings, SD 57007
(605) 688-4792

Tennessee
University of Tennessee
26211 Morgan Circle
121 Morgan Hall
Knoxville, TN 37996
(865) 974-1000

Texas
AgriLife Extension Service
Texas A & M
106 Jack K. Williams
Administration Bldg.
7101 TAMU
College Station, TX
77843-7101
(979) 845-7800

Utah
Utah State University
Logan, UT 84322-4900
(435) 797-0810

Vermont
University of Vermont
19 Roosevelt Hwy.
Suite 305
Colchester, VT 05446
(802) 656-8642

Virginia
Virginia Tech
101 Hutcheson Hall,
Mail Code 0402
Blacksburg, VA 24061
(540) 231-5299

Washington
Washington State
University
Ag Research Center
P.O. Box 646240
Pullman, WA 99164-6240
(509) 335-4563

West Virginia
West Virginia University
Room 817, Knapp Hall
P.O. Box 6031
Morgantown, WV
26506-6031
(304) 293-5691

Wisconsin
University of Wisconsin
432 N. Lake St.
Madison, WI 53706
(608) 263-2400

Wyoming
University of Wyoming
Dept. 3554
100 E. University Ave.
Laramie, WY 82071
(307) 766-5124

GARDEN PLANS

This section contains a series plans for gardens in a variety of sizes and purposes. In addition, there is a five-stage plan for making use of a "supply garden" in any garden area, and detailed plans for use of a cold frame.

PLANTING DATES

The planting dates shown in the crop lists are based on a growing season extending from an average date of last frost in the spring of May 10 to an average date of first frost in the fall of October 10 (our growing season in Connecticut). Determine your own frost dates to develop a realistic planting schedule for your growing season. Double-check your local frost dates with a qualified source of gardening information in your area.

ABBREVIATIONS

The form in which crops are placed into the garden is shown on the crop list as follows:

  B = planted as bulb or "set"
  S = sown as seed
  T = planted as transplant

SCALE

It was necessary to use different scales for different garden and container plans. In making up your own garden plan from any of ours, be sure to go by the same scale indicated on the plan. For clarity's sake, drawings do not always show the mature size of plants.

32-Square-Foot Elevated Herb Garden (8' x 4')

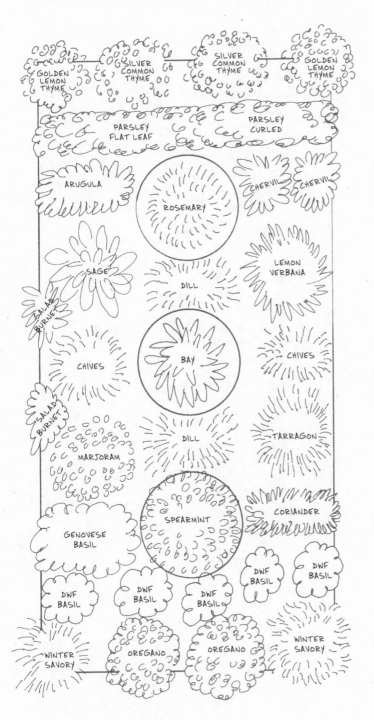

Arugula 4-15-S
Chives 4-15-T
Oregano 4-15-T
Sage 4-15-T
Winter Savory 4-15-T
Tarragon 4-15-T
Golden Lemon Thyme 4-15-T
Silver Common Thyme 4-15-T
Bay 5-1-T
Burnet 5-1-T
Mint 5-1-T
Parsley Flat Leaf 5-1-T
Parsley Curled 5-1-T
Rosemary 5-1-T
Spearmint 5-1-T
Chervil 5-15-T
Coriander 5-15-S
Dill 5-15-S
Lemon Verbena 5-15-T
Marjoram 5-15-T
Genovese Basil 6-1-T
Dwarf Basil 6-1-T

Plant rosemary, bay, and spearmint in 14" to
16" containers and sink to six inches above
ground level. Container will keep spearmint roots
confined and can remain in ground year-round.
Bay and rosemary must be dug up and brought
indoors in their pots for the winter.

3,000-Square-Foot Garden (50' x 60')

Early Spring
Garlic, Fall or 4-1-B
Shallots, Fall or 4-1-B
Peas 4-1-S
Onion Sets 4-10-B
Spanish or Bermuda Onions 4-10-T
Radishes 4-15-S
Swiss Chard 4-15-S
Mesclun Mix 4-15-S
Early Leaf Lettuce 4-15-T
Early Head Lettuce 4-15-T
Endive 4-15-T
Escarole 4-15-T
Chicory (Catalone) 4-15-T
Leeks 4-15-T
Beets 4-20-S
Beans 5-1-S
Spinach 5-1-S
Turnips 5-1-S
Snapdragons 5-1-T
Broccoli 5-1-T
Early Cabbage 5-1-T
Early Mini Cabbage 5-1-T
Cauliflower 5-1-T
Parsley 5-1-S
Carrots 5-1-S
Parsnips 5-1-S
Celery 5-10-T
China Asters 5-10-T
Gladiolas 5-10-B
Bibb Lettuce 5-10-T

Last frost date 5-10

Late Spring
Eggplant 5-15-T
Peppers 5-15-T
Tomatoes 5-15-T
Cucumbers 5-20-T
Squash 5-20-T
Cosmos 6-1-T
Basil 6-1-T
Beans 6-1-S
Spinach 6-1-S
Zinnias 6-1-T
Sunflowers 6-10-S

Summer
Beans 7-15-S
Spinach 7-15-S
Beets 7-15-S
Swiss Chard 7-15-S
Turnips 7-15-S
Brussels Sprouts 7-15-T
Late Cabbage 7-15-T
Cauliflower 7-15-T

Late Summer
Beans 8-1-S
Spinach 8-1-S
Broccoli 8-1-T
Kale 8-1-T
Fennel 8-1-T
Endive 8-1-T
Escarole 8-1-T
Lettuce 8-15-T
Radishes 9-1-S

First frost date 10-10

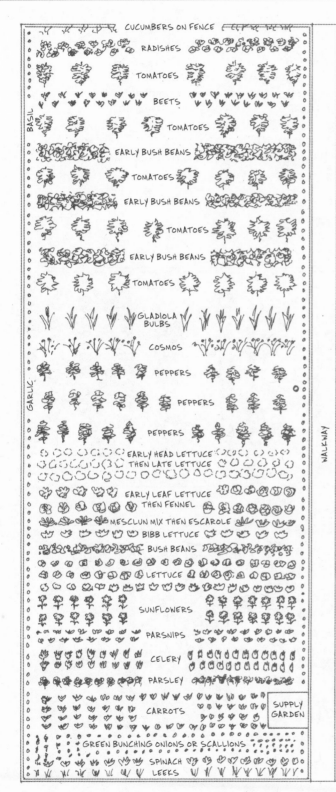

CUCUMBERS ON FENCE

RADISHES

TOMATOES

BEETS

BASIL

TOMATOES

EARLY BUSH BEANS

TOMATOES

EARLY BUSH BEANS

TOMATOES

EARLY BUSH BEANS

TOMATOES

GLADIOLA BULBS

COSMOS

PEPPERS

GARLIC

PEPPERS

PEPPERS

EARLY HEAD LETTUCE THEN LATE LETTUCE

EARLY LEAF LETTUCE THEN FENNEL

MESCLUN MIX THEN ESCAROLE

BIBB LETTUCE

BUSH BEANS

LETTUCE

SUNFLOWERS

PARSNIPS

CELERY

PARSLEY

CARROTS

SUPPLY GARDEN

GREEN BUNCHING ONIONS OR SCALLIONS

SPINACH

LEEKS

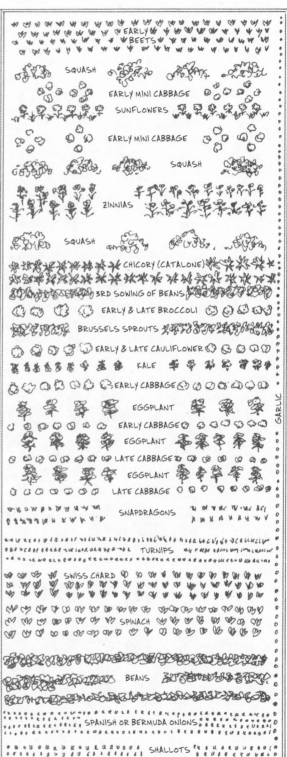

WALKWAY

EARLY BEETS

SQUASH

EARLY MINI CABBAGE

SUNFLOWERS

EARLY MINI CABBAGE

SQUASH

ZINNIAS

SQUASH

CHICORY (CATALONE)

3RD SOWING OF BEANS

EARLY & LATE BROCCOLI

BRUSSELS SPROUTS

EARLY & LATE CAULIFLOWER

KALE

EARLY CABBAGE

EGGPLANT

EARLY CABBAGE

EGGPLANT

LATE CABBAGE

EGGPLANT

LATE CABBAGE

SNAPDRAGONS

TURNIPS

SWISS CHARD

SPINACH

BEANS

SPANISH OR BERMUDA ONIONS

SHALLOTS

GARLIC

1,500-Square-Foot Garden (25' x 60')

Early Spring
Garlic, Fall or 4-1-B
Shallots, Fall or 4-1-B
Early Peas 4-1-S
Onion Sets 4-10-B
Spanish or Bermuda Onions
   4-10-T
Radishes 4-15-S
Swiss Chard 4-15-S

Mesclun Mix 4-15-S
Early Bibb Lettuce 4-15-T
Early Head Lettuce 4-15-T
Early Leaf Lettuce 4-15-T
Endive 4-15-T
Leeks 4-15-T
Beets 4-20-S
Snapdragons 5-1-T
Early Beans 5-1-S

Spinach 5-1-S
Turnips 5-1-S
Parsley 5-1-S
Carrots 5-1-S
Parsnips 5-1-S
Celery 5-10-T
Dahlias 5-10-Tubers

Last frost date 5-10

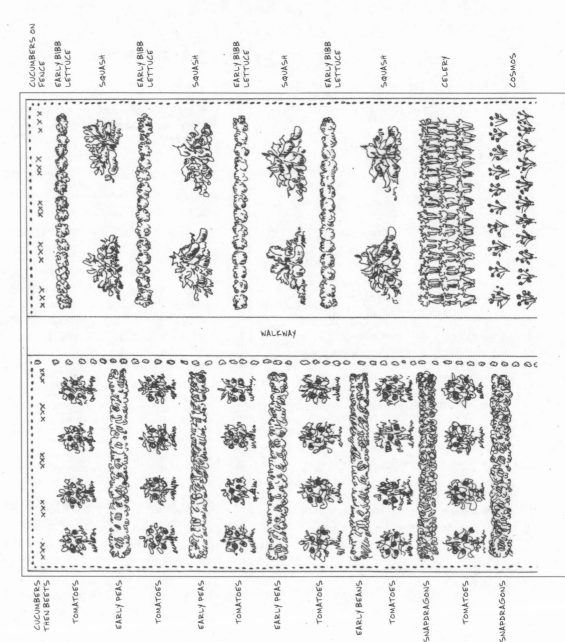

SCALE 1/5" = 1'

Late Spring
Eggplant 5-15-T
Peppers 5-15-T
Tomatoes 5-15-T
Cucumbers 5-15-T
Squash 5-15-T
Basil 6-1-T
Sunflowers 6-1-S
Zinnias 6-1-T
Cosmos 6-1-T

Summer
Beans 7-5-S
Spinach 7-5-S
Swiss Chard 7-15-S
Turnips 7-15-S

Late Summer
Kale 8-1-T
Fennel 8-1-T
Late Head Lettuce 8-1-T
Endive 8-1-T
Escarole 8-1-T
Beets 8-15-S
Radishes 9-1-S

First frost date 10-10

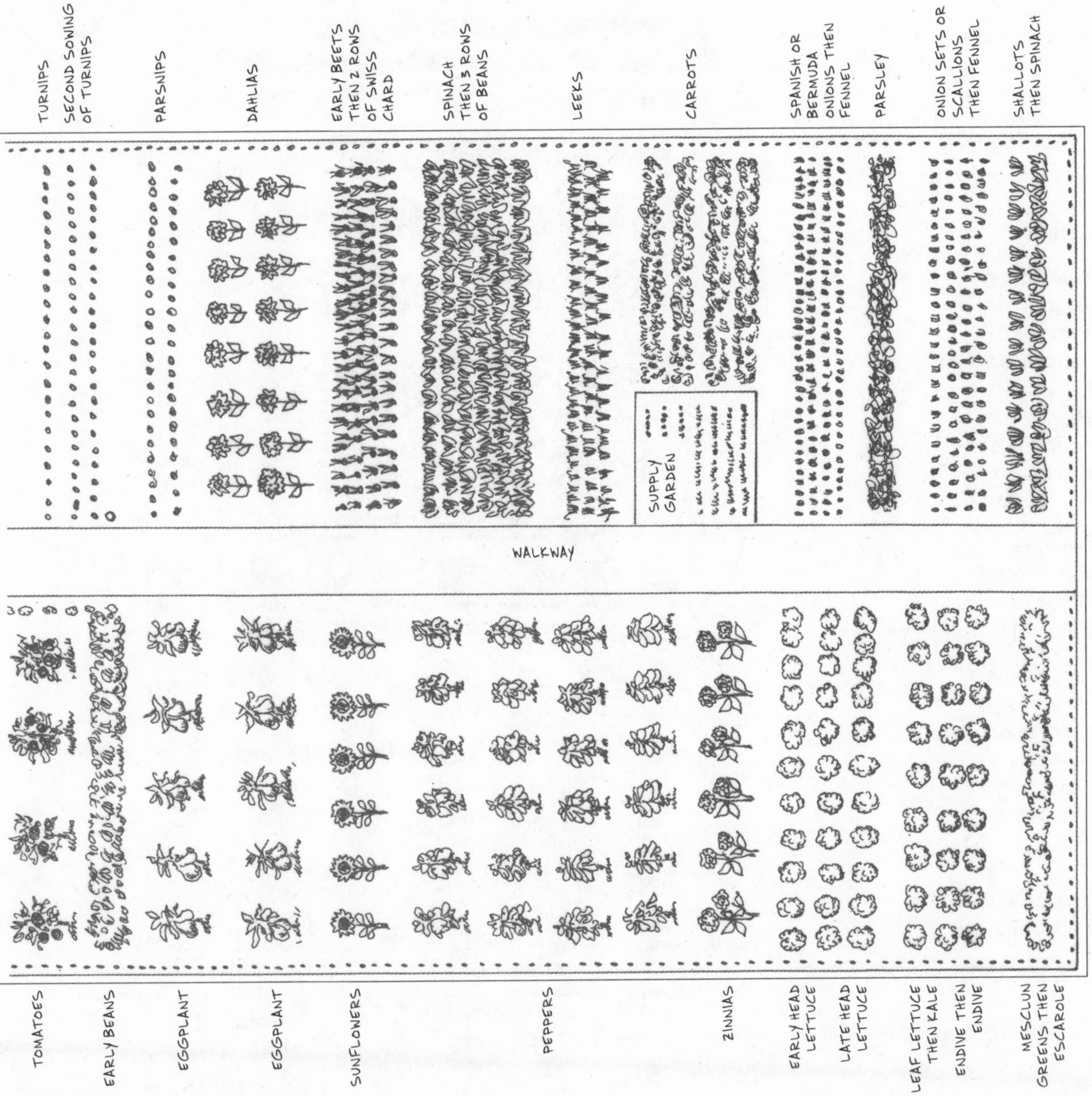
TURNIPS
SECOND SOWING OF TURNIPS
PARSNIPS
DAHLIAS
EARLY BEETS THEN 2 ROWS OF SWISS CHARD
SPINACH THEN 3 ROWS OF BEANS
LEEKS
CARROTS
SPANISH OR BERMUDA ONIONS THEN FENNEL
PARSLEY
ONION SETS OR SCALLIONS THEN FENNEL
SHALLOTS THEN SPINACH
SUPPLY GARDEN
WALKWAY
TOMATOES
EARLY BEANS
EGGPLANT
EGGPLANT
SUNFLOWERS
PEPPERS
ZINNIAS
EARLY HEAD LETTUCE
LATE HEAD LETTUCE
LEAF LETTUCE THEN KALE
ENDIVE THEN ENDIVE
MESCLUN GREENS THEN ESCAROLE

750-Square-Foot Garden (15' x 50')

Early Spring
Garlic, Fall or 4-1-B
Peas 4-1-S
Onion Sets 4-10-B
Radishes 4-10-S
Spanish or Bermuda onions 4-10-T
Lettuce 4-15-T
Early Beans 5-1-S
Beets 4-20-S
Early Spinach 5-1-S
Parsley 5-1-S
Carrots 5-1-S
New Zealand Spinach 5-10-S
Celery 5-10-T
Early Lettuce 5-10-T

Last frost date 5-10

Late Spring
Eggplant 5-15-T
Peppers 5-15-T
Tomatoes 5-15-T
Squash 5-1-T
Basil 6-1-T
Snapdragons 6-1-T
Zinnias 6-1-T
Sunflowers-6-10-S

Summer
Beans 7-5-S
Spinach 7-5-S
Beets 7-15-S

Late Summer
Beans 8-1-S
Spinach 8-1-S
Kale 8-1-T
Fennel 8-1-T
Endive 8-1-T
Escarole 8-1-T
Chicory 8-1-S
Lettuce 8-15-T
Radishes 9-1-S

First frost date 10-10

Note: Garlic should be planted in the fall.

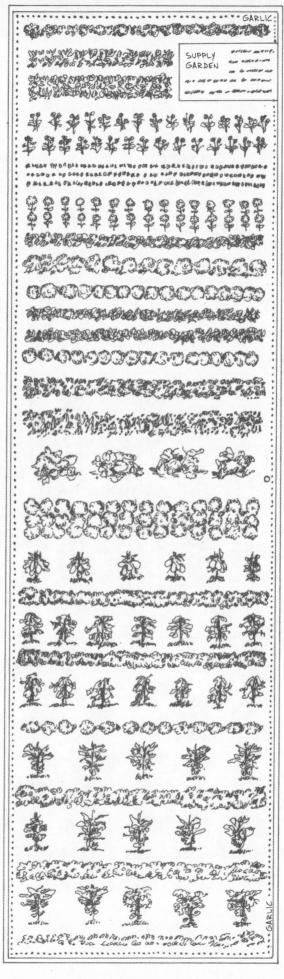

GARLIC
PARSLEY
CARROTS
SUPPLY GARDEN
CELERY
ZINNIAS
BEETS THEN BEETS
SUNFLOWER THEN KALE
SUNFLOWER THEN FENNEL OR ESCAROLE
BEANS THEN SPINACH THEN RADISHES
LETTUCE THEN ENDIVE
LETTUCE THEN BEANS
SNAPDRAGONS
LETTUCE THEN BEANS
NEW ZEALAND SPINACH
PEAS
SQUASH
CENTRALIZED WATER SOURCE
EARLY LETTUCE
EGGPLANT
EARLY SPINACH
PEPPERS
EARLY SPINACH
PEPPERS
LETTUCE THEN BASIL
TOMATOES
EARLY BEANS
TOMATOES
EARLY BEANS
TOMATOES
RADISHES THEN CHICORY
GARLIC

250-Square-Foot Cutting Garden (14' x 20')

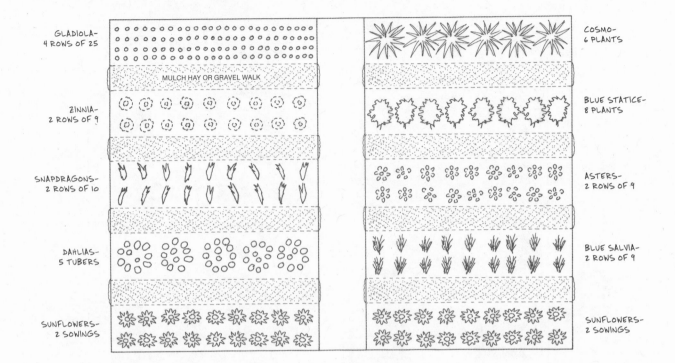

GLADIOLA-
4 ROWS OF 25

MULCH HAY OR GRAVEL WALK

ZINNIA-
2 ROWS OF 9

SNAPDRAGONS-
2 ROWS OF 10

DAHLIAS-
5 TUBERS

SUNFLOWERS-
2 SOWINGS

COSMO-
6 PLANTS

BLUE STATICE-
8 PLANTS

ASTERS-
2 ROWS OF 9

BLUE SALVIA-
2 ROWS OF 9

SUNFLOWERS-
2 SOWINGS

Asters 5-10-T
Cosmos 6-1-T
Dahlias 5-10-Tubers
Gladiolas 5-10-B
Blue Salvia 6-1-T
Blue Statice 6-1-T
Snapdragons 5-1-T
Sunflowers 6-10-S
       7-1-S
       7-15-S
Zinnias 6-1-T

400-Square-Foot Salad Garden (20' x 20')

SCALE ¼" = 1'

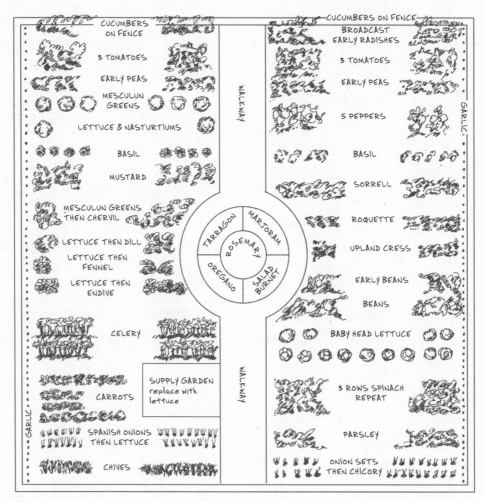

Early Spring

Garlic, Fall or 4-1-B
Early Peas 4-1-S
Onion Sets 4-10-B
Radishes **1** 4-10-S
Chives, Fall-S or 4-10-T
Spanish or Bermuda Onions
    4-10-T
Mesclun Mix 4-15-S
Lettuce **1** 4-15-T
Early Beans **1** 5-1-S
Spinach **1** 5-1-S
Mustard 5-1-S
Sorrel 5-1-S
Roquette 5-1-S
Marjoram 5-1-T
Oregano 5-1-T
Tarragon 5-1-T

Burnet 5-1-T
Upland Cress 5-1-S
Thyme 5-1-T
Mini Cabbage 5-1-T
Parsley 5-1-S
Carrots 5-1-S
Celery 5-10-T
Lettuce **2** 5-10-T

Late frost date 5-10

Late Spring

Cucumbers **1** 5-15-T
Peppers 5-15-T
Tomatoes 5-15-T
Rosemary 5-15-T
Dill 6-1-S
Fennel 6-1-S

Basil 6-1-T
Chervil 6-1-T
Nasturtiums 6-10-S or T
Lettuce **3** 6-10-T
Cucumbers **2** 6-15-T

Summer

Beans **2** 7-5-S
Spinach **2** 7-5-S

Late Summer

Radish **2**
Replace radishes with
    lettuce 6-1
Second sowing of
    spinach 7-1
Second sowing of beets 7-1

400-Square-Foot Soup Garden (20' x 20')

SCALE ¼" = 1'

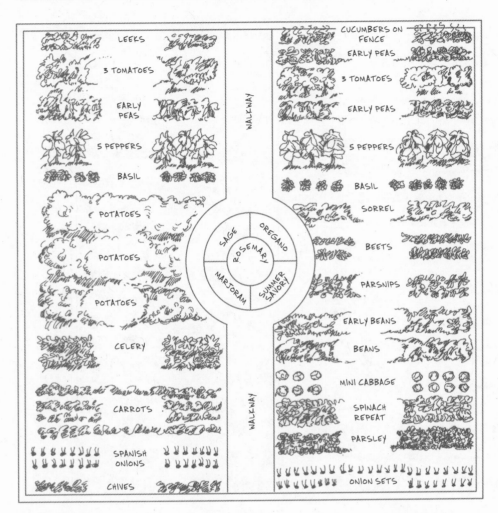

The illustration shows a garden layout with labeled sections:

LEEKS, 3 TOMATOES, EARLY PEAS, 5 PEPPERS, BASIL, POTATOES, POTATOES, POTATOES, CELERY, CARROTS, SPANISH ONIONS, CHIVES

WALKWAY

CUCUMBERS ON FENCE, EARLY PEAS, 3 TOMATOES, EARLY PEAS, 5 PEPPERS, BASIL, SORREL, BEETS, PARSNIPS, EARLY BEANS, BEANS, MINI CABBAGE, SPINACH REPEAT, PARSLEY, ONION SETS

WALKWAY

Central herb wheel: SAGE, OREGANO, ROSEMARY, MARJORAM, SUMMER SAVORY

Early Spring
Garlic fall or 4-1-B
Early Peas 4-1-S
Onion sets 4-1-S
Chives fall or 4-10-T
Leeks 4-15-T
Spanish Onions 4-10-T
Beans 5-1-S
Potatoes 5-1-sets
Beets 4-20-S
Parsnips 5-1-S
Spinach 5-1-S
Sorrel 5-1-S
Thyme 5-1-T

Mini cabbage 5-1-T
Parsley 5-1-S
Carrots 5-1-S
Marjoram 5-1-T
Oregano 5-1-T
Sage 5-1-T
Velery 5-10-T

Last frost 5-10

Late Spring
Cucumbers 5-15-T
Rosemary 5-15-T
Summer Savory 5-15-S

Peppers 5-15-T
Tomatoes 5-15-T
Basil 6-1-T

Summer
Beans 7-5-S
Spinach 7-5-S
Mini cabbage 7-15-T

First fall frost 10-10

400-Square-Foot Winter Garden (20' x 20')

SCALE ¼" = 1'

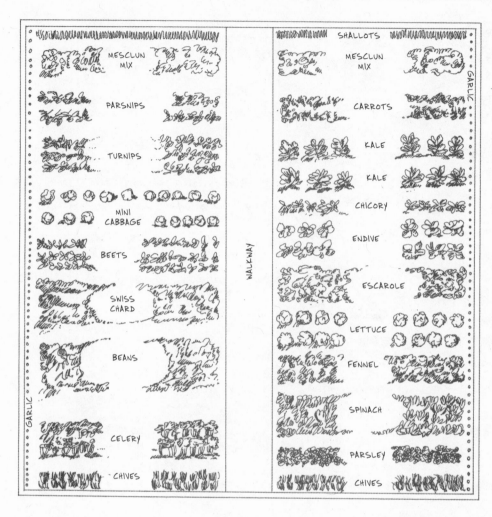

Fall
Garlic B
Shallots B
Chives S

Spring
Mesclun Mix 6-1-S*
Parsnips 6-1-S*
Parsley 6-1-S*
Celery 6-15-T*
Carrots 6-15-S*

Early Summer
Beans 7-15-S
Spinach 7-15-S
Beets 7-15-S
Swiss Chard 7-15-S

Turnips 7-15-S
Brussels Sprouts 7-15-T**
Lettuce 7-15-T
Cabbage 7-15-T
Cauliflower 7-15-T**
Broccoli 7-15-T**
Kale 7-15-T
Fennel 7-15-T
Endive 7-20-T
Escarole 7-20-T
Chicory 7-20-T

Late Summer
Lettuce 8-15-T
Radishes 9-1-S

First fall frost 10-10

* If time does not allow planting of these crops, they may be replaced with more of the others or with cauliflower, broccoli, or Brussels sprouts.

** Brussels sprouts, cauliflower, and broccoli are not included in the garden plan unless parsnips, celery, or carrots are eliminated because of space requirements.

All transplants for the late garden must be started early or purchased.

100-Square-Foot Sandbox Garden (10' x 10')   SCALE ¼" = 2'

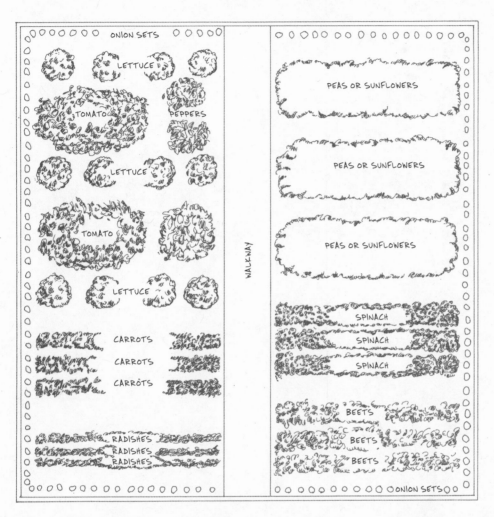

Plant onions the first day; peas the second day; radishes, beets and spinach the third day; carrots and lettuce two weeks later (5-1); tomatoes and peppers two weeks later (5-15); replace peas with beans two weeks later (6-1); replace radishes with lettuce 6-1

Plant onion sets so the scallions may be harvested throughout the season.

Plant row crops in threes to save space.

Second sowing of spinach 7-1

Second sowing of beets 7-1

Sunflowers: you may follow the peas with sunflower seeds on 7-1 or plant sunflowers.

• Metal box is not advisable unless the bottom is removed.

400-Square-Foot Raised-Bed Garden

HORIZONTAL VIEW

TOMATOES

TOMATOES

PEPPERS

EGGPLANT

SQUASH

BUSH BEANS

BABY LETTUCE

Ground level

Gravel or low-mowed grass perimeter

Mulch hay or gravel in dug out walk

Soil planting raised bed

Gravel or low-mowed grass perimeter

400-Square-Foot Raised-Bed Garden (20' x 20')

SCALE ¼" = 1'

OVERHEAD VIEW

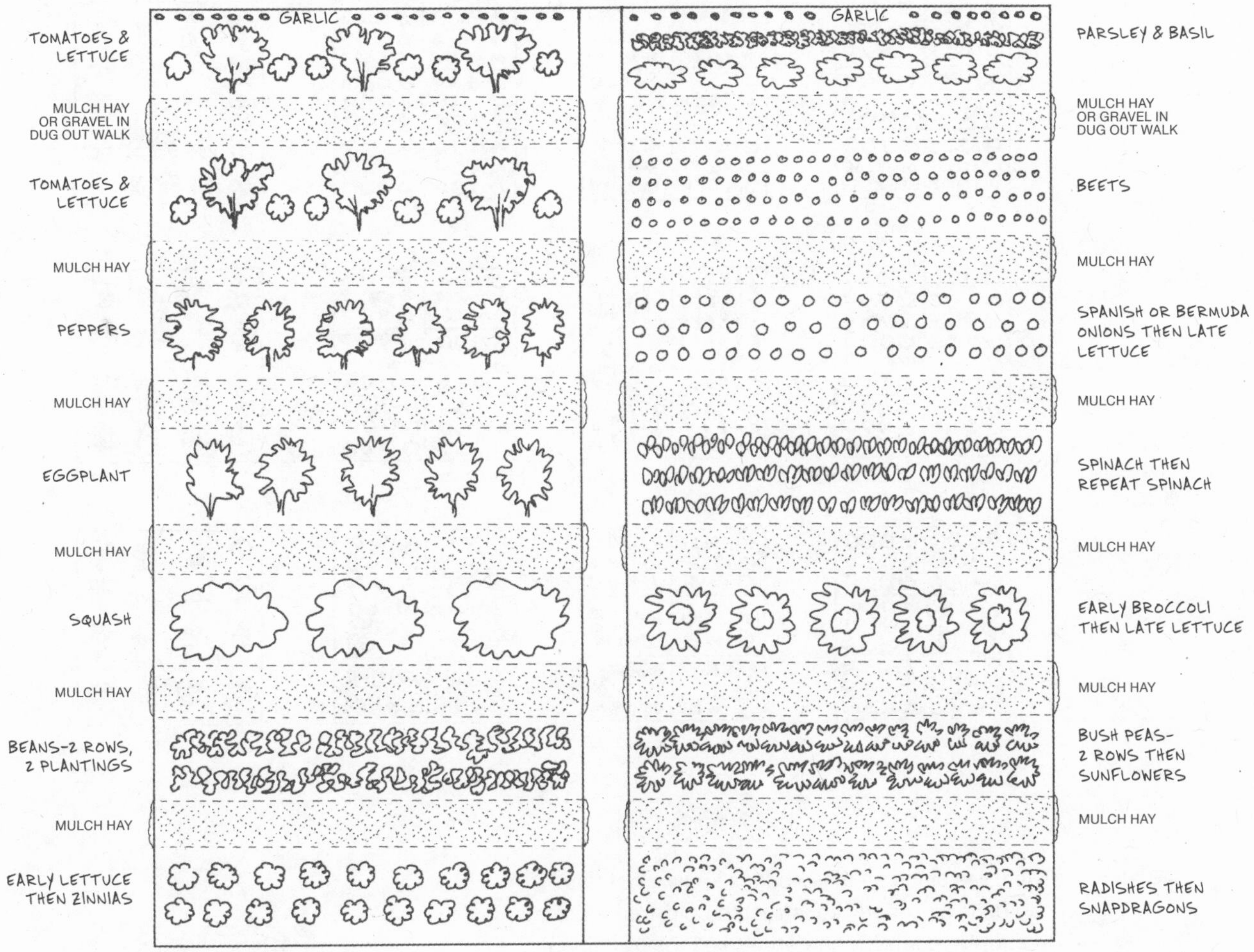

GARLIC
GARLIC
TOMATOES & LETTUCE
MULCH HAY OR GRAVEL IN DUG OUT WALK
TOMATOES & LETTUCE
MULCH HAY
PEPPERS
MULCH HAY
EGGPLANT
MULCH HAY
SQUASH
MULCH HAY
BEANS-2 ROWS, 2 PLANTINGS
MULCH HAY
EARLY LETTUCE THEN ZINNIAS
PARSLEY & BASIL
MULCH HAY OR GRAVEL IN DUG OUT WALK
BEETS
MULCH HAY
SPANISH OR BERMUDA ONIONS THEN LATE LETTUCE
MULCH HAY
SPINACH THEN REPEAT SPINACH
MULCH HAY
EARLY BROCCOLI THEN LATE LETTUCE
MULCH HAY
BUSH PEAS-2 ROWS THEN SUNFLOWERS
MULCH HAY
RADISHES THEN SNAPDRAGONS

Early Spring
Garlic, Fall or 4-1-B
Peas 4-1-S
Radishes 4-10-S
Spanish or Bermuda Onions 4-10-T
Early Broccoli 4-10-T
Early Lettuce 4-15-T
Beans 5-1-S
Beets 4-20-S
Spinach 5-1-S

Late Spring
Eggplant 5-15-T
Peppers 5-15-T
Tomatoes 5-15-T
Squash 5-15-T
Basil 6-1-T
Snapdragons 6-10-T
Zinnias 6-1-T
Sunflowers 6-10-S

Summer
Beans 8-1-S
Spinach 8-1-S
Late Lettuce 8-15-T

Cold Frame

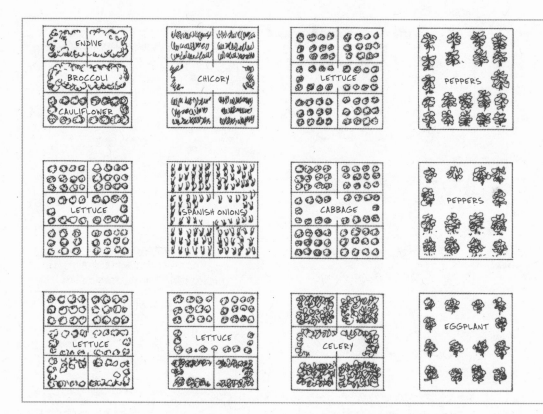

The three plans on these pages show what you can do in a properly constructed cold-frame area to supply your main garden with all the transplants required. The large fruit-producing crops—tomatoes, cucumbers, peppers, eggplant and squash—are started individually in 3-inch square peat pots or other suitable containers. All the other crops are grown in rows in 5" x 7" market packs. Use 15" x 15" carrying flats for convenience.

If space permits, the cold frame may also be used for direct sowing of crops such as spinach or mesclun mix salad greens, as shown, or lettuce or chicory. The cold frame remains cooler than the main garden area as summer progresses, so these leafy crops can be harvested over a longer period of time.

5' x 15' Cold Frame for 3,000-Square-Foot Garden

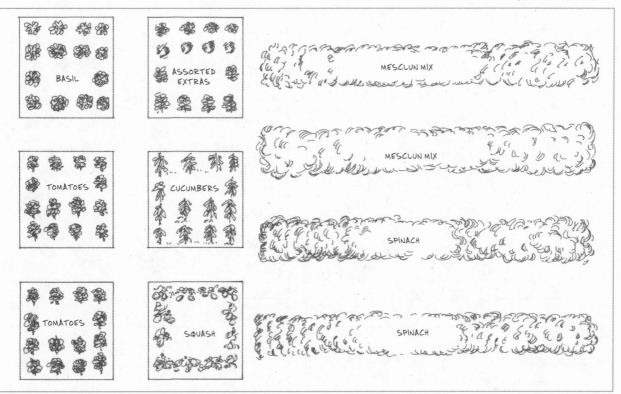

4' x 10' Cold Frame for 1,500-Square-Foot Garden

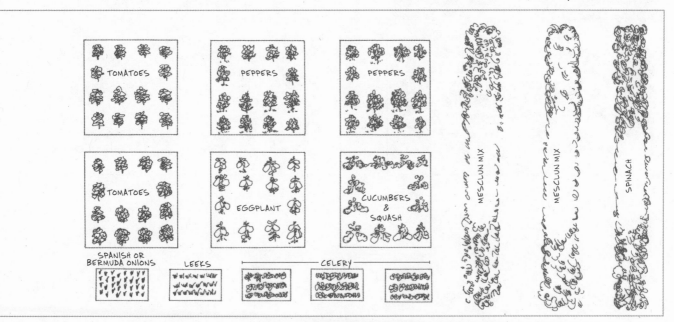

Supply Garden (3' x 3')

APRIL 15–MAY 15

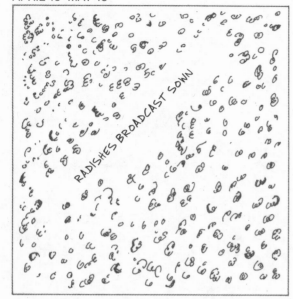

RADISHES BROADCAST SOWN

MAY 15–JUNE 15

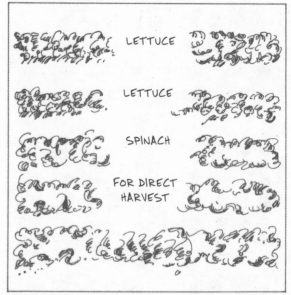

LETTUCE

LETTUCE

SPINACH

FOR DIRECT HARVEST

JUNE 15–JULY 4

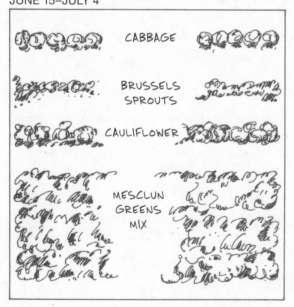

CABBAGE

BRUSSELS SPROUTS

CAULIFLOWER

MESCLUN GREENS MIX

JULY 4–AUGUST 15

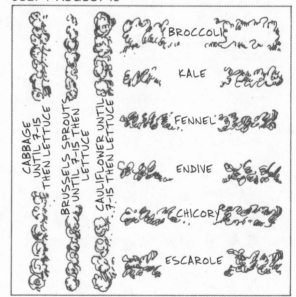

CABBAGE UNTIL 7-15 THEN LETTUCE

BRUSSELS SPROUTS UNTIL 7-15 THEN LETTUCE

CAULIFLOWER UNTIL 7-15 THEN LETTUCE

BROCCOLI

KALE

FENNEL

ENDIVE

CHICORY

ESCAROLE

INDEX